LOOKING UP WHEN LIFE LOOKS DOWN

Shattered Dreams, Medical Miracles, & Restored Hope

KIMBERLY WYSE

To Eliana, Charlie, and Redmond:
I adore every ounce of your beings.
You are my most precious treasures.
My God has answered decades of desperate prayers
with beauty, freedom, and wisdom.

To Rick:
The one who made this book possible.
Thank you for the seeds. The way you believe in me is humbling.
It is my great privilege to be your wife.

My precious ones, you were worth the wait.

TABLE OF CONTENTS

There are so many beautiful people to thank who helped to make this book possible.

Rick, John, and Sharon have done so much to help me cope with daily life and responsibilities. It means so much to have a mother-in-law who is willing to learn how to run tube-feeds, to put on special foot braces and shoes, and to happily change diapers. It means so much to have a father-in-law who says the best birthday present ever is to feed his two-year-old grandson and who gives the most generous gifts. Without their many games of ping ball and rides to see the piggies, I wouldn't have had the ability to pursue this dream. They've helped more than I can say.

Kristina has graciously kept things running smoothly when I didn't have the emotional capacity to handle one.more.thing. Her gentle nature and capable hands have blessed our family exponentially.

Many thanks are owed to my parents, who have always encouraged me to follow my dreams. They set the tone for this unexpected blessing and it has made every challenge so much easier to accept. They're always a phone call away with wisdom, unconditional love, and silly songs.

Katie, I'm so glad we have each other.

North Clinton, Christ Church, and all the prayer warriors who have shaken the gates of heaven on our behalf – thank you.

To my friends who have been editors and cheerleaders – Robin, Kristin, and Sarra – I appreciate you so much.

Orsi, thank you for your friendship and prompting. Get a table? Be a speaker? Let's go to a concert. Come over for dinner. Let's get ice cream.

Lastly, I want to thank Rachel Hollis. She gave me the courage to wash my face and stop the sin of complacency. Without her encouragement, I'd probably still be wishing my life away.

INTRODUCTION

A plan. I always had one. I had contingency plans, and contingency plans for my contingency plan. I liked to know where I was headed, how exactly I'd get there, and what I'd do once I got there. As a Christian, I wanted to honor the Lord with my life, and I thought I knew best how to do that. I saw God as someone who points in a general direction and then expects us to get ourselves there. That plan didn't work out so well for me.

While we certainly have the freedom to choose any path we desire, I discovered that I could make my life hard or I could embrace a more peaceful path. Through the journey I share in these pages, I have learned so much more about the nature of God. Like small children whose parents take care of everything and expect obedience when they give direction, my job is to relax into God's provision and follow His lead. My job is not to get ahead of Him, but to wait for His clear instructions and respond willingly. When I don't, I get hurt. Jesus wasn't kidding when He said that we are to have faith like little children.

When my plans failed, I had to learn a new way of being. I never planned to wait so long to get married. I certainly never planned to marry a farmer and live out in the middle of cornfields. It never occurred to me that I'd become a special needs mom who can insert a feeding tube when it gets pulled out, who doesn't freak out about vomit because I have cleaned it up often, and who knows exactly where to go in the hospital because we've been there so many times.

While I've been writing all my life, I had no idea this book was the one I'd finally write. I would have preferred to write a happy story of God's redemption to those who wait. But this story of tears - after I did wait so long and tried to be faithful - is the one I was given to write.

Even through this story of disappointment and very hard things, I promise you that our faithful God, who is patient with us when we are kicking against Him - this God is a God of redemption. This God we serve isn't one who prevents hard things from coming our way, but He gives us strength to make it through hard things. Not only that, He rushes to us in the middle of those things and allows us to feel the brush of angel wings against our faces.

During those times of struggle when we don't know how we're going to keep breathing, He breathes the holy, mighty breath of heaven into our spirits, and our lungs expand beyond anything we thought they could ever handle. We are lifted beyond the moment and graced with the magnitude of the power of the Lord, working in our small and insignificant lives, raising us to heights we might never reach any other way.

THIS story is the one I've been given to share. I've attempted to tell it with humor, grace, and a healthy dose of reality. I hope to draw you into the privilege I've had to get to know God in a deeper way, a way that may only come through suffering. This gift isn't meant only for me, and maybe you can experience God in a new way through my story. May it be encouragement for you through hard things. May reading it cause you to catch the fire of God in your bones, and may you be given the grace to help others through hard things.

As I share about the helplessness of seeing my newborn on life-support, supernatural miracles, grappling with a Down syndrome diagnosis, and learning a new normal, I hope that you will see how God graciously leads us, step by step, through the fiercest storms. May your heart be touched in deep and meaningful ways, and may you have a new perspective on the blessings in your life. I challenge you to see beyond the very hard circumstances you face to the joy that can be found in full submission to Christ.

And my dear sister, if you have been put in the terrible position of trying to decide what to do with a prenatal diagnosis of any kind, I extend my heart to yours. If you have been led by a doctor to end your pregnancy because of the overwhelming fear of that diagnosis, or if you are like me and feel a deep drive to always be in control, with tear-flooded eyes, my heart fills with compassion for you. You will find no condemnation here. What you will find here is a broken control freak.

I began this journey trembling and devastated and ashamed. Through the challenges I have faced, I allowed God's power to flow through my once helpless hands – rejecting fear, ruin, and shame. I chose to embrace the courage offered to me by The One who makes all things new. Then I decided to hold out my hand to let this power flow through me to anyone who will take hold of it.

God's grace is more than enough for both of us. Let me show you that God is good, even when circumstances are bad. He leads us to all He has for us. Lift up your weary head and see the grace of God poured out for you here.

1

SO MUCH WAITING

When I was eleven years old, our church, which was set right in the middle of rural cornfields in farming country, brought in a big name speaker for our mother/daughter banquet. Mom, my little sister, and I dressed up in our 1980's best, complete with shoulder pads and popped up collars, and excitedly went together. Some ladies in the church decided that the pastor's wife should be the one to announce the special speaker and welcome the attendees. In front of a large room full of women, my mother (who got a Bachelor of Science degree, rather than a Bachelor of Arts, so she could avoid the public speaking class) attempted to do what was expected of her.

She could barely stand for the shaking in her legs. My mother is a gifted musician who will gladly sit on stage and play with an orchestra; she once twirled her baton with the band during the Macy's Day Parade in New York City. She will organize a huge event and it will run smoothly without her so much as breaking a sweat. She will even stand in front of a group of college students or real estate colleagues and teach them how to run complicated computer programs like it's no big deal. But do not ask her to stand on a stage and use a microphone. That is a solid no.

My heart raced as she painfully struggled to get the words out and to keep from crying. Two of the women who had been so insistent that Mom make this announcement came and stood on either side of her to physically hold her up. I think every person in that audience was worried about her, willing her to get through it.

Then there was me. I could *not* figure out what her problem was. I thought, "Give me the microphone. I'll do it." Ah, the confidence of a child...

As I held my mother's trembling hand that night and tried to help her calm down, the speaker shared something I've never forgotten. She spoke directly to the daughters, encouraging us to pray for our husbands and children now. She said it's never too early to start. I soaked up her words like a sponge, and that night I started praying. I figured that a girl who starts praying for her husband and children when she's 11 years old is probably going to get the very best ones ever, because who does that? From that day forward, I prayed for all kinds of things specific to my life as a wife and mother.

I also prayed for wisdom. My dad regularly did family devotions with our family and I remember well the story of Solomon. Dad said that we could pray for wisdom like Solomon, and that it would affect every area of our lives. Wise people are successful people, so I prayed daily for wisdom.

Little did I know at that time that all my prayers were helping to save the life of a newborn baby I would have thirty years later. I thought those prayers were a great insurance policy against years of loneliness and sick babies. I wanted to have a comfortable and easy life, so I thought starting young was the best way to make sure that happened. I'll get back to that later though.

Adam, my baby brother, was born right before I turned 11. He was the answer to my parents' prayers and everyone adored him. My heart was completely taken with him and I treated him a lot more like a son than a brother. I carried him everywhere, did anything Mom would let me do for him, and resented the times she thought it was actually her job to take care of him. The audacity. I dreamed of the day when I'd have a baby of my own and I could be the one in charge.

My love for Adam extended to all babies. I started babysitting for other families, researched parenting methods, and listened with rapt attention to Focus on the Family and all Dr. James Dobson had to say about healthy families. In college, I arranged my class schedule so I could substitute teach at an elementary school. When I graduated from college and got my first full-time job, I supplemented my income by working as a nanny for a caregiver service. When I lost my job unexpectedly in my 30's, I was able to pay my bills by taking care of a friend's kids.

My parents encouraged me to major in elementary education in college, but when I read the course descriptions, my 18-year-old self was annoyed. I thought I already knew how to do those things and wasn't interested in taking four years of classes on something I felt confident about already. (I didn't consider the very practical need for an actual degree to do those things for money.) Instead, I chose to major in English. I love to read and write. What better thing to study for four years?

In fact, I knew exactly what I wanted to be: a pastor's wife. My husband could do the preaching, weddings, funerals, etc., and I planned to run things behind the scenes. I thought it would be awesome to teach Wednesday night classes, organize events, and run the women's ministry. A lot of pastor's kids resent church and hate feeling like they live in a fish bowl. I never felt like that. I loved church, even when I realized that it was made up of very broken people who were likely to lash out and hurt their leaders. My heart hurt for the broken and I wanted to help.

I spent my childhood chasing a few ideas – first, that I wanted to be a pastor's wife and mother, and second, that I wanted to make a great impact for the Kingdom of Heaven. How much of my dreams for my future were a result of the fact that my dad was a pastor – I don't know.

As a child, my dad got me started with a daily discipline of writing. He wanted us to read one chapter a day in the Bible and write down five things we learned. We had a spiral notebook to keep our "devotions" in. When we asked to go somewhere fun, he'd ask if our devotions were done. I'd run to my room to catch up as quickly as I could by writing things like "1. Jesus loves me." Then I'd bring my notebook to him. It seemed like a silly exercise to me at the time, but it taught me a great habit - devotional journaling. When I got older, I not only wrote down things that touched my heart, but I also wrote down my prayers. I filled dozens of journals with those thoughts and prayers. It was the beginning of my love of writing.

The summer between sixth and seventh grade, my life dramatically changed. Our family moved to Charleston, South Carolina. It was a culture shock to go from our rural, midwestern farming community to a genteel city in the southeastern United States.

It was hard for me to leave my friends and the only life I'd ever known, but it turned out that I loved living in the city. No one cared if I wore a short skirt or if I went to the mall on a Tuesday night. They were all busy living their own lives. It was so different from small town USA. I soaked up the beauty of the city – flowers everywhere, people dressed up and concerned with creating loveliness wherever they went, curving roads lined with trees, opportunities to go to the theater, and a smorgasbord of fantastic restaurants. A year after we moved to Charleston, we moved again. At the end of his sabbatical, my dad got a job in Greenville, SC. This move wasn't as hard because the wonderful new church welcomed us.

At this new church, I had the opportunity to learn about leadership and stage presence. As I moved through my middle, high school, and college years, I often sang solos. Whenever I thought the church needed a new program, Dad encouraged me to start it. I led the kinder-choir, volunteered in the nursery, performed in church musicals and dramas, was active in youth group, and eventually started the College and Career Ministry.

Because we moved several times and then I decided to attend a different high school than the one I started in, I went to five different schools in 13 years. I didn't like all the change, but I learned to be resilient and make friends quickly. I looked forward to settling into college and staying there for four years. I considered it a chance to really throw myself into social and academic life. I anticipated that I would travel with a choir, maybe do a musical, and find a husband. College was where I was going to thrive, I knew it.

A small, southern denominational Christian college offered me a scholarship. They were close to home, but not too close. The cost was high, but it was lower than most of the other schools like it. Although I wasn't a part of their denomination, they worshipped God the way I'd been taught to worship, and they had a great music program. A month before I left, I met a local girl who also planned to go there. She was the only person I knew on campus.

I thought everyone in college would be starting over like me and meeting new people. I was wrong. Because it was a denominational school, the kids from each state had grown up together at church activities. I quickly learned that within that denomination there was an unspoken rule that you married someone within the group. My ideas about finding a husband in college were frustrated. I got involved in music there and loved it, but I was too insecure to audition for the premier choirs, which were full of students who had won denominational talent competitions over the years they were in high school.

I'd also been surprised when I went to college to find out how different my family was from the other families represented there. I think it's a common realization for a college freshman in a totally new environment to go through some difficulty trying to learn a new normal. What wasn't normal was that I was having nightmares on a regular basis. I didn't want to tell anyone about them because I could barely stand to remember them, so I suffered in silence.

I woke up after those nightmares wondering what was wrong with me, why my brain would create such scenarios and play them out night after night. I couldn't get out of bed and face the world, so full of shame and grief. I begged God to take them away and tried to figure out if something terrible had happened to me as a child and I couldn't remember it.

I wracked my brain for answers, unable to recall any memory of abuse or abandonment. My family isn't perfect, but I had a good childhood. I grasped at straws, blowing things up in my mind as the possible source of the nightmares. I spent a lot of time in bed with the covers over my head, grappling with fear. When I went out, I tried to maintain the appearance of normalcy.

I did attempt to speak with the school counselor about it one time. She asked me some very personal questions that I didn't think had any bearing on my situation, then called me a liar and told me that if I didn't answer them honestly, she couldn't help me. I never went back.

Unable to control my dreams, I tried to control whatever else I could. I made plans for my life. Plans A, B, C, D, and so on. I had a plan for everything, along with contingency plans in case things I couldn't control didn't work out the way I expected. I often came up with "worst case scenario" plans to manage the anxiety that my plans wouldn't work out.

I went home for the summer and fell in love for the first time, planning to get married (not that I'd been asked) and work full time until he finished college. Then I planned to finish college. We'd have children then. He was in Bible college, so he'd be a pastor and I'd be a magnificent pastor's wife. Except that he dumped me when he returned to college in another state. I stayed home and spent my sophomore year at the community college, dealing with depression and a broken heart.

For the first time in my life, I had no plan. In my memory, I listened to sad country songs and cried every moment that I was alone. My mom offered to take me to counseling, but after my previous experience with the college counselor, I couldn't imagine why anyone went to counseling.

Things improved during my junior year of college. I changed schools for the third time, moving to Clemson University, which was about an hour from home. I got an apartment with a friend. Having my own place helped me regain some of my sense of control and I stopped crying all the time.

I'd gained a lot of weight during that bad year. I struggle with emotional eating and tried to soothe my aching heart with food. It was pretty bad, and my parents desperately tried to help me, but I was too afraid to admit there was a problem.

Since then, I have done extreme things to deal with the consequences of my choices. For a few years into my twenties, I binged when I'd had a bad day, then purged to get rid of it. But a friend lost her ability to carry a pregnancy from that foolishness, so I forced myself to stop. The threat of losing the ability to have children was a neon sign flashing "danger" brightly enough to stop me. I developed a special phrase that motivated me and I still use to this day: *I take responsibility for the food I put in my mouth.*

If I ate an entire pizza, I had to deal with it. I would not allow myself to purge. It worked. I haven't purged since my 20's, and while portion control may be an on-going challenge, I do not binge on food.

Various diet and exercise plans came and went. I fasted for spiritual reasons and lost 40 pounds, but it came back on as quickly as the other lost pounds had. I'd do well for a while, then something would happen to throw me into a tailspin and the weight would all come back on, plus some.

I turned to doctors, supplements, prescriptions, counselors, naturopaths, and personal trainers. Every time I thought I had gained control of my emotional eating, I found myself back where I started. I have often felt deeply ashamed and defeated.

College was not the dream I had anticipated. Clemson was good – with an excellent writing program and some wonderful opportunities to sing. But one of my dearest friends got deeply involved in a bad situation and I got myself right in the middle of it. Dealing with that challenge left me emotionally exhausted, and I worked a lot of hours in a physically demanding job. I didn't have much energy left for my classes.

When I graduated, I was thankful to have a degree and I didn't even consider my original plan of graduate school. I decided to move to Nashville. Music had become my niche. I performed with an acapella ensemble, sang solos in church, and often performed for weddings and special events. An acquaintance convinced me that if I wanted to be a professional musician, Nashville was the place to be. She promised to introduce me to the right people and help get me started.

After I moved, she didn't introduce me to anyone. She had her own issues to manage, but she got me there. I quickly found a temporary job in a Christian publishing house, working as a departmental assistant. I liked my boss and the organization, so I decided to stick around and get some experience there. I got a second job as a nanny for a service that sent me different places as needed.

I wanted to become a professional musician, but I had no idea how to do so. I had no connections, very little disposable income, and I had been taught that it was an absolute sin to promote myself.

My parents met at a Mennonite college. They weren't Amish, although many people confuse the two. Mennonites are pacifists who don't baptize infants (Anabaptist). They traditionally promote ideas like humility, simple living, hard work, caring for those in need, creating a peaceful world, and self-sacrifice. There are different groups of Mennonites, but many embrace modern conveniences like cars, electricity, and do not dress in a way that distinguishes them from others in a noticeable way. (In some groups, women wear head coverings and longer dresses, but the standard varies.)

Even though my parents left the Mennonite church when I was five years old, the theme of humility and self-sacrifice permeated my upbringing. I learned to work hard, not complain, and embrace classic style over trends. I could celebrate about anything I might be particularly good at with my parents, but in public I was to wait for others to notice and offer opportunities to use my gifts.

And I moved to Nashville, a self-promoting town where nearly everyone is a skilled musician. I can play enough piano to learn the notes to a new song, but not to accompany myself. I had very little confidence in myself as a songwriter. I also had such a fragile ego that I couldn't handle the constant criticism that entertainers face. Someone always has an opinion on their appearance and there's an expectation that they have perfect pitch or fake it well. After a few years of frustration at the lack of opportunities given to me (I would never ask for them), I decided to make music a fun hobby and not expect to become a career musician.

After about a year, I was promoted at work, then promoted again and started working as an event planner. Getting paid to make plans? I was thrilled to get that job! At 24 years old, I traveled all over the country, in charge of large events in full-service hotels. I wore business suits, negotiated contracts, planned event details, led meetings, gave directions to the hotel staff, welcomed up to 200 guests in our general sessions, and occasionally taught a session on marketing.

The job was amazing, and I felt like I was made to do it. The schedule was challenging, traveling every Tuesday through Saturday during the summer, then sporadically throughout the rest of the year. It was a great job with an exhausting schedule that wore on me after a while.

On the weekends, I hung out with my church single's group. Since I was getting good at planning events, I volunteered to coordinate activities for our large singles ministry. There were 400 of us who regularly met for a service, but at that time no other activities were planned. Eventually I found myself planning supper clubs, special interest groups, holiday parties, retreats, and Bible studies. I created and led a Wednesday night Bible study for singles, counseled with members who were hurting, and mentored young girls who needed accountability.

I was burning the candle at both ends and realized that I preferred the church end over the job end. I submitted proposals to the church to hire me full-time to run the singles ministry, but they didn't think it was necessary. What qualified me to do that anyway?

I spent about a year fasting regularly and praying about my future. I begged God to tell me what He had for me to do. I was looking for direction on a marriage partner, but instead God broke through my short-sightedness and pressed me to go to seminary at Regent University in Virginia Beach, VA. I'd balked at the idea, although it piqued my curiosity. I didn't think seminary was for women. I wanted to be a pastor's wife, not a pastor. For me, the word pastor was synonymous with male.

During this time, I was focused on one guy in particular. He was everything I thought I wanted and the idea of being his wife was exciting. That infatuation ended with a terrible crash that caused something inside me to shift fundamentally. As much as I loved the Lord and wanted to serve him, my expectations were so crushed that I lost my footing. I went into a tailspin. I looked to a man to meet my needs, rather than trusting God, and it didn't turn out well.

I didn't realize how vulnerable I had become. Heading into my late 20's, still single, I got panicky about the timeline I'd created for my life. I expected to have all my children by the time I was 30. My mom's last pregnancy was when she was in her mid-30's and I remember well the look of betrayal on her face when her body didn't respond to pregnancy as well then as it had in her 20's. Since I expected to marry a pastor and the supply of single, available pastors was pretty scant, my plans needed serious revision.

Panic and vulnerability are a bad combination and I got caught up in a situation that wounded me deeply. I turned to a guy I thought I might be able to convince to be a pastor. Plan B. Maybe we could *both* go to seminary? After a year passed with a lot of drama, we got engaged and had a date set and a house purchased, but my fiancé would not make the actual commitment. Once he knew he had my heart and had convinced me to compromise so much that was important, he withdrew. He didn't break up with me, but he wouldn't actually get married either. I had no contingency plan for that.

I made the excruciating decision to finally end it, only to have him return and beg me to give him a second chance. Hopeful, I allowed myself to believe he'd changed, only to suffer the same rejection all over again. It took everything I had to end a relationship that I thought had a strong possibility to end in marriage – especially with my timeline of marriage and children before the age of 30, but I was too broken to stay. It was January of 2004. In the wake of our breakup, I again went through significant depression and anxiety. My health suffered, and I felt like I'd reached the bottom of a deep pit.

What I didn't see was how God was working even through these devastating circumstances to prepare me for the future *He* had planned for me. He loved me and understood my desires, but He had something better. He was at work even in my pain. God graciously and lovingly reminded me that I was to be obedient to His plan. My expectation only needed to be that He was working on my behalf and bringing beauty for ashes.

I'd tried to do things my own way and I fell flat on my face.

Psalm 32:3-4 says,

> *"When I refused to confess my sin, my body wasted away, and I groaned all day long. Day and night your hand of discipline was heavy on me. My strength evaporated like water in the summer heat"* *(NLT).*

"Will you obey me now?" God asked.

It took every bit of courage I had to do what He asked me to do, but my answer was yes. I was exhausted from the hand of discipline that had been heavy on me.

It was time to go to seminary. The first time I stepped on the campus was to attend a preview weekend. It was March, 2004. I felt like I was raw and bleeding inside. I was smarting from the cancellation of my wedding and the end of that relationship. To make matters worse, a jealous co-worker had suddenly made my job almost unbearable. Several of my closest friends moved away that year, and I was still trying to recover from a bout with severe mononucleosis.

As I stood in line at registration, I struck up a conversation with the girl in front of me. She told me her name was Janna and she was nervous because she didn't know anyone either. We chatted through the long line, then discovered we'd been set up as roommates for the weekend. Relieved, we became fast friends. Everyone that weekend was so nice. During our first meal, one of the female professors sat with Janna and me. She asked me what my career goal was, why I wanted to attend seminary.

Before I could even think, I said, "I figure Beth Moore and Joyce Meyer will need a replacement someday." Then I laughed nervously, embarrassed that I'd said those words out loud. I'd told other people about my dream of becoming a Christian writer, teacher, and speaker in the past, but had been openly mocked and criticized. I'd been accused of pride. I hadn't spoken of that dream since then, much less considered it a possibility. To my surprise, her response was encouraging, supportive, and without a hint of mockery. With clear and honest eyes, she joined me in my dream at that moment and to this day she has never stopped believing in me. I knew I had found the place where I needed to be.

When I returned home, I left with a new friend, a new mentor, and renewed hope. That was good because things at work only got harder. What I went through in those last few months left me feeling like Nashville had spit me out onto the shores of Virginia Beach. While I knew that my jealous co-worker was wrong, when someone drills down on you like that and everything you do or ever did is put under a microscope, you can start to believe that you really are the terrible person they say you are. It was one of the most lonely and confusing times in my life.

I had a few weeks off from work before classes began, so I started writing. For hours each day, instead of packing like I was supposed to do, I wrote in my journal. Page after page was filled with my thoughts about the situation, prayers, things I was learning, and my very raw emotions. I wrote my way through that challenging part of my life and realized that I found great peace and contentment from writing. As I read back over what I'd written, I enjoyed reading it. Maybe I'd learned something from my college English degree? I wondered if I could become good enough to write books like I'd dreamed of doing.

In the fall of 2004, I enrolled in Regent University's School of Divinity, working toward a Master of Arts in Practical Theology. The School of Divinity is an exceptional place where the professors work in the field of ministry while they teach. It keeps them grounded in the present needs of the church, fulfilling the "practical" nature of the degree. Because of the comparison I'd often heard of seminary with a cemetery, and how out of touch theologians are with modern day issues facing the church, I was drawn to this practical degree.

As I look back on that time, it surprises me to realize the disregard I had for the *ministry* of a pastor's wife. Why did the idea of a woman earning a degree for the specific purpose of serving as an awesome pastor's wife seem like such a foreign concept? Just because the pastor's spouse isn't on the church payroll doesn't mean the job isn't extremely important.

As I sought God for my future, trying to come up with some sort of a plan, I began to realize that my desire to be a pastor's wife was more about wanting to be in ministry in the only way I knew how.

I struggled with Scripture passages that say a woman should not teach a man in the church when the rest of the Bible is full of stories of strong female leaders like Deborah, Huldah, and Junia. The only direction He gave me was to quietly whisper, "The ministry I have for you will not cause offense." I made the decision to stop focusing on my gender. I turned to the joy of getting to know my Savior better.

Regent welcomed me and soon I was immersed in my classes and working as a graduate assistant who helped plan events for student services. During my second semester, I was elected to student council. Although I'd started school with a disappointing 20% grant, within one semester 70% of my tuition was paid. Within two semesters, 90% of my tuition was paid: the student government position came with a 50% tuition scholarship, I received a 20% grant for women in ministry, and I also received a 20% J. Rodman Williams scholarship for academic excellence and leadership skills.

My two years at Regent flew by. In my mind, they are marked by tremendous personal and spiritual growth, as well as healing for my battered soul. I threw myself into classes, campus life, and a local church. The university had regular chapel services and I got to help lead praise and worship there. I met some great people, dated a little, made lifelong friends, and truly became grounded in my relationship with God. The professors wanted to make sure that their graduates had a firm foundation upon which to build when they left. I examined myself thoroughly, repented from sin, asked God to fill in any holes in my spiritual foundation that had allowed me to fall into repetitive sins, and set up some healthy boundaries as I learned how to be a woman of integrity.

One important thing I decided while I was there was that the man I married would be a godly man who refused to take advantage of any vulnerability he found in me. He would consider himself to be my protector and refuse to compromise his own values. Rather than expect me to be the one who was always strong, he would be full of the fruit of the Spirit (Galatians 5:22-23) because he truly worshipped God. I was done with men who claimed to honor God but thought little of trying to dishonor me.

During graduation week, I was surprised to find out that a meal where the professors prayed over us all was also an award ceremony. I glanced over the possible awards before things got started, noting which ones I might be eligible to receive. I laughed heartily when my roommate whispered to me that she hoped she didn't get any awards. She'd appreciate recognition for her hard work like anyone else, but she did *not* want to go up on stage in front of everyone. Just thinking about it made her face turn deep red. I told her I'd gladly receive hers for her and she laughed too.

As award after award was called, my name was unheard. I felt sick, flashing back to the awkward elementary school child who was always picked last for sports teams. As I sat with my hands in my lap, discouraged, I suddenly realized they had called my name. My dad, the only family member who attended that meal with me because the tickets were expensive, motioned for me to stand. I stood quickly, realized that I wasn't sure if I was supposed to be standing or what was going on, then sat back down. Everyone around me started shooing me to the stage. Bewildered, I walked up there, shook hands with the dean, received a plaque, and walked back down. I had no idea what I had been awarded.

Back at my seat, the people at my table and surrounding tables congratulated me. I grabbed the event program, looking for an explanation. I'd been given the top award, "for the student who showed the most potential for future ministry impact."

I still wasn't quite sure how I'd been chosen for that award, but I was on cloud nine for the rest of the weekend. It makes me smile today to think about it. The plaque hangs on my wall by my dresser where I can see it every morning, reminding me that while I'm in a season of focusing on my children, there are people who believe that I will impact others for the Lord. I truly pray that the time I spend at home right now will impact my children for the Lord, and that someday He will call me to impact others outside of my home.

Upon graduation, I moved back in with my former roommate and dear friend, Pamela, in Nashville. We knew the situation might be temporary, as

I was looking for a full-time ministry position and that might take me away from Nashville, but she let me stay with her until then.

The problem was that my big award and shiny new degree didn't mean much in the real world. I applied for all kinds of ministry jobs, shocked to find that many job descriptions actually said that the ideal candidate was male and married. Is that even legal? One job I applied for included a questionnaire that asked very personal information, like "Have you ever been abused?" and "Have you ever been intoxicated?" I spent all that time answering their questionnaire and they didn't have the courtesy to even respond. I was so mad at myself for taking the time to do the questionnaire.

While I spent hours, days, and months applying to and interviewing for ministry jobs, I went to work as an office temp. I wondered about my actual potential for future ministry impact. Had I made a total fool of myself by going to seminary as a single young woman? Many of my fellow male, married classmates had already taken secular positions when full-time ministry jobs didn't pan out. I could've accepted a long-term position doing administrative work, but why would I bother to go to seminary if I wasn't going to work in full-time ministry? My plan included work in some type of full-time ministry.

One evening I sobbed my concerns to the Lord in prayer, wondering if He had actually called me to do anything. Did I make this all up? If so, I was going to need to check myself into a mental hospital because I was totally delusional. After I cried my heart out, I decided to sing. Very quietly, and with a shaky voice, I squeaked out, "I will praise the Lord. I will praise the Lord. No matter what tomorrow brings, or what it has in store, I know I will praise the Lord."

I decided that even if I had made a fool of myself, I would praise and serve God. The next morning my phone rang very early. My swollen eyes didn't want to open as I answered. It was the Director of Women's Ministries at my church in Nashville. She told me that she was in the process of creating a job for me in women's ministry. She couldn't give me details yet, but she wanted to make sure I was interested.

Yes, please!

The senior pastor of our church had lost his wife to a long battle with a difficult disease. Now single, I soon learned that he had been quietly courting our beautiful and godly women's minister, Carol. They were engaged. He wanted Carol by his side as he moved into retirement. He planned to travel and preach at other churches, and he didn't want her distracted by other responsibilities. It took a few months, but I was hired with a fancy title of Creative Development Coordinator.

On my first day in the office, the senior pastor came in to speak with me. He told me that he'd hired me to take over women's ministries so Carol would be free to travel and minister with him. He said they'd transition us slowly, but I needed to quickly learn all I could from her so I could do a good job when she was done.

Within a year, I was given the title of Women's Minister. Carol was a blushing bride, gleeful and giddy, and I was thrilled for her. She waited a long time to feel that kind of love and she deserved to be adored as much as anyone I've ever known. The director of our department asked me to also develop our church's discipleship/small group ministry. I was happy to do so and launched Wednesday night small group meetings with curriculum I'd developed to go along with a study our pastor wanted everyone to go through. I was thrilled to write curriculum, and it helped that my work saved the church a lot of money in purchasing study guides.

We had all kinds of women's book studies, Bible studies, prayer classes, moms' groups, and mentor meetings. The pastor moved into retirement and the associate pastor replaced him. The new senior pastor licensed me as a congregational minister, and I took the call to pastoral ministry seriously. I knew that the license meant that my life would be different. That night I felt like I was taking marriage vows, committing to give my life to ministry. My friends got together and purchased a beautiful Bible, had it embossed with Pastor Kimberly Wenger on the front, and each wrote an encouraging word inside. It was a special night.

I worked as the on-call pastor once a week, plus spent a lot of time meeting with hurting women in the congregation. The amount of counseling I did with women who were suffering from mental illness, going through a crisis, or hurting from past mistakes was overwhelming. I only had one class in pastoral care and counseling in seminary, so I scrambled to educate myself on how to best help them.

I love to lead Bible studies and small groups, so I lead groups four to five nights a week. We didn't have a big budget for curriculum, so I wrote discussion guides based on the sermon each week for our leaders to use. One of my main goals was to develop new leaders within the congregation and I loved to see people who once felt timid and unqualified rise up as brave and excellent leaders. I worked closely with our Christian Education ministry to plan adult Sunday school classes and organize events that let the congregation get to know class leaders and learn more about each class offered. Encouraged by my director, I started writing a blog to offer spiritual encouragement to the congregation and help them get to know me better.

Then the pastor announced that a church consultant was evaluating our financial situation. The downturn in the economy in 2008 had greatly impacted our bottom line because people weren't in the same position to give as they once had been. Circumstances beyond their control forced the hands of the leaders. Our church had to cut 25% of the staff to get its finances in order. I was one of the last ones hired, so after four years I was thanked for my excellent service, given letters of recommendation, and laid off.

I had been taught that when you walk with God, obey His commands, and follow His lead, you can't help but succeed. If I wasn't following God's will for my life, I was unaware of the offense. Although far from perfect, I tried hard to be obedient, self-sacrificing, and humble - and I lost my job.

I had a choice to make. Would I allow my hurt and frustration to send me into a spiral in the wrong direction, rebelliously acting out against God in anger? That hadn't worked out very well in the past, but it was certainly a temptation. Another option was to see beyond the present hurt and apparent failure, trust God's heart, and embrace the change as His plan for my life. I'd recently spent 40 days in prayer and fasting, completely abstaining from food and limiting liquid calories, seeking the heart of God. I wanted to know Him better. I wanted to understand *His plan* for my life.

In that time I had come to trust the Father's heart for me in a way I'd never understood before. I became confident in His love. I found an inner strength from the Lord that I never knew was there, tried and tested. I came to understand that through the power of the Holy Spirit, I am fully capable of doing hard things.

Choosing to fast for that long caused me to draw on the strength of the Holy Spirit. I could quit at any time. Food was readily available all around me. I disciplined myself to do something hard. When hard things happened later, things that I didn't have a choice about, things from which I could never take a break - it was that strength that helped me remember that I was stronger than I thought. It helped me remember that God was right there, even when I couldn't feel His presence.

Even though I didn't understand or have a plan, I decided that God must have something else in store for me.

After I lost my job, I asked if I could keep my office at the church and volunteer in women's ministry. I continued to attend the church and help wherever I could. My attitude was completely different from the young woman who was deeply disappointed six years earlier. It wasn't a particularly fun season, and I spent a lot of time trying to figure out what exactly I was supposed to do next, but peace reigned over the storm.

One weekend during this time of transition, two women told me that God had been speaking to them about me as they prayed. They both said that God's provision for my life was already there, like it was in the room but standing in the shadows, waiting for the right time to step forward and be known. Another man in the church told me that I would have to sort through all the pretty boys before the man God had for me, he repeated, "the MAN", would make himself known.

2

MR. WISDOM

Right before I got laid off, I became extremely motivated to reduce my bills. I moved in with an elderly widow suffering from dementia. She needed someone around the house to help her out at night. My rent and utilities were covered, so I didn't have to worry about getting another full-time job immediately. That was a good thing because none of the hundreds of resumes I sent out produced even one lead. I didn't want to go back to full-time work. I wanted to get married, have babies, and focus on a home of my own. I imagined myself writing in my free time, finally free from the distraction of a job. (Because a husband and children aren't distracting to writers, right?) I'd been begging God to give me those things for years and my cries continued in vain.

As my severance pay came to an end, my sister invited me to go on vacation with her family for a week. It seemed ridiculous to leave when I needed to make money, but I had peace that something would work out. I went on the trip and enjoyed myself, singing pump-up music loudly the whole way to Myrtle Beach. On the way home, I let the Lord know that whatever He was doing didn't really have to be so dramatic. I needed to find some way to make money before I ran out completely. I was nervous, but I knew God must have something up His sleeve.

I'd been off the internet all week and when I came home, I took a few minutes to check Facebook before going to bed. Waiting in my inbox was a private message from a guy named Rick Wyse (pronounced "wise"). I didn't really know him, but I knew who he was because of a family connection. All he said was something like, "Hi! Remember me?" At that time I was constantly on guard against the advances of married men. The single guys I knew seemed to either not like me or not be a good match, but there were some married men who compared my best with their wives' worst and idealized me. I knew I was lonely and vulnerable, so I worked to avoid them. Although I didn't think Rick was married, his profile picture showed him with a couple of children. I responded to Mr. Wyse very directly: "Yes, I remember you. How are your wife and kids?"

Despite my guarded response, I went to bed that night, July 5, 2010, laughing at the thought that all my years of praying for wisdom might be leading me to marry a man named Mr. Wyse. I thought about how silly I'd feel if I found out that he was married, but something about that message caught my attention. God can be sneaky like that.

The next day, I discovered that Mr. Wyse had never been married and didn't have children. The children in his picture were his nieces and nephews. I'd never spent much time with him when we lived in neighboring towns, but I knew one of his sisters well. He'd heard of my blog through his sister, read a couple posts and liked them, then decided to get in touch with me.

A couple of days after that, my friend Beth asked if I would like to fill in for her nanny who was out of the country for an indefinite time. I gladly agreed to work 15 hours a week, helping around the house and taking care of her children. Her five kids were a delight to me and I fell madly in love with them. The missing nanny never returned, so for several months, I worked 15-20 hours a week for Beth.

Rick and I talked more, our phone calls got longer, and our conversations got much deeper. He told me that he didn't think women like me still existed. He couldn't believe I wasn't married. He said he liked me and wanted to pursue a relationship. According to him he wasn't that good at romance, but I said he might be better than he thought. He was quite a bit older than me, and I balked a little at our age difference, but he seemed young and full of energy. I told him that if he was serious about me, he needed to come to Nashville. I wasn't going to spend much more time on the phone with a guy who claimed to like me, only to have him meet me in person and change his mind.

Rick gathered up his courage and drove to Nashville for a weekend in late August. Accustomed to driving on rural roads with little to no traffic, the chaos of Nashville was a big challenge for him. Because he wasn't familiar with the area, I planned our activities. I was nervous that first day when he arrived with his friend Mike. Two farmers in Nashville to meet a girl - they were as nervous as I was. I invited them into the house, introduced them to the sweet woman I lived with and her daytime caregiver, and spent a few minutes chatting. Then we decided to go out and enjoy some fun in the city. As we walked out the door, Rick put his hand on the small of my back and a tingle ran straight up my spine.

"This man is your husband."

I heard the words like a friend who hurriedly whispers behind her hand a secret that makes you giggle, but you aren't 100% sure you heard her right. I'd been so wrong about the men I thought might be my husband in the past that I shook it off and went on with my day like I hadn't heard a thing.

We ate our first meal at the Hard Rock Café. It's on Second Avenue in the middle of everything, a casual and fun place that tourists enjoy. I figured he'd be happy to go there. I'll never forget how I could see his Adam's apple as he repeatedly swallowed hard over the $14 burger. He wasn't impressed. Before I could get worried that he was a cheapskate, he walked down Broadway and turned into a store that sold cowboy boots. He thought it was a shame that I'd lived in Nashville all those years and didn't have any, so he bought me a pair. And a hat. That was not a cheap gift.

As Rick and I got to know one another on the phone during the week, I learned that every winter when farming slowed down, he did mission work in third world countries. For the last decade, he had gone to Guatemala for six weeks every year. Although I'd long ago let go of the idea that I'd marry a pastor, I was drawn to his sacrificial work in missions.

He'd been to Europe to visit his sister when she lived in the Netherlands. He'd visited his brother in California and traveled to Phoenix by himself to visit his aunts. Here I thought he was a sheltered farmer, but it turned out that he had traveled the world. In one breath he told me wasn't very familiar with the city nearest his home, 40 minutes away, and with the next he said even so, he came to Nashville for me. When I thought I had him figured out, he surprised me.

With my work hours and his freedom to set his own hours, we could often spend time together on the weekends. I had three days off and no responsibilities at the church on Sundays. He planned another visit to Nashville around Labor Day, this time on his own, and we had such a good time together that we weren't ready to say goodbye when it was time for him to leave. I have no memory of how I got out of work, but he spontaneously invited me to come back to the farm with him and I agreed.

We rode together in his pickup truck, without air conditioning, and he taught me about farming. (I might have pretended like being hot and sweaty didn't really bother me.) He spent the next several days showing me around the farm. He was proud of his tractors and farm land. Although farming wasn't something I was interested in, I felt a sense of peace and belonging there. I had spent my childhood in the area and we often visited my grandparent's farm in Iowa, so farm life wasn't foreign to me.

I could see myself writing as I looked out over fields and the stream that runs through the farm. Rick is meticulous about the land and in the summer everything is lush and green - like a park with a large pond and mature trees. I could see raising children in a small, conservative community that values hard work and common sense. When Rick is in his element, he displays quiet confidence and a sense of satisfaction that's very attractive. He's worked hard and I respect him for it.

Rick and I went to his grain bins (what I'd unknowingly called silos, which are cement and hold silage or corn) and his barn, then climbed straight up a ladder that's 80 feet high and stood at the top on a platform that overlooks the whole farm. I'm not a big fan of heights, but I was excited to be up there with him. He was so happy, explaining that grain bins are metal and store different kinds of grain, and how the grain auger works to bring his crops from the grain truck into the storage bins. The platform at the top was built as a place to stand when the motor on the "grain leg" needs to be repaired.

He explained how they rotate crops, how various implements can be attached to his tractors to do different things, and how selling the grain at the right time to the right buyer is as much a part of successful farming as growing it. I understood that selling grain is like investing in the stock market. They must know when to sell and when to hold on to what they have. Sometimes they get it right and sometimes they don't. Farmers don't get a weekly paycheck. They get paid when they sell grain (or other commodity like livestock), which might be just two times a year.

Climbing down that ladder was almost worse for me than climbing up, but Rick went ahead of me and made sure I was okay. I couldn't help thinking that if I fell, I'd knock him down with me, but he said he'd catch me. I decided to trust him.

He has a horse that lives in the barn, so later that day I went for a ride, trying very hard to look like I was comfortable. I was much more comfortable as we flew around the farm on the four-wheeler that was like the one I grew up riding. He drove and I sat on the back with my arms around his waist, grinning like a little kid.

He took me to a combine derby at the county fair. It was so loud, but I was surprised to find how much I enjoyed watching the farmers as they drove beat up old combines, crashing into one another until only one remained and was the champion. Combines (pronounced with an emphasis on the first syllable), or harvesters, are very large tractors used to harvest crops quickly. Depending on the size of the combine, they can cost half a million dollars, plus the cost of the implement that goes on the front to lift the stalks, strip them of the grain head, and funnel them into a nearby grain wagon. Once they are too old to be useful, it's fun to crash them into one another.

I enjoyed talking to Rick's sweet and gentle mom, listening to his dad talk about the history of the farm, and meeting his friends. Rick took me to meet one of his best friends, Jon, and his wife, Jenny. He told me that Jon had been offended when he learned that Rick had bought his own tractors and hadn't told him. He figured Jon would be equally upset if he didn't introduce him to his girlfriend. I was a little taken aback to be compared to his acquisition of tractors, but I reminded myself that his tractors were a big deal to him. As we sat at Jon and Jenny's kitchen table chatting, Jon kept staring at me. It was a little uncomfortable, but I didn't blame him. Rick was 46 years old and had never had a serious relationship. Then he walks in with this 34-year-old woman from Nashville that he's never even heard about. Jon was trying to figure things out.

At the end of that week, I felt content and happy. A sense of peace and warmth spread through me and I couldn't believe I was considering marrying a farmer and moving to the country. Tears welled up as I prepared to fly home, missing him already. Then he whispered, "I love you." It was early in our relationship, but I knew he meant it. I loved him too. It was so hard to board that plane back home.

With my jobs and housing situation, I calculated that I actually had more spending money than when I worked full-time. I worked long hours every Monday through Thursday, but the jobs required very little emotional energy from me. Then I had every Friday through Sunday off. I had to laugh as I spent my weekends hanging out with Rick on the phone or in person and during the week wrote large checks to pay off student loans for my graduate degree while I answered phones, scrubbed floors, did laundry, and loved on babies.

Rick and I talked very early on about what marriage would look like for us. With our ages and the long-distance relationship, neither one of us felt like wasting our time so we laid it all out. He explained that he would never leave his farm. The land he owns is his livelihood. He loves his job and is totally fulfilled and satisfied in it. He and his dad helped one another a lot over the years, so he wasn't about to walk away from what they'd built. He told me that he wanted to get married and have children. He said he could afford to support a family. I could work if I wanted to, but if I wanted to stay home, I could do that as well.

I shared my dreams with him. I asked if he'd be comfortable with a wife who traveled as a speaker, who wrote books that might include stories about him, and who didn't really help farm. It was like he already knew me from the start. When I told him I was going to be a writer and a speaker, he said with quiet confidence, "I know." When I asked him if he'd be able to handle that, he grinned and said he'd be glad to put the babies on the tractor with him so I could go.

I had always wanted to be able to devote much of my time and energy to raising my children. I also wanted the freedom to write. Because of that, I hoped to find someone who was able to support a family. I was open to whoever God had for me, but it was something I hoped to find. It was an amazing idea to not be compelled to earn money and always wonder if I had enough money to pay my bills. What a man! He already knew my heart and he was happy to help me fulfill my dreams.

But the change that was coming into my life was costly. My sister told me once, "Nothing is free." She was right and I had learned by then that there's a cost to everything. The cost isn't always about money.

In order to marry Rick, I had to leave Nashville: my beloved city, a hub of music, entertainment, beauty, and publishing. It was the place of dreams. I thought, "Surely if I hang around Nashville for long enough, I'll meet a publisher who likes my writing." Pretty much all the female, Christian, devotional and spiritual books come out of Nashville publishers. It's the place to be for this industry.

I also needed to leave my friends. In the absence of family close by, my friends became the family I chose. It had been hard to find them and I nurtured those relationships. I leaned on them for support. Good friends like that, the ones you choose as an adult because you genuinely like them, don't come around every day. We were extremely close and the idea of leaving them about strangled me. I invited them to tell me what they thought of the guys I dated and expected honesty. I was greatly comforted when they all met Rick and loved him immediately. They'd been pretty vocal in the past when some guy didn't meet with their approval, so I was sure that they meant what they said.

Because the woman I lived with had an outside-access basement with guest quarters, Rick was able to stay at her house when he visited. I stayed with his parents when I visited him. We tore up the road between our houses, getting to know each other's friends, family, churches, and lives. Although he suggested it, I refused to move to his town unless we were married. After what happened with my previous engagement, I couldn't see giving up Nashville, my friends, and my income without the surety of marriage. How could I make a wise decision if I was dependent upon him for everything, but not even engaged?

For seventeen months I worked as a nanny, caregiver, and receptionist. I spent about every third weekend with Rick and lots of time with my friends. I wrote my blog, imagining myself looking out over fields while small children played in the yard, dreaming of becoming a full-time writer.

As soon as I began to feel really attached to Rick my anxiety flared up. I started panicking that he would leave me like I had been left before. He's his own person with a truly godly heart and self-discipline that refuses to waver, but I was terrified. He didn't hold his heart back from me or expect me to conform to his standards of perfection. He was proud to be seen with me, often commenting that he wanted to take me somewhere to show me off. He regularly complimented me and encouraged me to take good care of myself while not basing his love on my appearance. He often said he knew that women's bodies changed as they had children and aged, but that the true test of a woman is her commitment to the Lord. I love his values and how he makes me laugh. He's easy to be around. He is the solid and God-honoring man I had been looking for, but after so much loss I was terrified that I'd be left empty-handed again.

We were old enough to know what we wanted. I couldn't figure out what he was waiting for. My heart pounded with the fear that he'd realize he had my heart and decide I must not be that great after all. It felt a little early to him, but he saw the stress it caused me to keep waiting and moved up his timeline. On a warm night in May, he took me on a horse-drawn carriage ride in downtown Nashville and asked me to marry him. Our carriage driver turned around and started yapping on about some historical site in the middle of his proposal and I had to tell the man to be quiet and ask Rick to start again. I didn't want to miss a word of what he had to say.

He didn't give a big speech or make lofty promises. He simply told me he loved me and asked me to be his wife. The look in his eyes said it all though. He was anticipating our future together and that was all I needed to know. Both of us were nervous about the diamond that now flashed on my finger, and both of us were smiling from ear to ear.

As I've come to know him more, I've realized that he isn't a fast adapter and he was getting used to the idea after 46 years of singleness. Although I was eager to get married as soon as possible, suggesting a three-month engagement, I slowed down for his sake. When he looked at me, I saw love and tenderness and joy. There was no hesitation that I was the one for him. Finally able to relax and believe that he was truly my husband, we set a date seven months out.

I felt confident that Rick was the one for me. Not only was he the manly man I dreamed of, but he treated me with respect. Even after we got engaged, he was concerned that we avoid even the appearance of sin. Rick had learned to guard his thoughts and actions many years ago. He'd made a habit of avoiding anything questionable, choosing to focus on his work and volunteering with Youth for Christ. He was on the board of a homeless shelter and spent time with the guys on the weekends going to high school basketball games and Bible studies. Before me, he'd dated very little and had been concerned that girls didn't like him.

I knew that once we got married, I would have to rely on him to support us financially. While this idea once seemed like total luxury, I had never spent anyone else's money in my life. I got my first summer job when I was 13 years old, babysitting around 40 hours a week for a family friend's three children and sometimes my little brother too. My parents took good care of me, but it was important to them to teach personal responsibility. I'd worked to pay for much of my own clothes, entertainment, gas, car insurance, and so forth since I was 15 years old.

My parents taught me about tithing and saving, but I didn't have to ask anyone for permission to spend my money, and no one questioned my spending habits. Rick is not a spender, rarely buys clothes, and often drives old farm vehicles. He wasn't used to going out to eat or to concerts, preferring to relax at home on his time off. He's in a good financial position because of that. I was in the process of paying off credit card debt from my stupid spending habits in my 20's, plus student loans. I knew we were in for some conflict in that area.

Concerned that Rick be able to "leave his father and mother and cleave to his wife" (Gen 2:24), I was reticent to live close them for our first few years of marriage. I liked them, but I was aware of how involved they were in each other's lives and didn't want to create unhealthy habits early on. I also figured that I was moving over 400 miles from home for him, so he should be able to manage moving five miles away for me. As we discussed our options, Rick kept going back to the hassle it would be for him to drive back and forth every day from the farm. If we lived close by, he could come and go throughout the day with ease. If he needed to check on the horse at night, it wouldn't be a big deal to run down the road for five minutes. All I could foresee were long evenings alone in our house while Rick did whatever his dad wanted him to do. He thought the days at home alone while he was at the farm were what would make me lonely.

After lots of discussion and boundary-setting, I agreed to move into a house on the farm. To help me feel at home, his parents offered to remodel it to suit my style. During our engagement, I got to choose house details like paint colors and flooring. In one visit, I met with a kitchen designer and picked out cabinets, counter tops, knobs and drawer pulls. We went to the paint store and I chose paint colors for each room. Next, we decided on flooring. Then I went home, hoping the finished product would work. Thankfully, it's gorgeous and I love it to this day. But it wasn't easy to convince Rick that we should paint the 1950's woodwork that had taken on a distinctly orange tone. He was used to natural wood tones, carpet, and linoleum. I wanted white trim, ceramic tile, and shiny hardwood floors.

My parents remodeled most of the houses we lived in. They flipped houses and built church buildings from the ground up. I'd been there every step of the way, holding drywall in place while Dad screwed it to the studs. I'd helped my dad install counter tops, drive nails, paint walls, and anything else he thought I could do. I brought him tools when he worked on our cars, had been taught to change oil and tires, and drove a stick shift car aggressively. I've helped Mom recover chairs, install ceiling fans, and move our household many times.

Rick and his dad had a hard time believing me when I said the tile I wanted to install in our three-seasons-room wouldn't crack. They argued with me about how easy it'd be to close in a closet on one wall and open up the space in the room that backed up to it. When I insisted that my kitchen have a dishwasher, Rick didn't agree. His parents had a dishwasher, but it hadn't worked in years, and he didn't mind hand-washing dishes.

I said, "It's fine for three adults, but when you add in babies and toddlers, bottles and sippy cups, and three meals a day while feeding, changing, and caring for little people - it's different."

Rick bought a dishwasher without another word.

With all our differences, anxiety threatened me. I'd pray, begging God for clear direction. I was suspicious that Rick wasn't as good as he appeared and had some dark, hidden secret. As great as Rick seemed, I wanted to make sure we were actually right for one another. Would he always laugh at my ideas and think they were ridiculous? Would he always dismiss my experience as negligible, even when this woman knew more about a subject than he did? Was he a misogynist?

Peace would return then as I heard God reassure me over and over that He was leading me into a safe place, a stable place, a place of still water and green pastures. He reassured me that Rick's parents were wonderful people who cared deeply for their son and I could trust them. God reminded me that He gives His children good gifts. He brought to mind the verse He'd lit up for me years ago, "You will live in houses you did not build and eat from vineyards you did not plant."

Deuteronomy 6:10-12, referring to the Israelites after they were finally able to stop wandering in the wilderness (as I felt I'd been doing for so long), says,

> "When the Lord your God brings you into the land he
> swore to your fathers, to Abraham, Isaac and Jacob,
> to give you – a land with large, flourishing cities you
> did not build, houses filled with all kinds of good
> things you did not provide, wells you did not dig,
> and vineyards and olive groves you did not plant-
> then when you eat and are satisfied, be careful that
> you do not forget the Lord, who brought you out of
> Egypt, out of the land of slavery" (NIV).

My heart always swelled with this promise when I read the words as a single woman, wondering how long I'd have to wander in the desert before God would lead me to the promised land of marriage, children, and a home of my own. His farm had a grape arbor that Rick's mom uses to make delicious grape juice. There's a garden, water from a well, and natural springs on the property.

Despite the stress, we worked it out. On the morning of December 30, 2011, I awoke with a smile. I checked my heart, searching for any hint of misgiving or fear about marrying Rick. There was plenty of anxiety and concern about the details of our wedding day, about the move away from

Nashville, and about leaving my friends, but there was nothing holding me back from becoming his wife. Of that I was sure. Complications from trying to pull off a huge event on a limited budget swirled around me, but my heart was at peace in my choice to marry this man.

In fact, I'll jump ahead a bit here and share a story from our first days at home that strikes me as funny – now. When we first got back from our honeymoon, Rick didn't move many of his things into our house. He left nearly everything at his parents' house in his old room. He'd get up and eat breakfast in the morning, then go over there to discuss the plans for the day. After working all day, he'd go back to their house, take a shower, change into clean clothes, and then come home to me. He still parked his truck in their garage. I talked to him about it, but he didn't seem to get my point. In fact, as he reads this part with me today, he doesn't remember the story the same way I do. But since this is my book...

He made excuses like he didn't want to get our bathroom dirty after work, but we had a bathroom in the basement for the very purpose of cleaning up after a day of working in the field. Offended that he still hadn't moved his things to our house, one day I locked all the doors. When he came home, he was surprised to find that he couldn't get in. He had a house key, but he didn't carry it with him while he was farming. He banged on the door. I didn't make a move. He rang the doorbell. I waited. He rang again. Finally, I made my way slowly to the door, opened it an inch, and said, "May I help you, sir?"

He was totally confused. I explained to him that I lived in that house alone and needed to be cautious not to let a stranger in. He got the point. The next day he moved most of his things over. Within a short time, he had officially moved into our house. (Although I'm pretty sure he still has a few things at his parents' house today.)

But, back to Nashville! We got married on a Friday evening at the church I had worked in and still attended. It was important to us to include our family and friends in the celebration. We'd waited so long to find each other, we wanted a big party to celebrate with those who had waited and prayed with us for so many years. We opened the church's gorgeous play area with babysitters for the kids and laid out a holiday feast. My friend Reneé sang with her smoky voice – love songs and songs of praise to God for bringing us together at last. My pastor performed the ceremony, and my sister and friends stood beside me. My precious niece was our flower girl and she did her best to keep the congregation entertained, pulling up her dress, yanking up her tights, dramatically lip syncing with the soloist, and motioning for her grandma to come up on stage with her.

While we took pictures, my brother sang and played his guitar and guests mingled and ate light refreshments. The decorations created a winter wonderland – flocked Christmas trees, candles, snowflakes, and lots of shimmer and shine. My dress delighted me, simple and elegant with sparkly silver spaghetti straps and a few silver embellishments. Rick and his groomsmen wore light gray suits and my bridesmaids wore long, elegant, silver gowns. My sister was my matron of honor and with her tall, slim frame and dark brown hair, she stood out in a gold dress.

Rick and I were the last guests to leave that night. I always thought I'd want to be the first one to leave my wedding reception, anticipating the night to come. And I was anticipating it, but we had so many guests from out of town that had come for the wedding and we wanted to talk to them all. We were probably both also feeling a little nervous.

When we arrived in our hotel room that night, it was decorated with rose petals and candles. Our luggage had already been delivered and we spotted chocolate covered strawberries and champagne. I was so impressed, soaking up the romance and Rick's thoughtfulness. Then Rick laughed and told me he had nothing to do with it. His brother and sister-in-law had done all of that on their own. It wasn't the first time I realized that my husband was honest to a fault. It would have meant so much to me if he'd kept his mouth shut and accepted my gratitude, but that isn't him. He couldn't start off our marriage with a lie.

The months leading up to our wedding had been stressful for us both, so the next day we left for what I thought would be a perfect, restful week in the mountains of Tennessee. I didn't know my new husband well enough yet to understand that a restful vacation was a completely foreign concept to him. His annual "vacations" to Guatemala centered on work and sacrifice, eating strange food and sweating all day and night. He hadn't been on an actual vacation since he was a young boy. While I was trying to sleep in, he jumped out of bed in the morning, ready to tackle the day. When I didn't, he made my coffee and brought it to me in bed. When I invited him back to bed, he politely declined and asked if I wanted to go for a hike. It was January in the mountains. No, thank you.

We'd disagreed plenty of times before, but we had our first big fight that week. Rick's almost complete inability to say anything he doesn't believe is 100% true was eye-opening for me. When I asked him sensitive questions about how I looked or how he felt, he told me exactly what he thought and felt. It wasn't what I expected to hear and it really hurt my feelings. He was bewildered by my sensitivity.

I grabbed the car keys and my purse and left. I drove around for a while, crying and trying not to emotionally bleed to death. I ended up in the parking lot of a movie theater and thought I'd go in and watch a movie, let him wonder if I'd ever come back. It might help to put some distance between his words and my ears. As I sat there though, I heard God speak to me so clearly, "Go back."

"No way, God. Did you hear what he said to me? How can I ever go back? If You knew that's how he felt, why did You let me marry him?"

"Go back. NOW."

I put the car in gear and very slowly drove back, angry and reluctant and trying not to throw up. He was in the bathroom with the door locked when I returned. I sat on the couch, sulking. How could God expect this of me?

When he came out of the bathroom and around the couch, I looked up and almost choked. I didn't recognize him. He'd always had a short beard and mustache. I'd asked him several times to shave, but he always refused. In sorrow and repentance for how he'd hurt me, he'd shaved his face. He cried and apologized for his hurtful words. I forgave him, which didn't take away the hurt, but I learned not to ask him questions if I didn't want to know exactly what he thought.

My husband has two sisters, but he learned nothing from them about how to talk to women. It was like he'd grown up in a bubble. He had no idea what was acceptable to say to a woman. He always prided himself on his job as a farmer, stating boldly, "I'm no pretty boy." He was definitely rough around the edges. After seven years of marriage, I don't think I've ever asked him again, "How do I look?" Nope. I wait for him to compliment me if he feels like it.

After Tennessee, we flew to Costa Rica for 10 days. We'd found an awesome deal on the most amazing boutique hotel on the top of a mountain. It overlooked the ocean, and between the top of the mountain and the ocean was a rain forest full of exotic birds and animals. It was lush and stunning. Our room had a private balcony; none of the balconies were visible to the others. I was in heaven.

What we hadn't considered when we booked the hotel was that we were secluded on the top of the mountain and there were no restaurants or activities available to us besides the ones the hotel offered – unless we wanted to take a taxi into the little nearby town. The hotel had a private beach, hiking, a spa, and plenty of places to hang out during the day. It also had two restaurants – one more casual, and one more formal. The restaurants served amazing, unique dishes – and they weren't cheap.

My husband was not in heaven. He couldn't stand the idea of paying so much money for three meals a day, plus going on excursions that cost extra, and paying for a taxi to take us off the property. I had no idea what to do with him. I knew it wasn't that he didn't have the money and couldn't figure out what he expected. It never crossed my mind that his experience with travel was mostly mission work and youth group retreats. He'd never booked a full-service hotel or vacationed like that before. He had money because he rarely spent it on anything that wasn't a necessity, and I respected that about him.

After a couple of days of irritation that we'd reached a second location where we couldn't seem to relax and enjoy being together, we worked out a compromise that suited both of us. The next day, we took a taxi into town and spent the day exploring. Rick was surprisingly animated as we walked around the little town, pointing out things that reminded him of the place in Guatemala where he ministered. He seemed more comfortable there than in the nice hotel. We ate at a local restaurant and then went to a grocery store and bought snacks. We weren't sure what some of it was, but we made decent choices.

For the rest of our stay, we slept in and ate brunch, then had an early dinner. If we got hungry later, we had snacks in our room. We decided on the excursions that looked like the most fun to us and chose three. The last excursion was my favorite. We went on a waterfall hike, climbing through streams over rocks, climbing up the side of the waterfall with nothing but a rope to hold onto, and listened to a very interesting tour guide who drove us in and out of there on crazy roads.

We discovered a beach at the bottom of the mountain our hotel perched on. There was a shuttle to take us there, so we lounged in a private cabana. The scenery was breathtaking. One day we decided to skip the shuttle and hike down the mountain to the beach. I've been on plenty of hikes, so I wasn't worried about it. After we hunted around a bit for the beginning of the trail, we were surprised to find that it was not much of a trail at all. It was more like a narrow place where the grass had been worn away.

Some of it was at a dramatic angle with nothing to hold onto as we made our way down. I was up for the challenge, until I fell. It was near the top of the mountain and the trail there was so steep that I realized how easy it would be to lose my footing and really get hurt. From that point forward, my legs were rubber. My knee hurt from the fall. I went slowly and cautiously while my husband grinned and offered his hand.

At one point I lost my footing again. Frustrated and a little afraid, I sat down and had a pity party. Rick chuckled, which was not exactly a welcome response. When we started back again, we realized we were very close to the end. I was so happy to see the beach! We relaxed, charging piña coladas to our room and soaking up the sun, and then we rode the shuttle back up the mountain. Rick had timed our hike though, and all he could talk about was beating that time the next day. I invited him to try without me. I wanted to take a nap.

From that point forward, my husband challenged himself to beat his time every afternoon while I lay between the cool, crisp sheets and slept. We were both happy. He could do something physically challenging and I could have a little time alone. Ahhh....

We ended our honeymoon with three days in the Redwood Forest in northern California. We flew into Sacramento, and then drove up Highway 1 – along the coast. The Pacific coast was unlike anything I'd seen before. It was too cold to swim, but we enjoyed the scenery as we poked along in a rented red convertible. We had figured each other out more, learning that we didn't need to spend every second of every day together, and we were having fun.

At one stop along the way, we encountered a point where frustration set in again. We went to a restaurant and I couldn't figure out why Rick walked in and stopped in front of the door. He wouldn't walk up to the hostess station and request a table. He'd stammer about not getting in line before other people in the lobby or mumble something and I would get tired of it and go myself. I expected Rick to automatically take the role of leader. Because my personality is decisive and confident, he expected me to take over the role of leader. As we both stared at one another in frustration during a meal, I realized what was going on. I wanted to be a respectful wife and not run over him, but he has a more passive personality and at times he appreciates it when I take the lead.

Both of our fathers are strong leaders. They know what to do next, how to do it, and when it's the best time to go. We'd both grown up learning to let our fathers lead. There was no point in arguing. We had to go with the flow. It was necessary to our family dynamic that we do so.

There are no Christian resources that I've come across that address this issue between married couples. Husbands are declared to be the leaders and the ones who feel slighted when they don't have their wife's respect.

Wives are declared the followers and the ones who want to be loved. It's biblical. Husbands, love your wives as Christ loves the church. Wives, respect your husbands. (Ephesians 5)

But my husband wasn't comfortable getting a table in a restaurant. I didn't want to wait around forever (or more accurately, probably 30 seconds?) while he decided what to do. Our circumstances and personality traits make us who we are, and they help us know how to define our roles within OUR marriage.

I spoke to my mother about it, trying to quiet the rising frustration gathering in my throat. Very practically and with great wisdom, she said, "Kimberly, you're a leader. Rick is a follower. You lead." I couldn't believe it. My sweet, submissive mother, who had followed my dad's leading for years, told me to lead. I decided to try out her advice. When we walked into a restaurant, I looked to Rick to get us a table. If he didn't stride forward confidently, I took care of it. Not super romantic, ladies, I know. But it saved our relationship from years of frustration.

Concerned that it might be a sin to take the lead, I prayed about it. How could I accept a leadership role in our marriage when it's clearly the man's responsibility? God reminded me that Rick wanted me to lead in many areas. I wasn't actually *taking* the lead but following his lead by stepping into the role he wanted me to fill. I was leading with his blessing. He delegated that role to me, and I honored him by embracing it.

I consider the areas where Rick is the expert and has a strong opinion and step back in those times. He can be very opinionated and he's confident in what he knows well. It's not always obvious to me until I realize that he's struggling with me taking over his job. In those times, I've found that I can back off and he will take the reins. He does it well and gains confidence each time. It does my heart good to see the leader emerging in him. It also does my heart good to accept when he doesn't want to lead.

When it was all said and done – three weeks of honeymooning – we flew back to Nashville and my friend Shannan hosted a send-off party for us. Our parents had packed my things and had them delivered to our new home, so we only needed to put our luggage in the car when it was time to go. As we drove away from Nashville, my heart hurt a little. I was sad to say goodbye to so many dear friends, a good church, and the city I loved – but I was saying hello to the life I'd wanted for as long as I could remember. I was a wife. It was now possible to be a mother. I had a home waiting for me – decorated the way I wanted, waiting for me to put my touch on it. It was a good feeling.

We pulled into the driveway at Rick's parent's house first. After catching up with them, we went to see our house. The remodeling wasn't done yet, but it was ours and I wanted to stay there. We set my mattress up on the floor in the master bedroom and settled in. It was a few weeks before everything was finished, but soon it looked like a home. My home.

Rick's cousin Jon and his wife Jenny befriended me. Jenny came over and helped me unpack and set up the kitchen. I was still dealing with brain fog from the stress of all the new things happening and could not think straight. She laughed and went to work, deciding where things should go and reminding me of what I had in all those boxes.

Rick's family had thrown a kitchen shower for me during our engagement. It was through a popular gourmet kitchen company, so I was given a catalog and told to mark down what I wanted. I had gotten everything on the list, in multiples. The blessing of it put such joy in my heart. A couple years earlier, living in yet another home where I didn't need kitchen items, I had felt convicted to give it all away. The basement sat full of boxes of things I didn't need. I'd moved those boxes so many times, not opening them for many years. It was ridiculous. A friend needed kitchen supplies, so I passed them on to her. I heard God's word reminding me as I did so that He takes the little we have and turns it into much. I couldn't believe how much!

My kitchen was stocked with all kinds of awesome, brand new supplies. The paper finally came off our hardwood floors. We had a television, but no furniture yet. It would be a few weeks before the things we ordered got delivered. I decided to make do until that time by using a few of my old things.

Rick was out working, so I went down to the basement and located my four-foot-long folding table. It was heavy, but not big. I slid it over to the stairs, lifted it up on the staircase, then pushed it up. At the top of the stairs, I slid it into the living room and set it up. After I had it right where I wanted it, I very carefully picked up the large, flat-screen television and put it on the table. I plugged it in, turned it on, and felt very pleased with myself that I didn't have to view the TV on the floor any longer.

When Rick got home that night, I proudly showed him what I'd done. Instead of happy surprise, he got very upset. It was as angry as I'd ever seen him. Rick doesn't get upset with me about much, so this was new. He was furious that I'd taken a chance with the heavy table, thinking of what would've happened if I'd lost my grip on the stairs. He was aghast that I'd picked up the heavy TV and put it on the table. What if I'd dropped it? It was brand new and expensive.

I hadn't lost my grip or dropped the TV. It had all worked out fine. But Rick didn't see it that way. He felt like his job in our marriage was to lift heavy things and set up furniture. I tried to explain that I lived without anyone to do that for me for 18 years, so I'd learned to use my brain to maneuver hard situations like today. No, I wasn't strong enough to carry the table up the stairs, but I could certainly slide it. I wasn't strong enough to carry the TV across the room without dropping it, but I could lift it a short distance from the floor to the table top. Nothing I said mattered to him. We were married now and I was to let him do things like that in the future.

Okay.

For a long time after that, I wrestled with the idea of depending on him. My friend Shannan had gotten married when she was very young and had relied on her husband for all kinds of things. After 10 years of marriage, he was killed by a drunk driver. When he died, she had to deal with more than missing him and feeling sad. She had to deal with the shock of what it took to manage a household by herself. There was no one to carry heavy things for her. Many times I'd heard her exclaim about how hard it was to take care of the yard and her home alone. Her husband had taken care of all those things and she took it for granted. She looked forward to getting married again and appreciating the things her husband brought to the marriage.

I was used to doing those things by myself, so if Rick died, at least I wouldn't have that shock on top of everything else. I really didn't want to depend on him.

Every time Rick tried to do something for me, I balked. He persistently taught me trust as he easily depended on me to take care of things for him. After months of wrestling in my spirit, I finally decided that I had to learn to depend on him. I couldn't plan ahead for the possibility of being alone again. If he died, I would deal with the loss then. Until then, I had him right beside me, wanting to help. What a waste to not relax into his care and provision.

After I relaxed about that, I was amazed to find out how much easier life could be with him. There were things that never got done when I was on my own. Even though I thought I should get them done, they were so hard for me that I let them go. Those are the things that come easy to him.

Things that come so easy to me tend to be hard for him. We're a great team when each of us walks in our strengths and helps the other out.

Because I was 36 when we got married, I focused on the goal of having a baby as soon as possible. I knew so many couples who had faced infertility, and I needed to know that pregnancy was possible for us. I had researched all the ways to optimize our chances of conceiving, so Rick got to deal with my intensity right away in our marriage. In such a sensitive area. As usual, he handled me with patience and humor.

3

I WANTED TO DIE

Four months after we said I do, we saw that positive pregnancy test. I was elated. Rick was happy on the inside. I could hardly wait to tell everyone, but we kept it to ourselves for... oh? a day or two? I mean, we had to tell our parents. And my sister. And a couple of my friends. We did wait a while to announce it publicly, but I was so happy I thought I might float up into the air. I don't know how everyone didn't immediately guess.

Six weeks into the pregnancy, I threw up for the first time. I figured that a little nausea and vomiting were normal and was kind of pleased. It indicated a healthy pregnancy. But a week later, extreme nausea set in and I began throwing up everything I ate and drank, every day. If I didn't eat, I discovered something worse than vomiting – dry heaving.

I lay on the couch with a trash can beside me, which was one position where I didn't feel completely miserable. But if I had to get up to walk to the bathroom, I threw up once I got there. It was awful. I was too sick to clean up after myself and my whole body ached from retching. My new husband stoically took on the role of emptying the trash can when I threw up.

Friends had told me about how everything smelled bad to them when they were pregnant, and I thought it was cute. Oh, an extra sensitive sense of smell. That's adorable - until it happened to me. Everything stunk. The closets in my house smelled like dead bodies had been shut up inside them.

My kitchen smelled like trash. People who had recently eaten beef, whether they brushed their teeth or not, sent me running from the room due to their breath. No one else could smell those things, but I could smell when someone wore Depends. Strong smells caused me to gag and throw up.

I tried every old wives' tale remedy and nothing helped. My throat was raw with burns from stomach acid. I had no idea what acid reflux was or what was happening to me. When I asked my doctor if I could take Zantac, a stomach acid reducer, she looked at me oddly and shook her head. My sister finally said, "You are allowed to take Zantac while pregnant. I don't care what she said. You look it up, then you take some. This is ridiculous." I listened to her and Dr. Google told me it was safe. So, I took it. It helped a little, but not much. I later discovered that instead of asking my doctor about Zantac, I had accidentally said Xanax. My doctor didn't want me starting anti-anxiety medication while pregnant.

After week twelve, when I continued to throw up several times a day, I asked my doctor for some anti-nausea medication. She reluctantly agreed and prescribed Zofran. It did nothing for me. I called her back. She prescribed a stronger dose. Nothing. After eight weeks of constant vomiting, I was one step beyond desperate. I'd wanted to have a baby for as long as I could remember and had often joked that I'd have a smile on my face while my head was in the toilet, so happy to be pregnant. What a stupid thing to say.

I wanted to die. Horrible thoughts took over my brain. I could understand why women had abortions. The idea of having a miscarriage seemed like relief, except that I'd already worked so hard for 14 weeks to grow this child that I would be furious to have suffered for no reason. Friends came over to pray for me, I prayed for myself, and Rick pleaded with God to help. I threw up some more.

A chiropractor finally suggested that I take a stronger acid reducer that was safe for pregnancy. I tried to tell him that I didn't have acid reflux. I was clueless, but I figured it couldn't hurt. That ended the problem with my raw and burned throat. I thought that this baby better have a lot of hair because I'd heard that was the cause of pregnancy reflux.

My mom's family came into town for a little reunion and of course, I was in the bathroom loudly retching after every meal. My aunt asked me about Zofran and I told her it wasn't helping. She'd taken Zofran during her recent chemotherapy treatment for breast cancer and hadn't thrown up once. When I questioned her about it, she told me she took it like clockwork, every eight hours. She never missed one dose and it worked

48

perfectly. I had nothing to lose, so I set alarms on my phone and started taking it every eight hours. Within a day, the constant nausea was gone.

As soon as I got one issue resolved, new issues popped up. I started laughing hysterically one day when sciatica kicked in and the chiropractor told me it was due to the pregnancy weight gain. I was five months pregnant and I'd gained two pounds. Mom told me to stop thinking about it and go for a walk. I tried to ignore it and after a few minutes, I fell down. Sciatica made my leg go completely numb when I tried to stand on it for long. After that I had a mole removed because it was really bothering me. It was skin cancer.

My body does not like pregnancy.

Adding insult to injury, when I was 28 weeks pregnant, I did the blood glucose test and it became clear that I had gestational diabetes. That began the four times daily finger pricks (which hurt, no matter what anyone says), blood testing, and carbohydrate counting. I wrote down everything I ate, balancing protein and carbohydrates. I was grumpy about it, but as soon as I started doing it, I felt better.

I discovered that people are largely dismissive of those who have difficult pregnancies. My sister reminds me that I was once one of them, unsympathetic to her misery because she had what I so badly wanted and I wasn't about to feel sorry for her. They think everyone goes through what you're going through and you're just kind of a wimp. Even my husband thought he could have handled it better than me. However, I've tweezed some of his eyebrow hairs and learned how he responds to that kind of pain, so I'm pretty sure he'd be singing a different tune if pregnancy ever happened to him. I've also apologized profusely to my sister for my jealous dismissal of her pregnancy difficulties.

During my pregnancy, Mom found out she had breast cancer. Her sister had recently finished her breast cancer treatment and two other sisters found out they had breast cancer. Four sisters had breast cancer in a two-year time span. Mom had two kinds of cancer, so it required two kinds of treatment. My parents were also facing significant difficulties beyond cancer, and I hurt so much for them.

On the day of Mom's double mastectomy, I had a checkup and my blood pressure was high. I explained the circumstances, but my doctor wasn't impressed. I started having weekly non-stress tests (NST's), then twice weekly. My blood pressure continued to be higher than she wanted to see, so I ended up on modified bed rest. I spent the last six weeks of my pregnancy on the couch and at doctor appointments – NSTs on Mondays, doctor visits on Wednesdays, and NSTs on Fridays. Otherwise, I was only allowed to leave the house once a week for church. My closest friends and my sister were far away. Mom was suffering all the side effects of chemo and I was terribly worried about her. I cried a lot.

At 39 weeks, my blood pressure rose significantly and the doctor decided to induce me. It took about 26 hours, but when the doctor announced, "It's a girl!" I nearly burst with joy. I finally had my beautiful daughter in my arms. She was perfect. We named her Eliana (pronounced Ellie-Ah-na) Rose, which means "my God has answered with a beautiful flower." Her first name is a variation of my mom's name, Elaine, and her middle name is the same as Rick's mom's middle name.) How much more fitting could a name have been?

Three minutes before she was born, I was screaming, "Why does this hurt so much?!" But when she was placed on my chest and I looked at her squishy little face, every bit of love came rushing in. I was high, completely overwhelmed with a love I could never adequately describe. She was worth every bit of misery. As we gazed down on our precious daughter - 7 pounds, 7 ounces, and 21 inches that contained my deepest dreams come true - I looked up at Rick and said, "Let's do it again."

He looked at me like I was crazy, but I meant every word. For the first two weeks of Eliana's life, I sat on the couch and held her. I admired every part of her, wiping happy tears that she was finally mine. Mom had chemo scheduled for the week she was born, so she couldn't be with me until a week later. My parents came for Christmas and Mom said, "You're going to have to put her down sometime, you know." One day, yes, but babies don't keep. While I could, I was content to hold her.

I don't remember a more joyful or peaceful time in my life than those first few months after she was born. There were hard things that happened, including surgery to remove skin cancer, but I was in such a daze of happiness that it didn't really faze me. I'd been concerned that the pregnancy sickness would last forever, but from the moment she was born it left. After I recovered from the delivery, I felt fantastic. It felt like something heavy had been pushing down on me for months and had suddenly lifted, causing me to float up in the air freely.

The only real sadness I remember is that when she was born, I didn't have any of the people who understood how much it meant to me nearby. Those who had prayed with me for so many years weren't around to savor the depth of joy I felt with me. My closest friends were in Nashville, my sister couldn't come until Eliana was six weeks old because of work, and

Mom was sick. They all eventually came and were properly impressed, but I felt like I wanted to hold her in the air like Simba, but I had no rock to stand on.

Rick's parents were helpful with Eliana, and they lived so close that it was easy to drop her off when we needed to go somewhere. Grandma happily watched her while I got groceries and ran errands. Rick got up in the night when she cried, changed her diaper, and brought her to me to nurse. When she finished, he put her back in her crib. He didn't have much experience with babies, but I was determined that he would learn. He was the daddy and he needed to be able to take care of his babies. Even though it was hard, I left the room and let them figure it out when she cried because she preferred me.

One day, Rick looked up at me with a tender expression and said, "Thank you for trusting me with her."

He didn't have to say more. I understood. He grew up in a home that was overshadowed by tragedy, so they are very cautious people. "An ounce of prevention is worth a ton of cure" is one of their favorite sayings. A tiny, fragile baby in the hands of a rough farmer might have led some mothers to be concerned, but he was so careful and tender with her. I had nothing to fear. It wasn't long before her favorite place to sleep was with her head on his shoulder.

I stopped nursing Eliana when she was six months old so I could get pregnant again. We both cried for the first two weeks she was weaned, but I knew I made the right decision. Seven months after Eliana was born, we found out we were expecting again. We were delighted, but also aware of what was likely to happen again.

I worked like crazy, freezing meals and getting everything in order that I possibly could before sickness set in. I was very sick again. The whole time. Eliana was the sweetest little caretaker though. When I got sick, she'd come lay her head on me and pat me. She was a little slice of heaven and I prayed that she would love her baby brother and not feel jealous.

Again, I had gestational diabetes. On the day the baby was born, I'd only gained five pounds. My blood pressure went up some, but I had a new doctor who called me Mrs. Wisdom. He allowed me to go three days over my due date before he suggested induction. Because my pregnancy with Charlie came with new and terrible difficulties that only having him would allow me escape, I gladly went in for the induction, which went much faster than the first. Within a few hours, we heard the beautiful words, "It's a boy!"

Charlie Dean was 8 pounds and 12 ounces and 21.5 inches long. He was beautiful. Charlie is one of the friendliest names on earth. It means "free man". Dean is someone able to handle responsibility, like a university dean, or the head of a religious institution. I liked the combination of the names – a responsible, friendly, and free man! "So if the Son sets you free, you will be free indeed" (John 8:36, NIV). His middle name is the same as his Grandpa Wyse.

With Eliana, the epidural had been given late and not fully worked. This time the epidural went in too far and gave me a spinal headache. During labor and delivery, I could barely lift my head off the pillow, lying flat for some relief from the headache. After he was born, I could barely open my eyes to look at him, so I let my mom hold him minutes after he was born. I was happy to see this baby in her arms before he was an hour old. Mom had been declared cancer-free and it felt like an appropriate celebration.

God answered my prayers. Eliana adored her brother from the moment she saw him and to this day those two are peas in a pod. They fight like professionals, but they are truly best friends. I love the way they love one another, play together, defend each other, and comfort one another. Watching their relationship is one of the great joys of my life.

We brought Charlie home from the hospital while I still tried to recover from the headache and childbirth. While I sat on the couch holding him, I tried to pay attention to Eliana too. I couldn't explain it, but I was very emotional and concerned that I had displaced Eliana. She adored her brother, but I couldn't give her the time and energy I wanted to give her. I hired a teenager from church to come over and play with her. I watched them having a big time in the yard while I gave Charlie a bath in the sink. I had everything I'd ever wanted, but at that moment I wanted to be the one teaching my daughter how to use the new slide we'd gotten her.

Up until that point, I'd been the one to teach her all the new things she'd learned. (I'm sure Rick and his parents helped with that, but I considered them to be an extension of me.) Suddenly, I couldn't do everything for her. It was very painful. I had to shift my perspective so I didn't settle into depression. I decided that I would embrace all the gifts my children's caregivers could bring into their lives. The teenager who was playing on the new slide was carefree and silly. She picked grass and threw it in the air. She dug in the gravel driveway with Eliana, getting dirt under her fingernails. I would never do those things. I loved that Eliana had the opportunity to be spontaneous and get dirty.

When Charlie was about two weeks old, my father-in-law noticed that I had not recovered as well as we'd all hoped. He came over to talk to me about an idea he had. He said that when he was young, mothers always had helpers when they had babies. No mother was expected to recover from childbirth, take care of a newborn, and take care of the house and other children all on her own. My husband had been a big help, but it was getting to be his busy season and he wouldn't be around much. He said, "I hope I'm not overstepping my bounds, but would you mind if I found someone to help you out? If you'd trust me to find someone, I'd be glad to make that your baby gift."

Relief swept over me and I agreed quickly. Rick's dad found a jewel named Kristina to help us. What started as four weeks has turned into five years. Our amazing Kristina is now 21. She comes to our house three to four days a week and keeps us running smoothly. I love the godly, gracious influence she has on our children. She's the picture of modesty, humility, and fun – in a lovely package. She has won all our hearts. She got us through that first year of craziness without breaking a sweat. When things started to calm down a little, she worked fewer hours and I knew she'd become a luxury. We had no idea how much we'd come to need her again though.

Eliana and Charlie adore Kristina and she has taught them so much. She even potty trained them! We have delighted in the things they've achieved, smiling as they grow and hit milestones in an appropriate time. Rick and I are in awe of their perfect little bodies, their bright minds, and their individual personalities. They keep us laughing and my days are more meaningful than I even imagined they would be. (Most of the time. But for real, they can be little turkeys too.)

Eliana is full of energy and seems to never stop moving until the moment she falls asleep at night. She loves to run and tries to convince me that running is fun. When she was 18 months old, she saw a gymnastics competition where Simone Biles flew through the air on the uneven bars. Eliana never paid much attention to the television, but she saw that. She stopped her shenanigans and stared at the gymnast, then she started shouting, "And me! And me!" For weeks she ran around the living room shouting, "Me 'Mone Bibles!" I signed her up for Mommy and Me gymnastics soon after that and she hasn't stopped doing gymnastics since.

That little stinker could understand everything I had to say by the time she was 11 months old, and she started the "terrible twos" at that age. I was in shock and it took me a while to figure out what was going on. When she turned two, she immediately turned back into little baby sweetness, the frustration of the tiny rebellion she'd staged finally done. When she started kindergarten in the fall of 2018, she could speak as clearly as any adult, but she didn't talk very much until she was over two years old. We were concerned enough that we'd gotten a referral to a speech therapist but decided to wait a little while before we called.

It makes me laugh when I look back at that time. When she finally began talking, there was no stopping her. She used complete sentences and compound words almost as soon as she started talking. It's hard to even remember the days when she grunted everything she wanted and felt. Is it any wonder that the first negative report home from kindergarten was that she talked when she was supposed to be quiet? (If you know me at all, you'll know I couldn't really fault her. My parents report the same thing about me.)

Charlie, on the other hand, said his first words when he was eight months old. I had taught Eliana a little sign language at that age, so I thought I'd teach Charlie. One day I repeatedly showed him the sign for "all done." He flatly refused to do it, crawling around the house after me. Finally, he sat up and said as clearly as could be, "All done." Then He repeated it for the rest of the afternoon. His spoken language skills were far advanced, but he couldn't understand what I said to him.

Although Charlie talked early, he's quieter than his big sister. He's probably trying to get a word in edgewise. Charlie is a tender-hearted little guy. He will do about anything to accommodate his sister, until he won't, and that's when the fighting starts. Eliana gets so upset on the rare occasions that he doesn't let her boss him around. He's easy-going enough that he doesn't mind letting her be in charge, but when he feels strongly about something no one can change his mind. (He might be a little like his daddy?)

The other day Eliana wouldn't stop talking and Charlie had something to say. Very loudly to drown out his sister, he cried, "ELLLL-EEEE-AHHH-NA!" Everyone in the room got quiet and looked at him (most of us in amusement). He breathed a sigh of relief and said, "I want to say something!" And then he proceeded to tell us something that he thought was very important to say at that moment. I think it was about a toy. All the adults chuckled and our friend said sarcastically, "Nah, he's not a leader. He's shy."

Charlie can appear shy, but mainly he's observing his world and quietly drawing conclusions. He thinks about things until he's ready to share

54

them, which can make him appear to be shy. He's mechanically minded and at four years old could either fix broken things or offer a good suggestion for how to fix it. He gets underneath toys and takes them apart to see how they're made. He wants to understand how things work and the reasoning behind decisions we make.

He has plenty of energy, but his big sister is so overly energetic (and loud) that he seems relaxed. He started climbing on difficult things before he could even walk, making his way to the top where he'd dance a jig and scare me to death. He never fell when he was doing dangerous things though. We signed him up for a Little Ninjas class when he turned three. He has mastered the obstacle course training class and can't wait until he turns five and can go to the class for five and six-year-old boys.

If you ask Charlie what he wants to be when he grows up, he will immediately tell you, "A dad!" I've asked him if he wants to be a farmer, or maybe a fireman, or a pastor/writer, he shrugs. Maybe. When he's a dad he also plans to wear high socks, because apparently that's what dad's do.

Eliana will tell you that she wants to be a babysitter and a mom when she grows up. She does well in school, but her true love is athletics. She is currently asking me to take her out of her beloved gymnastics class because she wants to play basketball. Oh, and softball. Don't forget soccer. And mom, can I go to cheerleader camp too? I don't think I ever had that kind of energy and I admire it in her. But goodness, that child can wear me out!

I have to laugh when I think about how different they are from one another, but how close they are. We're planning for Charlie to start kindergarten in 2019, so they should only be one year apart all the way through school. We love it that they can be so close and support one another. That relationship has been especially helpful in the last several years.

When things started to settle down after that first year, both kids talking and walking, I got a little restless. I considered trying to teach English or composition at the community college. I looked into a second master's degree in creative writing, or maybe even counseling. I thought about trying to start a business in things I'd already been trained to do – like life coaching or spiritual direction. I went to a writer's conference before I knew I was pregnant with Charlie and started to work on becoming a professional freelance writer, but pregnancy sickness took over those ideas. I didn't have the motivation to finish a book. So many were started, but I lost interest before I got far.

I looked into returning to ministry, exploring my options for part-time pastoral work in the area. A job opened up and seemed like a good opportunity, so I went through a lengthy and challenging application process. I invested a lot of time and resources jumping through hoops to provide an acceptable application, only to be told that although I was well-qualified and had done nothing wrong, they were continuing their search. The sting of this rejection was deep. I was deeply hurt and frustrated.

Rick and I decided it would be good to get away for a few days and get some fresh perspective, so we went on a delayed anniversary trip to Chicago. It was February and we spent a few freezing days walking around the windy city, eating in yummy restaurants, and enjoying a posh hotel I found for a ridiculously low price. We watched a marathon of home remodeling shows on HGTV (we don't have cable at home, so it was a treat) and considered the idea of trying to have another baby. We agreed that our life was almost perfect with Eliana and Charlie, so we wouldn't be upset if we couldn't have another baby. But maybe we could?

We were relaxed and comfortable together, patting ourselves on the back for four good years of marriage. We went shopping and toured the Cultural Center where we giggled about toilet bowl covers stapled to the wall as art. We laughed as we tried to figure out how Uber works, feeling like country bumpkins. I'd been out of the city for long enough to feel awkward at how much things had changed while my quiet country life remained the same. It was a good trip and exactly what we needed to regroup.

Later that year, we decided that it was time to find a church that was more suited to the needs of our entire family. Rick had always attended the same church and he was happy there, but I found it difficult to fit in to the church culture. The congregation had a hard time adjusting to Rick's new role as husband and father, and while I had made some friends there, it was important to go somewhere that felt like home to both of us. We visited a number of churches in the area and really enjoyed several of them. When we found the church that was a good fit, it was a relief.

One of the things we immediately loved there was that the pastor preached a whole series of sermons on love, so we got to enjoy messages on marriage and relationships in general. We were challenged and left with things to discuss all the way home. We realized that we'd never heard a sermon about marriage in the entire time we'd been together and we were starving for it.

Even though it seemed good to both of us, Rick had a hard time leaving his home church. We met with the pastors and explained why we were visiting. We told them that Rick wasn't quite ready to leave his church, but I needed something different. I shared with them that I didn't want to become a member unless we could do it as a family, and I wouldn't force my husband to comply with my will. I wanted him to know it was the right decision also.

Every week I filled out the prayer request form at church with the words, "unity in our marriage." It seemed like a wild request, one that might never happen, but I had to ask. I wanted us to be on the same page about church. I didn't want Rick to comply with my wishes just to keep the peace. The change came slowly, but it was more of a roller coaster ride than I could have ever known.

In February of 2016, I went to my doctor, aching, in pain, limping, and miserable with myself for gaining weight. I'd been having fairly regular anxiety attacks. She ran tests and poked around but declared me perfectly healthy and in need of a vacation. She said I was under excessive stress. My chiropractor agreed, suggesting a significant change to my diet. She said, "You need to focus your diet on healthy meats, vegetables, and a little fruit. Avoid white carbs, sugar, and processed food. Your body is full of inflammation."

Rick agreed and we booked a large cabin in Gatlinburg, TN, for a whole week. We convinced Kristina to come with us. It was the end of March, 2016. We spent an entire week doing the unimaginable – sleeping through the night without interruption! Kristina and the kids slept on the lower level of the cabin where there was a game room and television. Rick and I had a master suite on the main floor. I turned off all my social media, which had been leading me to feel jealous and lonely. While we were there, I looked into anti-inflammatory diets and made a plan to change my diet when I got home.

That trip was so fun and relaxing that I cried when we left, wishing we could stay another week. I hadn't slept well in several years and the ability to sleep for eight uninterrupted hours a night for a week had been so refreshing. The break from social media cleared my mind and reminded me to focus on what I had – a giving and tender husband who loved me, a beautiful daughter, a darling son, and an awesome nanny! I was blessed! I saved our vacation photos until we got home, only posting them online when I was ready to wade into the complications of social media again. I made a promise to myself that I'd hide or delete anyone who stirred up jealousy or negative feelings in me. I was not going to allow Facebook to steal my joy. For the next few weeks, I boldly cut down my friend list and it worked.

I spent the next several months following a paleo diet that consisted only of lean, high-quality meat and eggs, vegetables, a little fruit, and some nuts. I drank water and black coffee. By the third week I had a revelation. The anxiety attacks I'd been having were gone. That was worth every sacrifice.

It took about four months for my energy to return. I found that I could easily bend at the knees and get back up with no problem, I wasn't limping any longer, and I felt great. I'd lost some weight too. I fully intended to stick with it for the rest of my life, allowing myself to have food freedom and eat other things when it was worth it to me, but all this healthy living did one more thing for me: I was pregnant. I couldn't guess how valuable my new knowledge of an anti-inflammatory diet would be for my baby.

4

LIFE & HEALTH, JOY & PEACE

Rick and I had been open to the idea of another baby for a while. After that vacation to Gatlinburg, I did everything I knew to do to get my body in the best condition it could be before I got pregnant the third time. I exercised regularly, getting the kids involved as we set up "yoda mats" (I couldn't bring myself to correct them) on the living room floor and did Pilates videos, and I worked with my doctor, a chiropractor, and a natural health practitioner to get healthy. Through their help and my diet changes, my tests came back with everything in normal ranges and lacking no nutrients whatsoever.

I'd been concerned about diabetes with the two diabetic pregnancies, but even those numbers were good. I took a high-quality multivitamin that contained folate. In addition to the diet changes, I worked on gut health by drinking Kombucha tea and eating Greek yogurt, which are full of healthy probiotics.

At 40 years old, I was in the best condition I'd been in for as long as I could remember. I worked hard to focus on my health. I exercised regularly, doing things I hadn't been able to do before (like jogging), ate whole and nutritious foods, slept pretty well for a mom with two toddlers, and felt great. I felt very hopeful that the third pregnancy would be the one I'd enjoy.

On the weekend we found out we were expecting, we did the unheard of and skipped church. Rick decided that we needed to do some fun things together as a family before the sickness set in. We spent a glorious July day at the zoo, soaking up the sun. I remember thinking that they were at the absolute height of their cuteness at ages two and three. We felt so blessed and lucky to have them. I spent the next two weeks preparing healthy, simple meals and freezing the leftovers for what I hoped wasn't to come.

What very few people knew was that in my heart I was fighting a battle. I hid it well, concerned that I was a little crazy, but from the moment the test came back positive, I couldn't shake the feeling that something was terribly wrong with this baby. The joy and excitement that had come with the first two pregnancies did not come with the third. I prayed hard, thanked God for the gift of another child, and tried to shake the feeling. Rick and I had made this decision together, asked God for another child, and I'd done everything I knew to do to prepare for it. Why wasn't it the amazing news I wanted to hear?

I tried to tell Rick, hinting around at the edges of what I felt. He told me that I was hormonal with the new pregnancy, kind of like how I needed to eat the very second I felt any kind of hunger and went a little nuts until I got food. I whispered my terrible thoughts to my dear friend Jenn, a licensed marriage and family therapist, and she replied confidently, "Hormones! You can't rely on your emotions right now. Your body is going through so much right now. Just relax."

I really hoped she was right, but when I couldn't get the thoughts to go away after nearly two weeks, I prayed a gut-wrenching prayer.

"Lord, if there is something terribly wrong with this baby, then I offer it back to you. I can't handle a disabled child. I'm sorry I was greedy or dissatisfied with the two amazing children You gave me."

The next day, almost unable to function for the fear I felt, I found myself sitting in the car in a parking lot, totally melting down. I felt like someone had their hands on my shoulders, pressing me into the dirt. Something was wrong and it was my fault and I'd ruined our perfect lives. I sobbed and bargained and pleaded with God to fix it. Please, Lord! How casual had I been with our blessed and easy life? Why had I decided to make it hard? I felt terrified and alone.

Finally, I calmed down enough to drive home, but it wasn't until I got in the shower later that day that peace finally came. As I continued my silent cries to God for help, suddenly my hand flew to my belly and the words, "Life and health, joy and peace" shot through all my anguish like a sword, separating bone and marrow. I dropped to my knees, humbled before the God who heard my cries and answered. As water poured around my face and washed away my tears, I repeated the words, feeling the calm and embracing this new life inside me. Throughout the entire pregnancy the fear whispered to me, but every time it got loud I spoke the words God had given me as a reminder and as a prayer, "Life and health, joy and peace."

We made an appointment with a midwife at our local health center. After two failed epidurals and two inductions, I hoped for a different experience this time. I wanted to wait until the baby came on its own; a simple and natural birth. I was hopeful that she'd take me on, even with my history.

I was about eight weeks pregnant the first time we met. I down played the concerns my doctors had during the last two pregnancies; explaining my healthy lifestyle and desire for everything to be as natural as possible. She said she would do her best to work with me, and I felt relieved.

Then she told me that we needed to schedule the blood work. She handed me a couple flyers with the names of different tests on them. Non-invasive prenatal testing. We needed to decide which test we wanted. She explained that it was to check for birth defects and that I could even find out the gender of the baby extra early.

We'd had a similar conversation twice before with doctors but had declined both times. Those doctors had shrugged, one had even laughed because the young people who didn't need it often wanted it and the couples who had higher odds of problems declined them. We told her we wanted to be surprised by the gender, and we weren't interested in the blood work. The look she gave us was something like a mix of pity and disbelief.

"With your ages and history, you need the blood work."

We explained that we'd already decided that we wouldn't terminate the pregnancy under any condition. With my anxiety issues, I didn't want to have a false positive, then worry the entire time and ruin the pregnancy. I'd heard all about the false positives. A good friend had been told that her daughter didn't have a brain. When she refused to terminate, her doctor was so awful that she found one who would work with her. They did extra monitoring, so she was able to see her daughter's brain form like normal (a little later than it should) and delivered a very healthy, precocious little girl. My precocious little friend Stefanie is thriving in middle school today and wouldn't be alive if her mama had listened to that doctor.

My midwife said that we must not realize everything that can happen and how bad it can be. She was right. We didn't realize, but we had a good idea.

When I was pregnant with Eliana, a childhood friend was also pregnant. We were about the same age. As Eliana was growing beautifully, despite all my challenges, her daughter was diagnosed with Trisomy 13. She had so many medical problems that it was unlikely she'd make it to birth and would have little quality of life if she did. Maribeth and Jeremy loved their precious girl through all the heartache and challenges. They prayed for healing, allowed the pregnancy to continue, and did all they could to give their daughter a chance at life. Maribeth carried her baby until almost 36 weeks. Then the baby stopped moving inside her and they knew she was gone. They went to the hospital and she delivered her baby sleeping. They named her Abbie Ann.

I told her that I'd seen a beautiful vision of grace and peace in my, and I knew what was possible. She agreed then that I certainly understood what I faced. She tried one more time to convince me, saying that if there were problems then we would at least know how to treat them and give our baby the best chance at life. I then made a decision I question to this day. I asked her if that would be obvious in the 20-week ultrasound and she agreed that anything severe should be. But 20 weeks was getting very close to the deadline for termination, so if we found problems we'd have to decide quickly. I stated very firmly, "Termination is NOT an option."

At the time, I feared a false positive and all the anxiety that would accompany it more than I understood the need to provide proper medical care to a baby growing with possibly life-threatening issues. If I ever were to conceive again, I would have the testing so I could provide the best possible care for my unborn child.

What we understood at the time was that a level two ultrasound with a maternal fetal medicine doctor would provide the information we needed. The midwife then told us not to tell anyone about the pregnancy yet because miscarriage is more likely before 12 weeks. In fact, it would be best to wait until 14 weeks to share the news. But I had been told, "Life and health, joy and peace," so we waited another week or two and then shared the news.

In spite of my efforts to get healthy, I was again struck with severe morning sickness and gestational diabetes. The vomiting began around 10 weeks this time, and I was diagnosed with gestational diabetes at 14 weeks. I immediately started testing my blood, logging my food, counting carbs and protein, and trying to figure out how to keep my blood sugar down. I'd been able to control it through diet alone before, but this one was different. If I wanted to have good numbers, I couldn't eat any carbs at all. I restricted them almost entirely, but still got higher numbers than they wanted to see. It was so strange to me because the standards had changed and what they considered acceptable with the first two was now considered high.

I met with the dietician and she told me that vegetables didn't count as carbs. I must have 45 grams of carbs at each snack and 60 at each meal. A total of about 300 grams of non-vegetable carbs a day! Diabetes is carbohydrate intolerance, so why did they want me to eat so many carbs? I decided to ignore their rules and do things exactly as I had with the other two. Despite my extreme restrictions, my blood sugar was rarely below the expected level for this pregnancy. Again, I gained very little weight.

On the day of my 20-week ultrasound, I was so full of fear that I felt like I was trying to walk through mud. My legs wouldn't move. It took every bit of energy I had to get dressed. I desperately wanted to cancel the appointment, but Rick made sure I got there. The baby was an active one! It moved so much that the technician had a hard time getting the pictures needed. After an hour, in which I felt like I'd forgotten to breathe, she finally said she had what she needed.

The doctor had been watching the ultrasound the whole time on her computer in her office. I was sure that the test had taken so long because they found a problem. The doctor started with small talk, then moved on to how my gestational diabetes wasn't well-controlled with diet and I was in ketosis. I couldn't concentrate on that though, so afraid to hear what they'd found. I finally told her that I needed to know if my baby was okay.

She stopped talking about diabetes for a minute and looked at me quizzically, "Are you afraid it isn't?"

I explained that I had some issues with anxiety and right now it was getting pretty bad. I needed to hear if she'd found any birth defects.

"No," she said. "Your baby is fine."

"FINE?" I needed to hear it again.

"Yes, he or she is perfectly healthy and very active."

Finally able to breathe again for the first time in over an hour, I clarified. "No Down syndrome?"

Her response was laughable to me, "Are you worried about that?"

Yes, I was worried! I told her how I'd been warned about the increased likelihood at my age. She explained that Down syndrome is sometimes difficult to detect in an ultrasound, but it didn't appear that the baby had it. She explained that at this point, our risk of a baby with Down syndrome was pretty low, but we could know better odds with a simple blood test, or we could know for certain with an amniocentesis. I thanked her for the information but told her I was content with our odds. The risk of miscarriage from an amniocentesis is small, but I have a friend who had one. I was not about to risk the life of my baby for any reason, and I didn't trust the blood tests.

She went back to telling me that I couldn't continue to avoid carbs in order to keep my blood sugar in check. She said that wasn't working anyway, so I had to stop. I told her about my paleo diet and how great I felt on it. She agreed that it was a great plan for someone who isn't pregnant with gestational diabetes, but since that wasn't me, I had to stop or it would be fatal to my baby. Fatal? I tried to pay more attention.

She said that I needed to eat the number of carbs prescribed by the dietician every day, and she knew about people like me who think they know better than her. To be sure I followed directions, she was going to have me pee on a stick every day to check for ketones. If I tested positive for them, I had to call her immediately. Ketones meant that my baby was starving in the womb. At that point I'd probably been in ketosis for nearly all the pregnancy and the baby measured a week ahead of schedule, so I couldn't figure out how they thought this baby was starving.

She also gave me a prescription to lower my blood sugar. Very sternly, she told me that it was my job to eat the way I was supposed to eat. It was her job to manage my blood sugar numbers. This lecture ran all over my distrust of western medicine. I *had* been taking good care of myself. It's not that I don't want a doctor's medical expertise in a crisis, to set a broken bone or tell me what prescription eyeglasses I need, but with so many things I have found that nutrition is the key to freedom. I'm skeptical of anything that doesn't start with a look at whole, nutritious foods as medicine first. Why mask the problem with pharmaceuticals when you can get to the root of it and heal yourself through good nutrition?

The next time I saw my midwife, she explained that if I ended up needing insulin that she would no longer be able to work with me. I begged her to help me stay off insulin and she said she'd do her best. Our insurance changed again and that maternal fetal medicine specialist was no longer covered, so the midwife agreed not to send me to a new specialist. She had her supervising OB see me every other time to monitor the diabetes.

He never asked for my blood sugar or food log though. He lectured me about bonding with my baby and getting a flu shot so my baby wouldn't have inflammation that could lead to autism. He decided that I needed a 3D ultrasound during one appointment. Rick couldn't make it that day, so he pulled me into a small room, stuck the wand on my belly, located the baby's genitals, and pointed to the screen. He said, "I can't legally tell you your baby's gender, but I think that picture is pretty clear."

Then he printed out several pictures for me to take home.

I couldn't hold back the tears on my way out of the office. The receptionist stopped me to ask if I was okay. I told her how we'd wanted to be surprised and how Rick and I anticipated finding out the baby's gender *together*, at birth. This secret was special to us and he'd stolen it – at one of the few appointments I went to alone. It wasn't an unwanted pregnancy. Why did he think I needed to bond and could only do so by knowing the baby's gender? How did mothers bond with their babies before they could know their gender? I was livid.

She told me that although the midwife was off that day, she was going to ask her to call me as soon as she could. I called Rick in tears. He was furious. He didn't want to know the gender, thinking it was possible that I'd gotten it wrong. I knew there was no way I'd misinterpreted that ultrasound. I double checked the photo. Nope. But I attempted to keep it from him for the rest of the pregnancy.

The midwife called me and apologized for his behavior. She told me later that she'd submitted an official complaint about it. I was really glad because I learned he'd done it to others too, but it was too late for us. That guy hated me after that. I wasn't too keen on him either.

For the rest of the pregnancy, I attempted to do what the dietician recommended. I felt very confused by the whole thing and really didn't want to go on insulin. I didn't want to be transferred to the OB who told me the baby's gender, and it stressed me out to think of finding a new practice at that point in the pregnancy. I was sick with various issues throughout the rest of the pregnancy, confirming for us that this was the last baby. We were satisfied with two, and three was a bonus.

Our family traveled to South Carolina at Thanksgiving, where my extended family gathered at my sister's house. Then my friend Laura traveled a couple hours for her family to hang out with us too. Laura and I always have so much fun together. We were both enjoying single life in Nashville when she met her Prince Charming.

Their youngest has a rare condition that caused him to have a mic-key button, which is a medical device that's surgically implanted in the abdomen in order to put in or take out fluid. They're typically used as feeding tubes or to give medicine. My friends were learning how to deal with it during that visit. I tentatively asked her if I could see it, wondering if she would mind. She was happy to oblige and showed me how they used it. I'd never seen anything like it before. We talked about the challenges they faced dealing with her son's medical issues, and I wondered where she found the strength to do so many hard things. I had no idea how God was preparing me for my future.

During one of our long talks that weekend, I started having contractions. I was only four months pregnant, so it really surprised me. I got up and walked around a little, then drank a large glass of water. The contractions continued, but didn't intensify. I finally fell asleep, unable to stay awake to keep timing them. The next morning, I was relieved to discover they were gone. That evening they came back and again lasted well into the night.

A pattern developed where I had contractions like that every day, but they'd be gone in the morning. During my next checkup, I told the midwife and the nurse about it. They looked at me a little funny, then went on like I hadn't said anything. I reported the contractions during every visit after that, growing more concerned because it was so early. Starting at 32 weeks, the midwife saw me once a week and administered a non-stress test (NST). During the first test, the midwife asked, "Do you know you're having contractions?"

I almost screamed my answer at her, but calmed down enough to say, "Yes. That's what I've been trying to tell you since Thanksgiving."

As she monitored me, the baby didn't move. I laughed and told her it was because it was morning. Mornings with this baby were very lazy. But after lunch this one started rocking and rolling, and the contractions came too. In fact, by this time the contractions were pretty much non-stop. As she jostled the baby, she had a troubled look on her face. She said that his heart wasn't doing what it's supposed to do. She sent me for an ultrasound and everything looked fine. I was to come back for another ultrasound at the end of the week.

When I went back for that ultrasound, the midwife said that I had excess amniotic fluid, called hydramnios. It wasn't so high that it needed to be drained, but if it went much higher, I'd need to go to a bigger hospital to have it drained. When I asked her why I had that, she said she wasn't sure.

She thought that might be causing the contractions, so she prescribed Progesterone to calm it down. I continued to have contractions around the clock. At the next appointment, she told me that it was likely a side effect of gestational diabetes and she'd continue to monitor it closely.

As tempted as I was to go to the internet for answers, I restrained myself. I didn't want to cause unnecessary stress and add high blood pressure to my list of challenges.

When I was six months pregnant, our niece, Rose, got married. She and her husband Tyler went to college near our home, so we saw them often over the four years they were there. We all adore them. Eliana was their excited flower girl and Charlie was their reluctant ring bearer. The wedding was in California, so we flew the family out for the wedding. I knew traveling at that point was questionable, so I didn't ask. The kids were fired up about their airplane ride and they peppered me with questions.

"Mom, if you throw up too much, will you throw up the baby?"

"Mom, will your belly get so big that it pops and the baby comes out?"

I explained that my belly will not pop, but the sack that the baby lives in – which is not connected to the place where the food goes - will burst and the baby will come out of a special place that's made especially for babies. They wanted to know where the special place was, so I said it was near my bottom. They were horrified.

"Mom, will the baby be covered in poop when it comes out?" I'm pretty sure everyone around us was snickering by then. Charlie wanted to get a good look so he could understand better. I told him that some things are better left a mystery. I was not ready to pull out diagrams and answer *those* questions for a two-year-old.

The distraction of warm weather and beaches in California was a welcome change. On the night of the rehearsal, I enjoyed myself as the kids played and I got to know Tyler's family. Then the contractions started again and became so strong that I had to go back to the room and lay down. I prayed desperately, kicking myself for having traveled this late in the pregnancy. Rick took the kids to his parents' room so I could relax. I drank lots of water, watched HGTV, and finally fell asleep. When I woke up, the contractions were gone.

I had contractions like that until the day the baby was born, but they never organized enough to throw me into labor. The baby's heart continued to do the same thing during the weekly NST, so they'd send me for another ultrasound and tell me the heart was fine. During one of those ultrasounds, they saw water around both kidneys (hydronephrosis). They weren't too concerned about it, but it was another thing to monitor.

During my 37-week NST, the baby wouldn't move at all. The midwife used an instrument with a gentle electrical current, but nothing happened. She tried several things with no luck. Concerned, she took me into ultrasound herself and stayed to see what was going on. As the ultrasound tech pushed on my belly with the wand, the baby finally moved, kicking gorgeous little legs in a beautiful motion that allowed us all to breathe again.

She said, "It's time to have this baby. Go home and do all the things to help labor along. Let's get this baby out."

Relieved, I complied with her instructions. That was Monday. On Tuesday, the baby moved even less. I kept poking my belly, jumping up and down, making loud noises like standing in front of the coffee grinder, and even drinking coffee to encourage some movement. There would be a little response, enough to make me think the baby was only running out of space in there, and I'd relax for a while.

The last time I tried to get things moving that night, I couldn't get a response. I tried for quite a while, telling Rick that we might need to get to the hospital. Rick had been through this with me before and wasn't convinced. Just as I was about to throw the bags in the car anyway and call Grandma, the baby moved a couple of times. Relieved, we went to bed.

When I woke up Wednesday morning, I was very aware that there had been no movement in the night. I hadn't slept soundly in months because this baby typically moved all night long, so in my sleep I was aware of the constant kicks and rolls and hiccups. But I slept hard Tuesday night, undisturbed by the baby's discomforting comfort. This was my third baby and I didn't want to be an alarmist, so on Wednesday morning I asked Rick to take Charlie to Story Time at the library. That was usually my thing, but I couldn't concentrate on much besides restoring the discomfort of tiny feet kicking my ribs and a head butting into my side.

I listened to a naturopath on YouTube talk about how to control anxiety. She was empowering and encouraging to me in those hours, giving practical tips and suggesting ways to deal with anxiety. As I listened to her, I suddenly realized that it was getting close to 11:00 a.m., and I still hadn't felt the baby move. I looked online to see how often the baby was supposed to move at this stage. It said to go to Labor and Delivery if the baby hadn't moved in an hour. Alarmed, I realized it had been about 12 hours since I'd felt him move. I called the hospital and talked to one of the nurses. When she heard how long it'd been, she said to get there immediately.

Because of Rick's hesitation the night before, I was ready for a fight. As soon as he walked in the door, I was fierce.

"The baby hasn't moved in over 12 hours. We're going to the hospital right now!"

Rick looked at me, surprised, and said, "Okay. Let's go!"

"Oh. Okay. Let's go." His response surprised me.

He laughed at my tension, reassuring me that he was fine with going in.

We called his parents to come, gave the kids hugs and kisses, and took off. I didn't truly believe anything was wrong. God had said, "Life and health, joy and peace." I trusted Him, and I had the experience of the previous pregnancies where it often seemed like the doctors were freaking out for no good reason. Everything had turned out fine then, but I didn't want to be irresponsible either.

My emotions were unstable though. Before we'd quite gotten into town, I let fear take over for a minute. The thought that I might have let my baby die because I didn't go to the hospital the night before started shaking its finger at me. What if he was already gone? Rick reassured me, calming me down a bit before we pulled into the hospital. He dropped me off at the front door. It was really hard to sit at registration and tell the lady that I wasn't sure if my baby was alive, but here – let me fill out all your paperwork. The hospital where I'd had our other two babies let expectant mothers go straight up and sent someone from registration to talk to them.

In the meantime, a nurse arrived with a wheelchair for me. I waved away the wheelchair. I needed to stand up and walk. For the first time in months I wasn't having contractions. Another nurse came into my room right away and pulled out the Doppler. Although I was joking with the nurses and laughing, she saw what I wasn't saying and wasted no time.

A second after she put the instrument on my belly, there it was. Life and health, joy and peace: thump-thump, thump-thump...

I closed my eyes as my nostrils burned and swallowed the dry lump in my throat. Tears of relief squirted out of my eyes as I worked to control my breathing. My baby was alive.

She had me put on a gown. She hooked up the NST machine and watched the report as it printed, then she left to call the midwife. When she came back, she said that Lisa, our midwife, would come over to see me soon. It was time. She planned to break my water and start an induction. I needed all the information repeated to comprehend what she meant.

"You're having this baby today."

I struggled to understand the urgency, thinking maybe they were over-reacting, but I also felt relieved to be done with the constant contractions and discomfort. In spite of my dreams of a natural childbirth, I was so ready to meet this new baby. I called my friend Michelle, one of the other moms that I'd connected with at church. She's the kind of person you want around in a crisis.

I'd called her months before about attending this baby's birth as a support person. She's a labor and delivery nurse at that hospital and I wanted her there. It was her day off and she said she was covered in dirt, helping her dad and husband with a farm project. It might be a while, but she said she'd come. Less than an hour later, clean and not quite dry from the shower, she walked into my room. She looked at the lines on my NST report that meant nothing to me and told me exactly what she saw. It didn't look very good. It was definitely time to get the baby out.

Lisa came in smiling and said, "Are you ready?"

I was ready. I was also getting nervous about an un-medicated birth. Lisa assured me that I could do it. I'd done it twice before and I could do it again. She checked me and I'd already dilated some, so she thought breaking my water would do the trick. But her little needle hook didn't work. Perplexed, she tried again. Nope. After multiple attempts to break my water, she finally left and came back with something else in her hand. THAT worked.

When I asked what it was, I was surprised to hear that it was the same kind of instrument she'd used before to try to get Redmond to move. It took an electrical current to break my bag of waters.

Very quickly, the bed was soaking wet. The floor flooded. Lisa jumped back and said she needed to change into scrubs. She hadn't been kidding about my high level of amniotic fluid. Rick and I laughed at the comic relief as nurses scrambled to save their shoes.

After months of contractions and concern for preterm labor, my contractions stopped completely. The nurse came in and attempted to attach a fetal monitor to the baby's head – inside me. But the baby had shifted and gone up as far as possible. She couldn't reach far enough. Without anything to numb me, I started to freak out. What she was doing to me was excruciating and I asked her to stop. She assured me that she was almost there, just a little further.

"No!" I screamed. "Get out!!!"

She didn't.

When I was pregnant with Eliana and thought I might be in labor, I'd gone in to get checked. The nurse who checked me was very rough. It felt to me like she had a diamond ring on her finger, scraping up the inside of the birth canal. I cried out and pulled back, but she didn't stop. Thinking that maybe it was supposed to hurt like that, I didn't insist that she stop. As Eliana descended the birth canal weeks later, I screamed in pain, feeling that place inside where the nurse had scraped me. The doctor said she didn't see anything, but oh how I felt it. It was close to six months before it stopped hurting. I had no intention of allowing that to happen again.

When the nurse didn't heed my warning, I lifted my foot and planted it firmly on her shoulder, pushing her away from me.

"Okay, okay! I'll stop!"

As soon as she stopped, I burst into apologies.

"I'm so sorry! Please don't be mad. I couldn't take it. I'm really, really sorry."

She was gracious about it. She assured me that she understood that it must have been very painful. She kept working with me that day and I was thankful that she didn't get offended. Rick knew better than to chastise me about it. He was there to help me, not boss me around. He'd learned that during the birth of Eliana when I threatened to leave the hospital and have the baby at home if the nurse didn't stop trying to make me lay on my back while I labored.

When I asked about drugs, Michelle told me that because the baby was in distress, I wouldn't be able to have anything. Panic set in. Nothing? With my other two, the babies had been ready to come out as soon as my water broke. There had been less than 30 minutes before I felt the urgent need to push. But nothing happened this time and the pain I'd just experienced unsettled me.

Michelle looked at the NST report again and said, "The things we don't like to see are these D-cells. The baby's heart is doing this weird thing and you're not progressing into labor. When we consider that, along with your age, gestational diabetes, and hydramnios, we get concerned."

I didn't know anything about d-cells, but I knew what it meant that I wasn't progressing into labor. I was so frightened of the pain of a completely un-medicated induced labor (much different than an un-medicated birth that progresses naturally) that a wave of calm washed over me.

"If I need a C-section, that's okay. I can handle it."

A relieved look crossed her face. She told me that it looked like we might need to do one. She explained the difference between a true emergency and an unplanned c-section. She said that in an emergency, they only have minutes to get the baby out. They put the mother under completely and get the baby out as fast as possible. She said this wouldn't be a true emergency, but in a few minutes, people would start coming in to prepare me for surgery. She explained what would be done to my body in order to prepare for surgery.

I told her I might prefer a true emergency. Some of that stuff sounded really distasteful and I'd rather be put out than endure the embarrassment. She explained that unplanned was much better than emergency because the surgeon could take his time and there was less chance of birth injury. I conceded my pride.

While people were doing mortifying things to my body, the surgeon came in to speak with me. He was a kind man I'd met a couple times in the office and I felt thankful that the other doctor who had told me the baby's gender wasn't performing the surgery.

I remained calm until they put me on a cold, steel table and strapped my arms down. Michelle hadn't mentioned the straps. I asked them why and as they rushed around, they explained that it could be really bad if I tried to move during surgery. They needed me to be immobile. Then a man I'd never seen before pulled my gown up past my breasts and rubbed something cold all over my belly and breasts. Taken totally aback, I recoiled. What the heck was he doing!? He said it was to sterilize the surgery site. Was he somehow confused about where the surgeon was going to cut?

He gave me a compassionate look and said, "There isn't much dignity in here, is there? I'm sorry."

Then he pulled my gown back down a little, leaving the bottom two-thirds of my body completely exposed. When I was in college, I suffered misconduct by a doctor and it robbed me of much of the trust most people have in doctors. This latest development left me feeling totally exposed and helpless, and it was more than I could take. Unclear on whether I'd just been assaulted or cared for, I started to panic.

A woman with clear blue eyes appeared over my head. She had on a mask and her hair was covered by a surgical cap, but her eyes were warm and calm. She had done my spinal a few minutes before. I decided that I loved her because it had gone smoothly. I don't even remember if it hurt. Her mannerisms set me at ease and it was a welcome change from the last time I had a needle stuck in my spine. She asked me how I was doing and I couldn't speak. I looked at her, mute.

"What's going on, Kimberly? Are you okay?" Her voice was soothing as she repeated the question several times, waiting for my response.

I didn't know how to say that I was freaking out about my completely immobile, pasty white and puffy body, completely exposed under bright and unforgiving lights, in front of so many strangers. I didn't know how to ask if what had just happened was normal. I was hyper-aware of the loss of all control – strapped down, paralyzed, and naked.

I finally choked out, "Anxiety."

She nodded like she understood completely.

"Can you give me something for it?" My voice sounded small and weird.

She assured me that she would give me something as soon as they got the baby out. It wouldn't be long. She'd be with me the whole time and it was all going to be okay. As we talked, the sheets went up, shielding my eyes from what was about to happen. Rick and Lisa came in with gowns, caps, and masks and sat beside me.

As the surgeon tested my skin to be sure I was numb, a new fear flashed through me: What if the spinal didn't take? The epidurals never really took. The sheet in front of my face made me feel separated from my body. I couldn't tell if I could wiggle my toes, couldn't test if I could move.

I had to force my mind to trust the process and remember what I knew. I knew the people in the room had done this surgery many times before. I knew Lisa and Michelle were right there with me and they understood what was normal. I knew that I didn't want to watch anyone cut me open. I couldn't think about the cutting part though, so I quickly shifted my mind into neutral and looked at Rick. Sometimes it seems like his main purpose in my life is to keep me calm.

Then the anesthesiologist asked me questions like my full name, address, and social security number. She already had all that information, but I knew she was trying to distract me, so I let her. I answered all her questions and did my best to let my mind float away and not think about what was happening to my body.

I heard the surgeon announce suddenly, "It's a boy! And he's breech!"

I expected them to lay the baby on my chest then and let me see him, but he was taken to the other side of the room where I could only hear quiet voices mumbling. I heard a tiny cry that sounded like a kitten and relief flooded over me. When Charlie was born, a host of witnesses were in the room because they were afraid that he'd swallowed meconium. We'd been told that if he cried right when he was born, he was okay. Charlie cried immediately and the extra people left quickly. Remembering that experience, I said, "Oh, thank God! He's okay! He's crying!"

Someone said, "Well, no, he's not okay. He's very sick. We need to go now so we can help him."

And with that, my baby was whisked away. Rick was holding my hand tightly as I struggled to understand that I couldn't hold my newborn son. Suddenly, the whole world turned upside down. It felt like the table tilted with my feet up and my head down and someone was crushing my chest. I felt like I couldn't breathe.

I gasped, "Help me. I can't breathe!"

The anesthesiologist replied calmly, "You can breathe. If you're talking, you're breathing."

We repeated the same conversation several times, with her adding reassurance that she was helping me. I hadn't eaten in hours, which had caused my blood sugar to drop right at the time that my blood pressure dropped from the spinal. Panic seized me, causing an actual seizure, and I passed out momentarily. When I came to, I could breathe freely again and the shaking stopped. I quickly regained my composure, issuing orders to Rick.

"You go be with the baby right now. He just got ripped away from the only comfort he knows. He's in a cold room, naked, with strangers messing with him. You get in there. You let him hear your voice. Hold his hand. But don't you stop talking. He knows your voice. That will comfort him. I don't care if you have to recite the alphabet. You keep talking."

I don't remember anything about being sewn up or returning to my room except that I felt very sleepy. I couldn't keep my eyes open. I knew my baby was close by, struggling to breathe, but there was nothing I could do about it. So, I let sleep come. Michelle came in to talk to me, and I listened groggily. She asked for my phone so she could take some pictures. Touched by her thoughtfulness, I gave it to her before I went back to sleep.

She came back in and woke me up so she could show me my baby boy. It's really odd to see photos of your newborn, never having smelled his baby freshness, never having looked into his eyes or felt his breath on your skin. I didn't get to have the normal high of emotions that surge as you stare into the most beautiful face you've ever seen (no matter how funny they look). Instead of a baby swaddled tightly in a little hat, the photos showed a naked baby whose face was puffy, eyes squeezed closed, and his arms and legs splayed out to the sides. There was something like plastic wrap on his chest and a cone shaped thing over his face. His belly button bulged, bright red, and there was a thin tube sticking out of it. His tongue hung out oddly in one photo. In another one his face was scrunched up from crying. Newborn babies are funny looking, but that one looked the best to me. I texted it to my family, letting them know that he'd arrived.

Rick came in to see me, asking what we were going to name him.

Redmond Samuel Wyse. It was a name we'd been tossing around for a while, looking to see if we found something we liked better. We hadn't, and I knew we'd get used to the odd way it sounded on our lips right then. Rick chuckled and asked if I was sure. I was sure. I sent him back to the baby.

"His name is Redmond."

A nurse asked me how to spell it and wrote it down. I told her that the name Redmond means "wise protector" and Samuel means "my God has answered" (like Eliana). He's named in honor of my dad, Samuel, whose very favorite color is red. Dad is so passionate about the color red that he has had every church he's pastored decorated with red, only drives red cars, and thinks we should all appreciate red as much as he does. We all get a kick out of his love for the color red. I like it too.

My God has answered with a wise protector. But right then, Redmond was the one who needed protecting and saving. I repeated the promise from God under my breath, "Life and health, joy and peace."

"Redmond Samuel Wyse, you're going to be okay." I whispered it into the empty room and fell back to sleep.

Michelle came back in. She said she wanted to let me know that it looked like Redmond might have Down syndrome. She explained that he was floppy and had striking single lined creases on each hand. Palmar creases are a sign of Down syndrome, but not a diagnosis. She said he had a fat pad at the back of his neck, called a nuchal fold, and almond-shaped eyes.

I looked back at the pictures again. I'd never seen a baby with Down syndrome, so I didn't know what to look for. I thought back through all the ultrasounds we'd had. My friends whose babies had shown the smallest sign of Down syndrome had been warned far in advance that the shortened nasal bone or slightly thick skin on the back of the neck might mean Down syndrome. Their babies had been fine. My baby showed absolutely no signs on the extra-fancy ultrasound. I'd had two ultrasounds a week since 28 weeks, so how could they miss that? So, I told Michelle that he didn't have Down syndrome. He was puffy from the c-section and all the stuff they were doing to him. She agreed that it was possible, but she wanted me to be prepared. I forgot that most babies are curled up in the fetal position.

She let me know that the hospital had already called the nearest neonatal intensive care unit (NICU) and a transport team was on the way to get Redmond. They'd take him to the closest children's hospital that night so the NICU team could support him. I expected to be put on the ambulance with him, but I was not allowed to leave. I had to stay in the hospital and recover from the major surgery I'd just had. I begged her to let me see my baby before they took him. She told me that they planned to bring him in to me for about 10-15 minutes before they left. Relieved, I went back to sleep.

She came back later and told me that something had changed. No one told her why, but they were leaving *now* with lights and sirens. There was no time for me to hold him. She quickly wheeled my whole bed out into the hall and started pushing me fast. She blocked the door to the room where they had him in a clear, acrylic bed on wheels with a lid. As several people dressed all in black with the word "TRANSPORT" written across their backs wheeled him into the hall, she stopped them. She opened one of the port holes in the side and had me put my hand in and touch him.

I tried so hard to see his face, but he already had a ventilator in his mouth and so many things were taped to him that I couldn't tell what he looked like. I spoke into the crib to him. I told him how much I loved him and I couldn't wait to hold him. I squeezed his chubby little hand and told him we'd be together again soon. Tears streamed down my face as they took him away, and in my heart I cried out to God to supernaturally protect him from the trauma of separation.

Michelle had grabbed my phone without a word and passed it around for each of the nurses to take pictures for me. My heart felt like it had been ripped out of my chest. Rick couldn't go with him in the ambulance because there wasn't enough room, so he was taken away from everything he knew just hours after birth.

Exhausted and grieving, we tried to decide what to do. Should Rick stay with me or go with him? Michelle said Rick should stay with me and get a good night's sleep. There was nothing he could do in the NICU. Rick called his parents and worked out a plan. His dad would go with him in the morning for an hour, then he'd go home and get cleaned up, spend some time with the kids, and come back to the hospital to see me. I told him an hour wasn't long enough.

I'd spoken to both of my parents, but I couldn't bring myself to tell them the suspicion of Down syndrome. I was too fragile and I didn't know how they'd respond. They had not been happy when I got pregnant again. Knowing how hard pregnancy was on me, and that it only got worse with age, they had advised against it. If they said something like, "I told you so," I would lose it. My sister called to check on us soon after Michelle told me. I forced myself to choke out the words, "They think he might have Down syndrome."

I have no memory of her response, but I know that it was compassionate, positive, and affirming. Nothing about that conversation let me feel sorry for myself or that my child didn't deserve to be here. She thought I was crazy for having another baby, but once he was born it was nothing but love. Knowing her, she probably prayed for us before she hung up. I asked her not to tell Mom and Dad.

Rick and I slept hard that night. I was drugged with pain medication, anxiety relief, and Benadryl to stop the horrible itching as the spinal medication left my body. It felt so odd to sleep soundly while my baby fought for his life an hour away, but it was exactly what I needed. The next morning, my midwife and OB came in to check on me. I asked them about Down syndrome and they agreed that it was possible, but they weren't sure.

While I spoke to them, a nurse from the NICU called to ask if they could put in a PICC line. She explained that a PICC is a long, flexible tube (catheter) that is inserted through a small vein and threaded into a larger vein. It stays in longer than an IV and allows them to take blood and give him medicine without having to stick his arms and legs repeatedly. A needle is used to insert it, but then it's removed and only the soft tube remains. They needed my permission to do it.

I gave my consent, familiar with the procedure and glad to know needles wouldn't be constantly sticking him. Soon after that call, another nurse called to talk to me about how he was doing. As she spoke, I repeated what she said and the midwife wrote it down. It was a lot and most of it made no sense to me. I understood that his blood sugar was unstable because of my gestational diabetes. (I felt terrible about that.) I understood that he wasn't breathing well. They were having a hard time getting him stabilized.

Before we hung up, I swallowed the huge lump in my throat and forced out the words that wanted to stick there.

"I was told that it looks like he might have Down syndrome. Is that right?"

She was completely silent for a moment and I knew. My whole body went numb and the sound of rushing water filled my ears as she quietly said, "We won't know anything until we get the blood test back in two weeks, but that's the theory we're operating under."

I thanked her and hung up, nodding "yes" to Lisa and the OB. Their eyes filled with tears and compassion.

Crying, I tried to wrap my head around it. I couldn't make the words fit. Redmond was fighting for his life, I'd never even seen his face, and I had to process the diagnosis I had so feared.

"What are we going to do?" It was a genuine question. I looked at Rick, who was maddeningly calm despite the raging storm. We were completely unprepared to handle a baby with Down syndrome.

The OB, who had been very quiet and reserved up to that point, suddenly spoke up. With a strong, clear, and reassuring voice, he told us, "You're going to be fine. If he makes it through this medical crisis, you will have a wonderful baby boy to love and nurture. He was born in the best time possible for him. There have been so many medical and cultural advances in the last 20 years, you have nothing to be afraid of. You can do this. God called YOU to be his parents, and you will do a terrific job. Don't be afraid. He's just a baby boy, and Down syndrome isn't that big of a deal." He then proceeded to preach me a sermon, full of Scripture and insights that struck me as profound. I wish I could remember one word of it, but I have an overall impression that he was clearly a godly man, anointed for this moment, appointed by God to deliver our baby, and I loved him.

My midwife gave me an adorable hat that she'd knitted for him. It was his first baby gift. She told me she would be praying for us, and she wiped tears as she left. I called my parents. I told them the medical update first, and then I gathered all my courage and told them about Down syndrome. They told me that Katie had already told them, and they were going to love that little boy with all their hearts. He was going to be a wonderful addition to our family, and God had created him and gifted us with him. I was so surprised. I felt a surge of fierce love for my parents, followed by feeling totally foolish for doubting them. Emotion flooded me and tears of appreciation and fear and sadness fell. Mom and Dad comforted and encouraged me, never allowing me to fall into despair.

God bless my sister for her wisdom. She ignored my instructions and gave my parents some time to process the information before they talked to me.

Over a year later, my dad told me that when he first heard the words "Down syndrome," he'd been transported in his memory to when he was a child. A seed salesman had come to talk to his dad and he was nearby, helping on the farm. He said that he'll never forget their conversation. My grandpa had asked the man about his newborn baby. He'd responded with sad news. The baby had been born with Down syndrome. They hadn't even brought their baby home but turned the child over to a home. He said his wife was having a very hard time grieving the loss. Dad was a little guy, but he had wanted to scream, he was so shocked and horrified. They just threw their child away?

He said that he was so afraid that Rick and I wouldn't be able to love him. He begged God to put His love in our hearts for Redmond. He begged God not to let us throw him away. He was desperate to let me know that we could love him. He said that as he prayed, he had the impression of a happy, carefree young man who brought joy and laughter to our home. He was to be the delight of my life. He was to bring more joy to our family than we'd ever known.

Rick called then. He'd talked to Redmond's doctor, who'd spoken frankly with him. Redmond was the sickest baby in the NICU. They couldn't get him stabilized and he might need to be transferred to a higher level NICU for the one treatment he couldn't get there. I'd been assured by several people that the hospital he was in had an excellent NICU. But this other one was one of the top in the nation. If the doctors he currently had couldn't help him, he might have a chance there. Rick and his dad ended up staying with Redmond for hours. His dad couldn't bear to see his grandson hooked up to so many tubes and wires. He had to sit in the family room. Rick went back and forth between his dad and Redmond. Rick's dad was so afraid we'd soon be having a baby funeral. He was grief-stricken.

My sister texted around 11:00 a.m. "There's a non-stop flight that leaves at 2:00. If you want me to come, I'll be on it." I started to thank her but tell her I'd be okay. I wasn't going to ask her to leave her own family and responsibilities. Before I hit send, another message popped up. "If it were me, I'd want you to come."

I called her back. When she answered, I sobbed, "Please come. I want you to come."

She said she'd be there. She dropped everything – work, husband, and two kids of her own – spent an exorbitant amount of money and jumped on that plane. She reserved a hotel room, flew into a nearby airport, rented a car, and was able to get to Redmond's side before I could.

5

FEAR & SHAME

The obstetrician said I needed to stay in the hospital for three days to recover. I begged him to let me go sooner, but he refused. I couldn't understand how doctors and insurance companies and hospitals can expect a newborn to be separated from its mother for the first three days of its life. It's unacceptable. Why can't the mother be transported by ambulance to the new hospital and admitted there to recover near her baby?

I was told that no one wants to pay for it, but it felt inhuman. Like it wasn't enough that he needed major medical intervention, but to be surgically removed from my body and taken from the only comfort he'd ever known while all that happened to him? I ached with the pain of knowing he would be affected by that trauma forever. I desperately and repeatedly begged God to protect his heart and mind.

Rick's mom brought the kids to see me in the hospital. I told them that I'd be there for a few days. Grandma had explained that Redmond was sick and was at another hospital, so they didn't expect to see him. They were fascinated with the IV in my hand, the hospital bed, the TV remote, and all the new things in the room. While they explored everything and Rick's mom reminded them to be gentle with me and not jump on the bed, I talked to her. She was her usual gentle, sweet, accepting self. She said that if he did have Down syndrome it wouldn't matter. We'd love him just the same. The kids got restless pretty quickly, so she had them give me goodbye kisses and very gentle hugs before they left. They expected to see me again in a couple of days.

A few minutes after they left, Michelle came in. She was working that day, and she'd convinced the obstetrician to let me leave. She'd told me that she'd shared with him what the NICU doctor said, and he agreed that I needed to go be with my baby. She got me up and in the shower. She helped me get dressed, pack my bags, sign the paperwork, and get down to the car. She put my things in her car and drove me home, stopping to pick up my prescription medications first. Unbeknownst to me, she'd sent the prescriptions home with Rick's mom, who had dropped them at the pharmacy an hour earlier.

At home, she unloaded my things and got me inside. While I tried to think of what to pack, she talked to the kids and Kristina. In a fog of Percocet and shock, I threw in a few maternity outfits, some toiletries, pajamas, and socks. Rick came in the house and packed. He went to feed the horse and check on things around the farm, and then it was time to go. Eliana and Charlie were overjoyed to have us home, but now we had to leave again and they did not understand.

It was awful. Charlie clung to Rick's leg, begging us not to leave. He sobbed and screamed. Kristina had to peel him off Rick's leg and carry him forcefully into the house so we could pull away. Rick was in tears. I was torn between the children I knew and the baby I had yet to hold. As we drove away, Charlie and Kristina waved from the kitchen window. We ached for Eliana and Charlie. What would their lives be like now?

Rick dropped me off at the front of the hospital and ran to park the car. I don't remember it, but his mom tells me that I walked into the hospital and she chastised me. I was supposed to be in bed. I thought I was fine, but she asked the security guard to get me a wheelchair. She commanded me to sit. Rick ran from the parking lot and wheeled me to the NICU, banging into walls and door frames while I winced and silently questioned the wisdom of a wheelchair. (It's tougher than it looks to maneuver a wheelchair down narrow halls and through doorways.) When I entered Redmond's room, I saw Katie sitting beside him, holding his hand. She hugged me and said, "His breathing gets better when I sing. Watch this."

She showed me the number on one of the many monitors to watch. She softly sang "Jesus Loves Me" and the number immediately jumped up. When she stopped, it went back down. Singing made it better. Silence made it worse. We laughed. He is a Wenger (my family). We all love music.

I looked at him, drinking in his body and his face, trying to imagine what he looked like under the white tape that covered much of his face. He had adorable little feet with some crazy toes, like his big sister had as a newborn, and his legs were crossed at the ankle. He was chunky, with full, adorable cheeks and perfect fingers. His eyes were closed and I was happy to see a little dark hair on his head. He looked like a normal, healthy baby to me. I thought, "He doesn't have Down syndrome."

I pulled up a stool and sat beside him, unsure of what to do with myself. Rick hovered on the other side of the isolette. We rubbed his feet, touched his soft skin, and kissed his tiny toes. I introduced myself to him.

"Hi baby. I'm your mom. Remember me? I'm here like I promised. You don't worry about a thing. Just get better."

My arms itched to hold him close, feel his baby softness against my skin, to snuggle him on my chest and inhale the scent of his head. A nurse came in and introduced herself. She told me what was going on at that time, and then she pushed a large blue box on a stand with wheels toward me. She had a big plastic bag full of stuff with her and I got that as well.

"Pump," she commanded.

Pump? Pump what? I stared at the machine in front of me, at the bag, at her. What did she mean?

She clarified that it was time for me to start pumping breast milk for Redmond. They couldn't feed him yet, but he needed my colostrum and milk to be ready when he was able to eat. She showed me how to pull the curtain over a couch at the far end of the room and told me to pump for 20 minutes. She showed me how the machine worked and left.

I'd completely forgotten about breastfeeding. There were no nursing bras in my suitcase, or even at my house. The top I'd packed for the next day was a soft, gray maternity sweater with a high neck and a tight belt at the top of my belly. We all laughed about it. I had obviously not thought that through! Charlie had only nursed for five months, and a couple of those months I had to pump and bottle feed him because he simply refused to nurse. He got two teeth when he was four months old and started biting me hard. Nothing I tried worked to keep him from biting me, so that was the end of that. It had been a long time since nursing was on my mind.

Katie went to Target and got me a few nursing-friendly tops and supplies, plus a plethora of snacks. She'd always been my personal shopper anyway. When we were younger, I could give her money and send her shopping for me and she always came back with things that fit and looked better than anything I found on my own. She said situations like this one call for snacks.

The first time I pumped, I sat there for 30 minutes and got about one milliliter of colostrum. When I brought the tiny amount to the nurse, she cheered and said, "Good job!" We put a label on the bottle and stuck it in the fridge. It became my job to pump milk for Redmond every three hours. It seemed so foreign and silly – pumping milk for a baby who I'd yet to hold. Miraculously, my milk came in and I never had any shortage. I wasn't an over-producer, by any means, but I had exactly what he needed.

The doctor came in later that night and stared at me in surprise.

"What are YOU doing here? *In jeans!*"

Before I could go home, Michelle had me shower and get dressed in the going-home outfit I'd packed: my most comfy pair of maternity jeans, a thin maternity sweater, and a cardigan. I wasn't sure what else he thought I should have on, totally clueless that other NICU moms were wheeled down from recovery in their hospital gowns, disheveled and looking like they'd been through battle. While Rick had driven the hour from our house to the hospital, I'd put on some makeup. My hair wasn't particularly styled, but it was clean and dry.

"Where else should I be? My baby is *here*."

He nodded, then he looked Rick in the eye and spoke authoritatively.

"She just had MAJOR surgery and needs to rest. It's fine for her to walk a little here and there; in fact, it will help her heal. But she is not to walk up steps or much more than from here to there." He pointed to the elevators, about 100 feet away.

Then he looked at me. "You need to rest. Sleep when you can. Take naps. Do not push yourself. If you do, you risk infection and re-opening your sutures. Then you're no use to your baby at all. You have one job right now – to take care of yourself. We're taking care of your baby. Get plenty of rest. Eat good, nutritious meals. Then rest some more."

Rick and I nodded at him and promised to obey. Then he looked at my sister and said, "Make sure she takes her pain medication. Don't let it get out of her system."

Katie had c-sections with both of her children, so she knew what he meant. She kept track of what I needed to take and when, handed me pills and bottles of water, and kept the medicine in me. It was painful for me to get out of bed, to stand up and sit down, and anything else that required the use of those abdominal muscles that had been cut. But beyond that, I was really fine. It shocked me that I felt so good. It was way better than the way I'd felt after my other two children were born. (No one gave me Percocet then!)

The doctor asked us if anyone had spoken with us about genetics. We told him that we were aware of the suspicion of Down syndrome. He told us that it was hard to tell at this point, so we'd have to wait until we got the blood test results. He explained that it was called a karyotype, and that in a lab somewhere a technician was sorting out Redmond's chromosomes and matching them up in pairs. The lab would look for an extra copy of the 21st chromosome. Then they'd let us know the results, which would take a couple of weeks. He said that he couldn't tell us one way or the other at this time. He'd been sure a baby was positive for Trisomy 21 (Down syndrome) and been wrong. He'd been sure a baby was negative for T21 and been wrong then too. Only the blood test could give us the answer.

The nurse handed me a form to fill out, explaining that we could stay at The Ronald McDonald House. It was close and free, plus they had food and other things we might need there. Then she shooed us out of the room, assuring us that she'd take wonderful care of our baby overnight. We needed to sleep.

It felt so strange to leave my newborn baby with complete strangers, but I was also a little relieved to sleep in a bed, rather than deal with beeping monitors and uncomfortable furniture all night. We checked into a hotel-like room at The Ronald McDonald House. There was a queen-sized bed and a pull-out couch, a television, nightstands, and a large window that looked out to the hospital. We had a private bathroom that had plenty of toiletries we might need, plus a sound machine to drown out the noises in the hall. There was a stack of clean sheets for us to make our beds, and when we left we were to clean up the room for the next guests. We were happy to do that.

Katie commanded me to sit in the wingback chair while she made our beds. Rick brought our things in and took a shower. All I wanted to do was sleep and sleep, but I needed to get up every three hours to pump. Rick unpacked our things and put them in drawers. He put the suitcases in the closet and we all went to sleep. The nurse had my phone number if she needed to talk to us about anything.

The next morning, I woke up with a start. Where was my baby and how was he doing?! I felt awful for leaving him. I got ready as fast as I could and Rick brought me over to the hospital to see him.

Redmond had not had a good night. The doctor couldn't get his blood sugar stabilized. Guilt pressed down on me. If only I'd followed my instincts in managing the diabetes! I wished that I had been strong enough to ignore the instructions that seemed ridiculous to me and do what had worked in the past. Or maybe I should have followed the doctor's orders more strictly and had them put me on insulin? My mind reviewed all my decisions and choices, all with a finger of shame pointing at me for failing this child.

I knew that nothing I did during the pregnancy caused Down syndrome. It's a genetic anomaly, present at conception. A baby either has Down syndrome or they don't. But unstable blood sugar was definitely a result of uncontrolled diabetes, and I could not escape the accusations pounding in my head.

Redmond had a ventilator tube down his throat. It was hooked up to nitric oxide, which is used to help open the lungs when they won't receive blood from the heart to oxygenate it like they should. He got as much as they could give him without blowing his lungs out. The problem was that the numbers flashing on the screen weren't where they needed to be. For a while, they'd been able to turn the nitric down to 15, but then they had to crank it up to 30, which was the highest they could push it without pediatric surgeons on call to repair his lungs if they blew.

That Friday, we sat in the room and watched the numbers on the screen. We talked to him quietly and sang, waiting for the news that he was better. I'd known a lot of people whose babies had to be in the NICU for a few days because of breathing difficulties. While the nurses and doctors bustled around, warning us that he was in critical condition, I often felt calm.

We had been told that if he made it through the first 36 hours, he'd be out of the woods. Every 12 hours there was a shift change. New doctors and nurses made new plans, trying different things. The nurse on Thursday night had been warm and nurturing, allowing us to sit around his bed and touch him, talking and laughing as we passed the time. The nurse on Friday clamped down on the rule that only two people could be in the room with him at a time.

She told us we were welcome to sing quietly (we'd never been loud) and touch him, but she showed us how to cup our hands and place them firmly on the top of his head and his bottom. We weren't to stroke his skin or do anything that could irritate him. Although he wasn't a preemie, she said he was very sensitive to light, touch, and sound. The lights in the room were dim, the curtains pulled, and everyone spoke in whispers. This rule struck me as hilarious, since machines beeped and buzzed non-stop. Alarms went off in sharp, loud tones and no one bothered to shut them off, but we needed to sing quietly.

Rick's parents and his sister came to visit. My sister-in-law, Jackie, a college Bible professor, hadn't been able to visit my other two babies in the hospital. This time she cancelled one of her classes and drove an hour to meet her nephew. Pastor Brad, the congregational care pastor at our church, came to visit. He prayed over Redmond and stayed with us for a while in the family room. Rick and I rotated between the family room and Redmond's room. My sister continued to hand me pain medication and water, made sure I ate, and sent me back to The Ronald McDonald House to take an afternoon nap.

When we were alone, Rick and I talked about the possible diagnosis and how we should handle it. Rick said we'd love him no matter what, and we'd be okay. It was all going to be okay. We talked about how we were going to pay for all the medical bills. We have health insurance, but we knew that hundreds of thousands of dollars in expenses were accumulating. Rick said it didn't matter. We'd sell farm land if we had to. Redmond needed everything they were doing for him. (I couldn't believe he said that. His farm land means so much to him.)

On our third day in the NICU, the new doctor came on with the shift change and decided that Redmond might, in fact, need bright lights, loud voices, and activity in the room. He encouraged us to move into the room with our guests and make some noise. We obliged and hoped for good results. 12 hours later, a new doctor and nurse came in and glared at us, turning down the lights, shooing us out, and returning his room to soothing quiet. I felt bewildered. Having never been in the hospital for more than labor and delivery, I didn't realize how much of a voice I had in the treatment plan.

After our visitors went home that night, the doctor came in to speak with us. He said that Redmond had almost made it through the first 36 hours and he was hopeful that he was on the mend. It was still a slight possibility that he'd need to be transferred, but it looked a lot less likely. He encouraged us to go back to The Ronald McDonald House and get a good night's rest. We went to bed with hopeful hearts, thinking we'd be able to take him home in a few days.

The phone rang before 7:00 a.m. the next morning, jolting me awake. I answered groggily, fighting through the haze of sleep when I saw the NICU number on my caller ID. A nurse's urgent voice said that Redmond hadn't had a good night and needed to be transferred to the larger hospital. I needed to get over there immediately to sign papers so he could go. Shocked and in disbelief, I dressed quickly. Rick drove the short distance to the entrance, parked the car in the drop off zone, loaded me in a wheelchair, and took me up as fast as he could, banging into doorways and walls the whole way. Ouch.

A doctor with fire in her eyes met me at the door. She introduced herself and explained that she'd been working on the night Redmond was brought in, but then had several days off. She was stunned when she came back that morning to discover that he was still there. She said that he should've been transferred the next day. She was furious with the other doctors for not doing so and couldn't understand what they'd been thinking.

She explained to me that he might not need ECMO, a life-support system that would give his heart and lungs a break to heal and get stronger, but if he did they needed him to be in the other hospital. They might not have time to transfer him otherwise. Her face was grim.

As wave after wave of shock washed over me, I realized that things were much worse than I'd realized. I signed a bunch of papers, not reading a word, and wondered why in the world people weren't moving faster if it was such an emergency. They explained that the Level Four NICU was trying to make space for him. They'd move him as soon as they got the word. I asked if I could go in the ambulance with him and was denied. There was no space for me, the EMTs, and all the necessary medical equipment.

Rick went back to The Ronald McDonald House while I stayed with Redmond. He and my sister quickly packed our things and loaded them in the cars. Rick left before everything was quite done so he could be with me and Redmond while Katie finished up. The staff at The Ronald McDonald House told us not to worry about the room, just to go.

When the transport team finally arrived, dressed again in all black with the word TRANSPORT in large white block letters across the back of their shirts, they brought a new isolette. The nurse began unhooking lines and tubes to move him. I wasn't doing well at all. There were so many things hooked to him! Once she had him all unhooked, she looked at me and asked if I wanted to move him into the new bed. Oh, how I longed to hold my baby! But all the things attached to him scared me to death. She said she'd help me, so she picked him up and laid him in my arms. Sobbing, I took a couple of steps and put him down in the new crib. The transport team worked quickly to reattach all the lines and tubes.

When I picked him up, I saw that the blanket his little head had been lying on was covered with tiny hairs that must have rubbed off. I'd been told that it was helpful to hold something that smelled like him when I pumped. It would cause my milk to let down. I asked the nurse if I could have the blanket, knowing they didn't normally let anyone take their linens home. She agreed immediately, then not only gathered up the blanket, but every piece of linen he'd used, including a small pillow to elevate his feet. Rick arrived to get me right before the nurse handed me the clear, plastic bag marked PERSONAL PROPERTY. I knew without question that she believed he wouldn't make it and this was all we'd have to remember him by.

Rick and I stood in the hall and watched the transport team roll him away from us. He held me while I sobbed. Then he guided me in the wheelchair with a bag of the milk I'd already pumped, a few papers, and Redmond's bed linens. We went down the elevator and out to the car in a zombie-like state. We drove over to meet Katie, and then followed her to the bigger hospital.

On the interstate, a car cut in front of us and dramatically slammed on the brakes, nearly causing us to rear end it at close to 80 mph. We had no idea what had upset the driver, but it was too much for Rick. He honked and honked at the driver, yelling like the other guy could hear him. It was so unlike him, I began shaking uncontrollably, begging him to calm down. We didn't need to add a road rage shooting to the list of bad things happening that day. He apologized and calmed down, but it was clear to me that as calm as he appeared on the outside, he was not handling the emotions of this crisis any better than I was.

Jenny, the parent advocate from the new NICU, called us on our way there. She introduced herself and told us where to park. She gave us directions to get to the NICU and explained that there were nesting rooms right in the NICU where parents could put their things and rest. Two of her babies were NICU graduates, so she understood a little of what we were feeling. I think Rick and I both felt our blood pressure drop to a more normal level after that call.

We followed Jenny's instructions and weaved our way through the enormous state university campus, dodging students who walked everywhere with little thought for the cars on the roads. We pulled into the main entrance of the children's hospital and Rick found a wheelchair for me. I waited there while he and Katie parked the cars. I couldn't believe the number of cars driving through and all the people who streamed through the front doors. Security officers stop each person who comes in, asking if they've been out of the country or exposed to any diseases. They ask if you have a cold or cough, and if you pass their screening, they give you a sticker and directions.

I watched as parents pushed children in wheelchairs and special strollers, managing oxygen tubing, tanks, and other medical equipment that I couldn't identify. Children with all kinds of medical issues passed by as I waited. Rick and Katie finally found me and we went through screening, went down the hall, and entered the waiting area for the six elevators. It was jammed with people and my wheelchair was obtuse. We finally made it onto an elevator and went to the ninth floor. Bang, scrape, bang, bump. My incision seared as I tried to brace myself for the impact of the wheelchair on walls and doorways. Rick apologized again as Jenny greeted us.

She wrung her hands and explained that we'd beaten Redmond to the NICU. Puzzled, we couldn't figure out how that had happened. So many things had delayed us. How could the "lights and sirens" ambulance not yet have arrived when we'd left almost an hour after him?

Jenny said she didn't know because that never happens. She suggested that we go on a tour of the NICU. Unsure what else to do, we agreed and followed her around as she showed us nesting rooms, the family waiting room, bathrooms and showers, and the pumping rooms for mothers. After we'd seen everything at what felt like a very slow pace, she got a message that Redmond had arrived. We went to room 38 and saw the transport team wheeling his isolette into the room. They quickly opened the top and started attaching his tubes and wires to machines in the room.

We walked out to give the team space to move around in the small room. Jenny showed us a little seating area near our room and explained that it was for parents when rooms got a little crowded. I went back to look at Redmond while Rick and Katie asked Jenny about meals and accommodations for parents. Everyone in the room was moving quickly, and the look on their faces told me something was very wrong. I noticed a nurse with gray hair squeezing a bag that was attached to his ventilator tube. I knew from watching television shows like ER that she was "bagging" him. Alarmed, I asked what was going on. She looked up at me and said sharply, "We're just getting to know him."

I realized that my presence in the room was not helping. I went back out to the seating area and waited with Rick and Katie. Exhaustion set in. I hadn't eaten anything all day. Jenny provided me with a room service menu and explained that nursing mothers receive three meals a day while their child is a patient. I looked it over and picked out something simple. She had the food delivered to us and I dutifully ate.

Redmond's room had calmed down by then, so I went to the nesting room to take a nap. I lay there for a few minutes, trying to calm my aching heart and racing mind. I had no words for prayer but a groaning cry. Romans 8:26 promises that when all we have are wordless groans, the Holy Spirit prays for us in our weakness, and I clung to that promise.

Before I could fall asleep, there was a loud knock on the door. My sister had my wheelchair and told me to get in it now. They were going to put Redmond on ECMO and they needed me right away to sign the consent.

I had to quickly absorb medical information that was difficult to understand. I learned that ECMO stands for "Extra Corporeal Membrane Oxygenation." It's a treatment that uses a pump to circulate blood through an artificial lung back into the bloodstream of a very ill baby. This system provides heart-lung bypass support outside of the baby's body.

I'd been so sure that the local doctors were exaggerating, and that the new doctors would figure out what he needed to get better. Hearing that he really did need ECMO was another shock that day. A nurse handed me a stack of papers and I glanced over them, but I had to stop reading. What I saw said that ECMO could save Redmond's life, but it might also cause all kinds of other problems. Hearing loss, vision loss, mental and developmental delays, and so forth jumped off the page at me. But what else could I do? Crying, I showed the papers to Rick and he agreed, so I signed the papers without reading the rest.

Rick held me and prayed, "Lord, please help this treatment to do only good for Redmond. Please protect his mind and body from negative side effects."

Katie called Mom and told her that she needed to get to us right away. Mom had a ticket purchased for a flight in three weeks. She'd been planning to wait until then, but Katie told her she needed to come NOW. Mom listened to her and was there the next day.

We found out about a year later that the reason we arrived at the hospital before Redmond was because he died in the ambulance.

His heart stopped beating more than once. The transport team had to pull over so the driver could assist in resuscitation. They wisely chose not to tell us that news, realizing that it would only upset us more than we already were.

I believe that the Holy Spirit chose the members of that transport team and empowered them with wisdom, skill, and strength to provide exactly what Redmond needed. They were terrified and wanted the transport team from the new hospital to pick him up, but that would've taken longer, so the local team had to transport him themselves.

I look forward to the day we can thank them for bringing our baby back to life. When I think about them now, I continue to thank God for them and pray blessings over each of them for the blessing they were to us.

Of course, we knew nothing about it on the day of transport. We were scared enough with the information we had. The fire we were about to walk through was hotter than we needed to know.

6

LIFE SUPPORT

Before the surgery for ECMO started, an extremely tall woman approached us, introducing herself in impersonal, clipped tones. She was a resident and talked to us about what she was about to do. She wore a white coat and had crazy stuff attached to her, including a long tube that emerged from under her coat and followed behind her like a hissing tail. Goggle-like eyewear perched on her forehead and she looked a little like an alien. It was the gear she needed for surgery, but it took me by surprise. In the middle of that high-pressure situation, I nervously giggled a little, thinking maybe she was aware of how odd she looked. She did not crack a smile.

Maintaining total focus on the task before her, she explained that she was going to make an opening at the base of Redmond's neck, then insert two large tubes, called cannulas, and connect them to his heart. The tubes would allow them to remove blood from his heart, oxygenate it artificially through a machine, and then pump it back in. One tube was for blood going into the heart and one tube was for blood going out of the heart. She thought it would take about 15 minutes and they'd do the surgery right in his room.

Rick and I waited together with my sister, Katie, on bright orange furniture down the hall from his room. Large windows overlooked the biggest cemetery we'd ever seen. While we waited, I called the church office to ask them to pray. My sister and I tried to find the humor in the situation. We're normally particular about having our hair and makeup in place for photos, but we took a selfie with our disheveled hair and lack of makeup. She posted it to Facebook with a sarcastic comment about how lovely we looked. When I see it today I think about how surreal it was that we were going through such a horrible crisis and I still tried to smile.

The curtain to Redmond's room stayed closed for a long time.

Finally, Redmond's nurse practitioner, June, came out to talk to us. She explained that the surgeon had struggled to get the tubes to go in far enough. There was something blocking them, but she kept working until she found a way. They weren't in as far as they liked for them to be, but they thought it would work. The way they described his ECMO cannulas was "positional." His body position determined how effective they were.

Since the surgeon's hands were in his body, I couldn't understand how some unknown thing blocked the tubes. What was it? To this day, I don't know.

At least 45 minutes after they began surgery, the curtains finally opened. The surgeon came to talk to us, repeated what June had told us, and warned us that they might have to redo the tubes if it didn't work. We nodded like we understood, but we were clueless.

June came back to talk to us. She explained that Redmond's heart had several holes in it that shouldn't be there. His lungs appeared to be well-developed and healthy, but they hadn't "turned on" yet like they should've when he was born. I knew that was a possible complication of c-sections because there is something about the baby squeezing through the birth canal that causes the lungs to turn on. Without the squeezing, the body doesn't necessarily get the message. Women's bodies are designed in amazing ways to communicate with the baby's body during the birthing process.

Our hearts pump blood into our lungs. The lungs oxygenate this blood and give it back to the heart. Then the heart pumps the oxygenated blood throughout the body. When the blood has gone through the body, it returns to the heart and lungs for more oxygen before it goes back out again. Redmond's lungs couldn't receive the blood, so his heart had created holes that kept it from exploding. Even though the holes weren't good, they were his body's way of trying to stay alive.

As concerned as I was, I marveled at how amazing it is that his body had taken care of itself like that. June asked me if I had any questions. Terrified, my mind raced with the questions I wanted to ask but couldn't say. Finally, I forced out words that seemed the best: "Is it recoverable?"

She looked me right in the eye and without hesitation said, "Yes. He can recover from this. ECMO works and he can go on to live a full and good life after it."

I searched her face as she spoke and there was not a hint of a lie. She believed what she said and that was enough for me. I sat back, took a deep breath, and thanked her. Friday, March 4, 2017, was the worst day of my life, but God sent me an angel named June. She continued to wiggle her way into my heart as the days wore on. In fact, I was repeatedly surprised by how much love I instantly felt for some of Redmond's medical team.

I whispered prayers for Redmond's lungs to wake up and start receiving the blood from the heart. I recalled the song, "Great are You, Lord," by All Sons and Daughters, that I'd sung with all my heart in church during my pregnancy. (I can't legally quote the lyrics here, but you have access to YouTube, right?) The lyrics beautifully tell of God's power to restore broken hearts and breathe His breath into our lungs. The song's authors surely had something else in mind when they wrote it, but I became emotional as I remembered how I'd been thinking about and praying for my son's heart and lungs long before birth.

I asked June if we should let Eliana and Charlie see him. I became hyper-aware of how critical the situation was, and the terrible thought that came to me was: How could I explain that we didn't have a baby to bring home if they never saw him?

They'd anticipated their baby brother or sister with excited expectation. We needed to make sure they met him while he was alive. June encouraged me to have them come. She said it was absolutely the right decision. Rick's parents brought the kids to the hospital that day, arriving moments after the surgical team left Redmond's room.

I sat alone at the end of the hall in the orange chair, my brain still foggy and my body in shock from the events of the last three days. Had it only been three days? Katie had left to check into her hotel and Rick had gone down to the lobby to escort his parents and the kids through security.

I wanted so badly to feel God's presence, to feel His arms comforting me like I'd heard other people talk about in times of crisis, but I felt nothing. I clung to the words that I'd felt so strongly were a prophecy over this child – *life and health, joy and peace* – but nothing that was happening felt like a fulfillment of that promise.

In my heart I cried out, "Where are You, God?"

I didn't hear an answer, but I knew God and my heart reminded me of the answer I'd learned through other hard things.

"I'm here."

I believed God was with me. I understood that He'd prepared me ahead of time for these terrible days; but in the moment, I struggled to feel my spirit connect to His. I could've blamed God for not making Himself known to me at that moment; but in truth, **I had curled up in a tight ball inside. My spirit hid from God, fighting back the acrid fear that God might require me to give up my son for His plan on earth to be fulfilled.**

Years before, on that day when I was first licensed as a congregational minister, then again when I was ordained as a pastor, I had made a choice to submit myself to His will without question, no longer demanding that He do things my way. (That had never worked anyway.) I knew how much God loved me. I knew He had a plan for my life that intersected His plan to run the universe, so my personal happiness in any given moment was much less interesting to Him than my willingness to trust Him. **He does things for our good and His glory. But what did He require of me through this trauma?**

Parenting Eliana and Charlie had shown me the heart of God so beautifully. Of course, I want them to be happy and free, but I also have to teach them to be responsible, considerate, gracious human beings. They have to learn to follow the rules so they don't hurt themselves or others. They have to be disciplined by me now in the hopes that they'll one day understand how to discipline themselves and be productive members of society.

Sometimes their hearts will be broken, by me or by something I can't control. I can't be with them 100% of the time, so I have to trust that God will protect them and take care of them when I can't be around. How can I expect my children to trust me if I can't trust God? God has given me these little blessings for a season, but ultimately - *they belong to Him.*

If God chose to take Redmond before I'd even had a chance to cuddle him next to my skin and kiss his face without tape and tubes blocking me from touching his lips, it was His right. He is God and I am not. But even as I type these words nearly two years later, I can't hold back the tears. There's a picture on the wall facing me as I write, Redmond at six months old, held in my arms, face to face with me, smiling as we look into one another's eyes. It's so precious to me because of the triumph of that gift.

I trusted God to do what was best for me, but I was terrified of what that might mean. The words from Scripture banged around in my head, "He spared not His own son, but gave Him up." Would God require me to give up my son? Who was I to deserve anything better than what God went through for me? I was submitted to His will for my life, but the fear of what that might mean so overwhelmed me that I couldn't receive His comfort in that moment. God was right there with me, and I understood that cognitively, but my heart had closed its iron gates.

I'd been leaking tears all day, unable to get myself together. Then, just as I felt my sanity slipping away, my older children came bouncing around the corner. As soon as they saw me, they lit up and called out, "MOMMY!" Eliana broke into a run and threw her arms around me. Charlie, not about to be left behind, followed closely behind her. Rick and his mom called out after them to be careful with me. They crawled up into my lap and hugged and kissed me. It was exactly what I needed to come back from the brink.

After I got my fill of hugs and kisses, Rick pushed the three of us in my wheelchair to the room and looked through the glass wall at the machines and tubes that seemed to cover the room, nearly concealing the baby in there. We'd brought in two soft, cotton blankets for him – one solid red and the other with a red and white owl print. The red stood out in the middle of all the chaos. The nurse that bagged Redmond earlier was still on duty and she looked at the kids in alarm. I explained to her that June had encouraged us to bring the kids in to meet him, but I could tell that she didn't think it was a good idea.

She reluctantly consented, but only one at a time, and only for a few minutes each. Rick carried Eliana in first and held her as she looked down at her baby brother. I watched nervously from the door, wondering what she'd think of all the tubes and wires. She didn't even seem to notice them. Eliana smiled with all the love of a big sister for her new baby brother and very softly reached down and held his hand. I could hear her cooing softly to him, like she had done with Charlie the first time she met him.

After about a minute, Rick brought her out and picked up Charlie. Charlie mimicked his sister, looking lovingly at the baby and carefully touching his hand. They both spoke softly to him, chiming in as Rick introduced them. Charlie had questions about the tubes and wires. He wanted to know where they went and what they did. Rick explained a couple things, but then told him they'd have to talk more about it later. Their time was up.

Rick and Charlie left the room and the nurse stopped scowling and returned to bustling around in the room. What we didn't discover until a year later was that Redmond's heart stopped during surgery and they'd had to resuscitate him again. His life hung by a thread that was even thinner than we realized. She was scowling at us because she desperately wanted to keep our baby stable and alive. The NICU staff knew better than to upset us with unnecessary information, and I'm thankful that they kept us in the dark. Our precious nurse carried the trauma home with her that night and never let us know how close we'd come to losing him that day.

The children's hospital has a great indoor play area for patients and their families, so we took the kids over there to let off some steam. I went in a wheelchair and Eliana and Charlie sat on my lap for the ride. I wrapped my arms around their healthy little bodies and thanked God repeatedly for the miracle of their health and wholeness. As soon as we got in the play area, they jumped down and explored all the fun things they could do.

I sat in that wheelchair and cried. It hurt so badly that I couldn't get up and play with them. I wanted to run and catch the balls they were throwing, sit down on the floor and do the big puzzle, and catch them as they went down the slide. But I had to let their daddy do those things by himself because my body was as broken as my heart. All I could do was sit there. I cried because my newborn baby wasn't at home, nursing every few hours, keeping me up at night and teaching me about what he liked and disliked. I longed for the luxury of that exhausting first six weeks with a newborn.

Redmond lay in a hospital bed with huge plastic tubes inserted in his neck, pumping his blood out of and back into his body. His chest didn't rise and fall. There was no breath in his lungs. He looked like a doll, medically paralyzed and lifeless. It was so odd. I wanted to take him in my arms and let him know I was with him. And here were Eliana and Charlie, full of life and energy, begging me to play with them and I couldn't do that either. I remember feeling so embarrassed that I couldn't stop crying, wondering what Rick's parents must think of me. In hindsight, what else was I supposed to do? Not crying in that moment would've been really weird.

My sister had sandwiches from a gourmet shop delivered and we sat at a table in the play area and ate. The food felt like gravel in my mouth, but it was my job to eat so that I could produce milk to pump for Redmond. I ate as best I could and listened as Eliana and Charlie explored each new toy and showed me their treasures.

After a while, Rick's parents were ready to go. It was time. The kids went home with them happily, on an adventure with Grandma and Grandpa. Kristina had gone home for the weekend and their Aunt Jackie planned to visit them the next day to help her parents. They were to spend the night at their grandparents' house and were excited about the fun day they had planned for the next day.

I cried because they left. I cried because they didn't even seem to mind leaving us. If they had acted like it was hard to leave us, I would have cried over that. There was simply no end to the tears that day.

Rick wheeled me back to Redmond's room and I sat in the bright yellow recliner, the only piece of furniture that could still fit in his room with all the ECMO equipment. I knew Redmond couldn't see me, and without a heartbeat or air in his lungs I wasn't sure where his spirit was, but I hoped that he could sense my presence in the room. Did he know if I was there or if he was alone with strangers?

I wondered about the state of his soul when his body was run by machines. I wondered where his mind was, where his subconscious took him in that fragile state. Was he truly alive if he wasn't breathing on his own, if his heart wasn't beating? Did our voices comfort him because he was used to hearing their muffled sounds from inside the womb? It was too weird to try to figure out, so I gave up and decided to treat him like he could hear us and knew who we were. I decided to believe that although his heart and lungs were resting while a machine did the work for them, his spirit remained in his body and he was alive.

I felt guilty for leaving him at night, but there was no space in his room to sleep comfortably. There were four people in the room caring for him around the clock, and they needed to talk and work freely. I could try to sleep on the couch in the brightly lit hall, but I had to get up every few hours to pump and staff walked the halls constantly. There'd be no rest there. So, we left every night, torn and uncertain about what we were supposed to do, wondering if he even knew we'd been there. I'd stand beside his bed, bend at the waist to get as close to his little face as I could, and I'd whisper a prayer.

"Goodnight, sweet baby. We love you so much. We'll be back in the morning. Jesus, please take care of our boy. Please, God, let us keep him. Please don't take him away from us. We ask You to send angels to stand charge over him, protecting and keeping him safe. God, we ask that he'll have sweet dreams. Cover him up with a blanket of Your peace. Please, Lord, let him know how much we love him and that we're not far away. Amen."

That night, Rick wheeled me upstairs to a small room in The Ronald McDonald House. It was actually in the hospital – up two floors from the

NICU. There was a key to get in the main area, which had an office, a living space with couches and a TV, and a kitchenette with a small table. Bins of snacks were organized on the kitchen counter and a refrigerator held milk and leftovers.

Through another door was a long hall with doors. Our room was the first one on the right. Our little haven was barely large enough for the twin bed, narrow recliner, and nightstand. It had a small bathroom where everything was automated. It had an automatic flusher that sounded like an airplane taking off, which really startled us in the middle of the night. The sink came on automatically when you put your hands under it, dispensing warm/hot water only. It was odd to brush our teeth in hot water. The shower was tiled and had barely enough room to turn around.

Because I was recovering from the c-section, we decided that I should sleep alone in the twin bed and Rick would sleep on the recliner. It had been a very long day. We stumbled around, getting ready for bed through half-asleep eyes, and tried to get some rest. My phone was always on in case the NICU or our kids needed us. Every few hours, I'd wake up with a start, soaked with sweat and freaking out. My thoughts were out of control as I tried to sleep. Wild, scary dreams plagued me. I'd forgotten about all the sweating during post-partum recovery. I'd done the same thing with the first two – raging hormones and excess fluid causing my body to flush it out while I slept. The result was that I'd wake up completely drenched, hair wet, clothes stuck to my body, shivering as soon as I threw off the covers. It didn't matter how cool the room was, my body had a job to do.

The next morning, Saturday, March 5, 2017, Rick wheeled me down to the NICU where we heard that Redmond had had a hard night. He'd been setting off alarms all night, only settling down an hour before we came down. His nurse was edgy, speaking briskly to the ECMO specialists as they adjusted things. Because it was my job to eat, I sat down in the recliner and ordered breakfast. Suddenly aware that I was no longer diabetic and there was no lack of space in my belly, I ordered an enormous breakfast: French toast, bacon, coffee, cranberry juice, oatmeal with brown sugar and raisins, and a bagel with strawberry cream cheese. Relieved that he had settled down, I ate every bite of that delicious, carbohydrate-laden food while nurses and specialists buzzed around me.

My sister came mid-morning and sat beside me on an uncomfortable chair, shifting occasionally to stand beside Redmond's bed for a while and sing quietly, "Jesus Loves Me." His room was always really full though – there was an ECMO specialist and a nurse, and usually there was a second nurse and a second ECMO specialist in training. Runners constantly came by the room with the latest blood gas numbers, which told them something about his lung function at that moment.

Every four hours they did his care - changing his diaper, repositioning his body so he wouldn't get sores, checking over his entire body with a flashlight, and a bunch of other things I didn't understand. Every time they moved him, alarms went off. Then the nurses and ECMO specialists scurried around until they figured out how to get his numbers back where they needed to be. When the alarms started going off, I'd leave. I couldn't handle the tension. It didn't seem like having me in there helped them either, so I walked down the hall to the seating area that overlooked the cemetery. We hung out in that area a lot those first few days.

Redmond had to be catheterized for ECMO. The catheter had gone in hard and caused him to start bleeding right before surgery. He was on blood thinners for ECMO, so his body didn't have a chance to heal. Every time they changed his little diaper, there was blood in it. It terrified me, but they reassured me that it was just a tiny amount and wouldn't cause a problem. They were on constant alert for a brain bleed, so I figured if they said it wasn't a big deal it really wasn't, but I didn't like it.

Katie went to the airport to pick up Mom then. I ordered lunch and ate it outside the room. Chicken quesadillas with sour cream and salsa, tortilla chips, a cheese and fruit plate, and two miniature Diet Cokes. I could have caffeine! I could eat almost anything I wanted without fear of gestational diabetes and hurting the baby! The food was delicious and again I ate it all. I couldn't believe my appetite. The scale was never far from my mind, but I didn't care right then.

Rick went down to the hospital cafeteria for lunch almost every day. While he was downstairs eating, Mom arrived and I took her in to meet Redmond. She was determined that he would get better. She talked to him and questioned the nurses. Relieved she was with me, but thoroughly exhausted and on edge from night terrors and the sound of alarms going off, I waited until Rick came back and then excused myself to take a nap. Rick wheeled me upstairs, then he went for a walk to explore the hospital. Mom and Katie stayed with Redmond, catching up and worrying about me.

My nap wasn't very successful because I kept jolting awake with dark and morbid thoughts. I finally gave up and called Rick to come back. We went back to Redmond's room together, my wheelchair scraping against walls and catching on door frames. When I told Mom and Katie what was going on, Mom asked if I was on Percocet. When I confirmed that I was, she said that she'd had the same thing happen to her when she took that after her mastectomy. She hated the stuff and stopped taking it.

I was more afraid of the pain of the c-section than the sleep problems though. After I figured out what caused it, it stopped bothering me. I'd jolt awake with some crazy dream/thought, then remind myself that it was just Percocet and immediately go back to sleep.

As I sat for hours upon hours in the NICU, waiting to see how Redmond would respond to ECMO, I realized I was in a state of shock. I noticed weird things, like how the shape of the lights on the ceiling mimicked the shape of one of the pieces on my breast pump. Colors stood out to me, like the bright orange and yellow furniture. They are two of my favorite colors, but they aren't soothing. They aren't typical colors for couches and chairs. My husband kept mumbling on about the windows that overlooked the cemetery below. I don't know that I would've considered how morbid it was to overlook a cemetery while my child's life hung in the balance if it hadn't been for him and his keen powers of observation.

I was appalled at the filth in the hospital. I thought hospitals were supposed to be clean, but at times it was disgusting. Redmond's blood spilled on the floor around the ECMO machine and no one bothered to clean it up for days. Dried spatters of blood all around his bed drove me batty. If it hadn't been for the pain I was in from the c-section, I'd have been scrubbing the floor myself. I finally said something about it to one blessed nurse who was fastidiously cleaning everything at the beginning of her shift. She couldn't see it from her vantage point, but when she came around to where I was sitting, she immediately cleaned it up.

I observed as once every three to four days someone from environmental services entered his room, ran a wet mop quickly over the floor without moving anything, wiped off the counter, emptied the trash, and moved on to the next room. An enormous machine went down the halls every so often to mop the floors, but I never saw anyone clean a bathroom or the pump rooms. I began looking for those anti-bacterial wipes in every room I entered. If I had to pump, first I got a wipe and covered every surface I'd be likely to touch. Trash overflowed the small cans next to each chair and spilled drinks congealed on the floor. One day it was so bad that I reported it. Three hours later nothing had changed. I used those wipes on my chair in Redmond's room, on the counters every morning, and on the chairs in the hallway. The filth got to me.

But when a patient left a room, I've never seen anything quite like the scrub down those rooms received. The doors closed and soap and scrub brushes completely covered every surface from floor to ceiling. Few things are as shiny as one of those rooms when a new patient entered it. Anything that touched the floor in our room immediately went in the trash. Anything that had been used once went in the trash. We couldn't believe the number of things that were thrown away every day. When we asked about it, the response was, "Hospital germs are much worse than home germs. We don't want to risk contamination."

Another family also hung around the hallway chairs while we did. Their daughter was in room 34, and she was also on ECMO. In fact, there were four babies on ECMO on our hallway that week. Our two families were the only ones who stayed throughout the day though. We got to know one another as the days dragged on. The mother was close to my age and walking slowly as she recovered from childbirth, her belly still swollen like mine. Her husband was exhausted from working and taking care of their other children while spending time at the hospital. As the weeks wore on, we became friends, cheering on one another's children and waiting together for test results and through surgeries. She handled her daughter's extended NICU stay with tremendous grace and resolve, helping me to remain calm and steady.

Mom, Katie, and I made the most of our time together. We learned many years ago that in the worst of times, you get through it by finding the humor in the situation. While Redmond was going through surgery for ECMO, my sister made me laugh through the tears. As we waited outside in the hall while alarms clanged and beeped, while ECMO specialists and nurses bustled around to find a way to help Redmond, we found things to laugh about together. It was surreal – trying to distract ourselves while we sat helplessly waiting to hear if he'd be okay.

On Saturday night, Mom and Katie went back to their hotel for the night and Rick and I reluctantly left Redmond in the care of the fantastic nurses to get some sleep. That night I had nightmares I couldn't shake. I'd wake up, try to shake off the thoughts and sort of go back to sleep, but the dream continued.

I could see King David in 2 Samuel 11-12 as he wept and prayed for God to save his newborn son. This child's life hung in the balance and David fasted and prayed for days, begging God to spare the child's life. But God didn't save the baby, and when David's servants came to tell him they were afraid of how he'd respond. They were shocked when he got up, washed his face, and ate.

When questioned, he said he'd done everything he could do while there was a chance that God would save his baby. The child would not be saved, so there was no more point in asking. (The Bible never says how Bathsheba responded, by the way. I have a feeling she didn't get up and wash her face and eat.)

In my dream, I believed that Redmond died and I had to get up, wash my face, and go back to daily life. I had to accept that this trial was God's plan for my life and get on with it. It seemed a totally rational, even spiritual, dream. Forgetting that David and Bathsheba had conceived the child in sin and God would not let that sin go unpunished, I allowed shame to wash over me. God would take my son like King David's son. "He spared not His own son," so why would He spare mine? He owed me nothing. Muddled and confused, sure that God had already taken Redmond and no one wanted to call and tell me, I got out of bed and quickly dressed. Rick opened his eyes and asked me what time it was. It was ridiculously early and he hadn't been having nightmares, so he didn't have my sense of urgency.

I left the room without Rick, completely forgetting that I was supposed to be in a wheelchair. I walked down the hall to the elevator, went down the two floors while trying to catch my breath, then made the long walk from the elevators to Redmond's room, which was as far as one could get from the elevators. By the time I got to his room, I was shaking, hyperventilating, and my mouth was so dry I couldn't swallow. I fully expected him to be gone, a lone social worker waiting to tell me what had happened. "While you were sleeping, he was dying" was the phrase that rang in my mind.

When I finally got to his room, I saw the now-familiar ECMO machine at the foot of his bed, the specialist sitting in front of it with his laptop, and two nurses at their station inside the door. Redmond's body lay exactly as it had been – on his little red blanket in the clear, acrylic crib. I looked at them incredulously, stammering out the dreaded words,

"Is he alive? Is he okay?"

Realizing that they had a mother freaking out on them at that moment, they snapped to attention and came to my side.

"Redmond is fine. He had a good night. He's stable right now. Come see."

The nurse drew me over to the side of his bed, showing me his little body, still hooked up to all the lines and tubes, like he'd been when we left the night before. My nose burned and tears flooded my cheeks as I stared at him, relief nearly knocking me over. I could breathe again. I could swallow. I could live. He was okay.

I looked at her and whispered, "I was so afraid."

She nodded with understanding and slipped back to her station, giving me space to calm down. I caught the look the ECMO specialist gave the nurse as she walked away – eyebrows up, concerned. I didn't care.

In that moment, the Holy Spirit washed over me and sanity returned. My mouth opened and words poured out of me that had never crossed my mind before. I believe they were directly from God, given to both me and Redmond in that moment.

"Redmond Samuel Wyse, you are a gift from God. Every moment of your precious life is a gift. And whether I have you for six days, six months, six years, or a lifetime, I will be grateful for every single moment. You are an answer to my prayers, and I cherish every moment I've had with you – every moment of that horrible pregnancy, and every fear-filled, terrible moment since you were born. You are a gift and I'm grateful for you."

With those words that I hadn't felt moments before, things changed. Love rushed in and bubbled over my heart in a refreshing stream, replacing once and for all the numbness and thoughts that it might be better if he didn't make it. Love knocked down walls I'd built to protect my heart from the pain of losing him. Love reminded me that in Christ, every life is precious and worthwhile, even the lives of babies with Down syndrome, congenital heart defects, and pulmonary hypertension. Love washed over every part of me, reminding me that God is greater than any fear, any doubt, and any lie from Satan.

Until that moment, I'd been carrying around terrible guilt and shame. When Rick and I conceived our first child, I was 36 years old and he was 47. We had been warned then that birth defects were more likely as we got older. Down syndrome had been mentioned to us with every pregnancy. **The idea of what people would think of us, would think of him, and how they would treat our other children had lurked in my mind. I couldn't get past it. But in that moment, my love for this precious child overruled any concern for the opinion of others and I felt only total adoration and love.**

7

CONSIDERING DOWN SYNDROME

The hardest thing I write as I share this story is that we truly didn't think God would do that to us. Down syndrome and birth defects were things that happened to other people. We'd been more faithful to God than a lot of people we knew, so we imagined that we were somehow protected from hard things. My spiritual pride was as deep a sin as any other, although I did not see it then.

The doctor suggested genetic testing when I got pregnant the first time at age 36. She wasn't worried about my ability to have a successful pregnancy but thought it would be wise to check for birth defects. We declined. When I had our second baby at age 38, we were again told that we had an increased likelihood of birth defects. But when we went in for Redmond when I was 40 years old, to be 41 when he was born, the warnings were much more severe.

Our babysitter, Kristina, has 9 siblings, the last of whom was born when her mother was 48 years old. When I mentioned the doctor's concerns to her mother before Redmond was born, she responded thoughtfully.

"You have plenty of years left to have children. They warned us too, but all 10 of our children are healthy and strong. To be fair though, my best friend was expecting a baby at the same time as I was expecting our youngest and her son is not okay. We don't know why God chooses what He does and that's been hard."

For her, hard meant the guilt she faced at having 10 healthy children while her dear friend faced the difficulties of a son with multiple diagnoses that make their lives very different.

Guilt pressed down on me and I squirmed under the weight of it. I'd been warned, but I thought we were safe under the umbrella of God's protection. When a person steps out from under that umbrella by living in willful disobedience to God, they open themselves up to the consequences of sin, which is death. When I heard things like, "we live in a broken world and broken things happen," I basically plugged my ears and shook my head, refusing to acknowledge it. I confused my spiritual pride with faith in God's protection.

In the first NICU, a social worker named Kim approached me during a rare moment when I was alone in the family lounge. Standing in front of the door, I stared blankly at a poster while questioning accusations raged in my mind. What had I done to our perfect family? Why hadn't two healthy, happy kids been enough for me? What were people going to think of us? Was there some unrepentant, deliberate sin in my life? Why hadn't God protected us? Protected innocent little Redmond who surely had no sin in his life? Unknown pain and tragedy loomed before me; fear threatened to swallow me up.

"Are you Redmond's mom?"

The question caused me to shake my head to clear the anxious thoughts. She invited me into her office to chat. It was like she could read my mind and realized exactly what I'd been thinking.

"How are YOU doing? How are you handling this crisis?"

Totally embarrassed, but also unable to hold it back, the tears broke like a dam. Sobbing, I answered her questions without the need to say a word. She had an intern with her, and she quickly went to find Rick. He came and sat down beside me, bewildered. Kim brought him up to speed quickly, and he took my hand.

When I'd calmed down enough to speak, she asked, "Did you know there were any issues with the baby?"

"No. We had some slight concerns about his heart, but the ultrasounds kept showing that everything was fine. We really weren't concerned about his health at all."

She asked then, "How are you feeling about it now?"

I shared with her and Rick (and that poor, stunned intern) about the guilt I felt and the thoughts I couldn't silence. *It's my old eggs. This is my fault. I'm greedy and selfish. I ruined our perfect lives.*

She nodded as I spoke, hearing me and acknowledging the pain I felt. Instead of trying to assure me that Down syndrome wasn't my fault, which would've gotten her nowhere with me, she asked me another question.

"Did you know there was an increased chance of birth defects at your age?"

"Yes," I whispered, unable to look up.

"So why did you decide to try for a baby anyway? Why didn't you have the tests to find out if he had Down syndrome?" She asked her questions compassionately and with genuine interest in my answers. There was not a hint of accusation.

"We knew there was an increased risk and we didn't care. We discussed the possibility and agreed that we'd love any child God gave us. We wouldn't have an abortion under any circumstances, and we didn't want to worry throughout the entire pregnancy about something that we couldn't even be sure about until the baby was born." As those words left my mouth, I began to feel like I could breathe again. The accusing voices in my head quieted down.

"So, you knew it was possible, but you didn't care because you valued the life of your baby over your own comfort and convenience?" With those words, an encouraging smile spread across her face.

"Yes. I guess that's right," I replied.

Kim asked Rick if he blamed me. Of course he didn't, and he was sad to know I'd been blaming myself. We talked about our uncertainty of what the future would look like and how our older children would be affected. Kim encouraged us that it would be okay. She talked to us about people she knew with Down syndrome, about how they went to school with their typical peers, had friends and jobs, even lived with some independence. Neither one of us had known many people with Down syndrome, but Rick reminded me of a young man at church. I hadn't even realized that was his diagnosis. He's handsome, speaks clearly, and completed high school at a Christian school that didn't have a special education program. He has also taken many college courses. Encouraged, I dried my tears and left her office with a better outlook.

It would still be a while before the guilt and shame left completely. Sometimes these things happen a little at a time.

One thing we didn't discuss until later was that both of us wondered if Redmond *should* make it. What would his quality of life be? What would our lives be like with a child with Down syndrome? We were clueless. The obstetrician had told us that if he made it through this medical crisis, our lives would be good. We weren't sure about that. Nevertheless, we prayed for God to heal him completely and for him not to have Down syndrome. We really wanted their suspicions to be wrong.

A nurse in the first NICU handed us a thick, white 3-ring binder, provided by the Down Syndrome Association in our area. The first page was a copy of a copy of a copy of an essay entitled, *Welcome to Holland,* by Emily Perl Kingsley. I read it slowly and tried to let the message sink in. Basically, it said that I had been planning a beautiful vacation to Italy, but when I got off the plane, I found that I was actually in Holland. Holland is beautiful, but very different from Italy. I was unprepared for Holland, so I needed to start learning about windmills and tulips and stop yearning for gigantic plates of pasta and Roman architecture. I'd probably always wonder what Italy would be like, but I needed to settle into Holland and start appreciating the unexpected beauty.

I thumbed through the rest of the binder, which appeared to be an enormous list of resources like doctors and social programs for disabled kids. I closed the book and didn't open it again for months. I couldn't wrap my mind around the need for those resources. At that time, it would have been helpful to see photos of adorable babies and toddlers with Down syndrome, stories from parents about how wonderful their children were, and so forth. It was depressing to see a list of medical specialists and medical equipment rental companies.

Another nurse handed me a slip of paper with the first name and phone number of a mom whose son has Down syndrome. She said that this woman was happy to talk to me if I had any questions. I thought, *there is no way I'm calling some stranger to talk about her son with Down syndrome. What if her son's situation is awful and it depresses me? We don't even know for sure if Redmond has it.*

We decided to wait to share the news publicly until we had the results of the blood test. Our parents, siblings, and a few close friends knew of the suspicion. Nearly everyone responded positively. One of my dearest friends had the hardest time with it, telling me in disbelief that there was no way. God would *not* allow that to happen to us. When she said it, with very good intentions, something in my heart shifted. It almost felt physical. I knew she was wrong. Still, we didn't have the results yet and I prayed that she was right.

There was another concern I had with sharing the diagnosis publicly. Within the Christian community, there are those who believe so strongly in the confession we make with our mouths (the words we say out loud) that to them, announcing a medical diagnosis removes the possibility of healing because we have "claimed it." It's called the faith movement and to them, if we have enough faith in the power of God, we will make a positive confession of that faith. If we confess healing and wholeness, we will have healing and wholeness. If we confess sickness, we will have sickness.

The movement demands that God respond to us according to the way we understand His will. I know some very sincere believers who have accepted this teaching as truth. When their "good confession" doesn't produce the desired results, they believe it's because someone didn't have enough faith. They insist that we haven't prayed hard enough, or we haven't had enough faith to bring about God's perfect will. If the person praying has enough faith but their desired outcome still doesn't happen, then someone else must not be praying with enough faith. But Romans 8:26 says that when our prayers are weak, the Holy Spirit prays for us with groanings that are too deep for words. So is the failure of healing the Holy Spirit's fault?

I grew up around the fringes of this movement and bought into parts of it without even realizing what it meant. Hard and confusing circumstances in my life have caused me to question the validity of this idea. Although imperfect, I believed I'd done the best that I knew to do and the results still didn't line up with my expectations. **My experiences have led me to realize that God doesn't operate by formulas.**

I knew there had to be some other truth. As I looked around at the faith-filled believers whose lives were hit with as much difficulty (perhaps more) than someone with no faith whatsoever, I came to a new determination. I cannot manipulate God's plan through saying just the right prayers or having the right thoughts. The heart is desperately wicked anyway, so who besides Jesus has exactly the right thoughts?

God is running the universe and His plan is much better than mine. He can choose to say a word and obliterate disease from the face of the earth, but He doesn't. He can choose to allow disease to wipe out our entire race, but He hasn't. He could strike all unrepentant sinners with disease and keep all Christians totally healthy, but He doesn't.

It's my job to be obedient to what His word tells me to do and leave the results to Him. Period.

As I study Scripture, I see many examples to support the reality that God is mysterious and not to be placed in a box. While Jesus walked the earth, His cousin John the Baptist, who was chosen to announce His coming and prepare the world to receive Him, was beheaded by a government official. Why didn't Jesus, who could calm the sea and raise the dead, stop that from happening? Why didn't God send an earthquake to shake the prison where he was held and loose his chains like he did for Paul and Silas, or send an angel to set him free like he did for Peter? While he languished in prison, John the Baptist himself asked Jesus if He was indeed the Messiah or if they should look for another. Was that a lack of faith?

Sometimes giving our entire lives to the work of the Holy Spirit means that we will lose our lives (or lose our plan for our lives) in mysterious and underserved ways. We may not be beaten and imprisoned like Paul and Silas, we may not be crucified upside down like Peter, we may not have to run for our lives and live in the wilderness for years like King David; but we may find ourselves raising a medically fragile child or a child with special needs.

We may find ourselves unfairly dealing with family members who make our lives miserable. We may do something brave like adopt a child out of foster care and discover that the child suffered such serious damage from previous trauma that our lives become unbearably hard. Maybe we have a perfectly healthy and happy child, only to have a serious accident that leaves them permanently disabled.

Stories of godly people who are dealing with very hard things abound and every one of the examples above is from someone I know personally. No one is exempt from suffering.

It would be understandable if the people in these examples chose to question the goodness of God. Instead, what I overwhelmingly see in them is a strength that rises from somewhere deep inside. They become examples of faithfulness in the midst of suffering. **It's a breath-taking strength, like steel, and a fire that only the Holy Spirit can light, that drives them deeper into their relationship with the Lord and spills over into everyone they touch. They are the warriors, scarred and often battle weary, who stand as champions in the kingdom of God.**

Oh, to be like them. To stand on the top of the mountain I am climbing and plant a flag that says to everyone who sees it, "By the grace of God, I made it; and by the grace of God, I will stand."

John the Baptist leapt in his mother's womb the first time he was in the presence of Jesus. He knew who Jesus was before he was born. His expectations that his cousin, the Messiah, the Savior of the world wouldn't allow him to suffer like that were unmet. I'm struck by the fact that *God never bothered to explain Himself* when it came to John the Baptist. Jesus didn't say, "I know you're there and I have a really good reason for not rescuing you. Here's my plan."

God doesn't have to explain Himself to us.

What makes us think that we deserve an explanation every time something doesn't go the way we think it should? What truth from Scripture causes us to believe that if we sacrifice our convenience to serve God that He is required to give us an easy life? This message will be offensive to many, but Jesus was sent as a stumbling stone and a rock of offense to those who try to pursue righteousness based on works (Romans 9:31-33).

I cannot think of one example of a hero of the Bible who did not suffer in spite of their commitment to the Lord. I'm not saying that God causes suffering, but we have plenty of examples of how He allows it. How are we going to handle it? Will we become angry and bitter? Will we turn away from our Creator because our expectations have not been met? Or will we adjust the lens through which we look at our circumstances, get back up and straighten our crowns, and ask God what He would have us do to bring Him glory through our circumstances?

Recently, an idea has been growing slowly inside me. A question, really. What if suffering itself is a gift from God? What if the roots that go down deep during times of difficulty, the ones that anchor us to the Lord in a way that couldn't come without suffering, are the gift? Not a consolation prize that God allows us because we're suffering – but the gift itself. What if suffering is the gift that God gives us as He leads us deeper into our relationship with Him, as He lavishes His love upon us? **What if an easy life is exactly the opposite of what we need?**

When Redmond was born, we hadn't worked out our thoughts on the role of faith in suffering yet because we had never really had to. We chose to wait to share the suspicion of Redmond's diagnosis until we had confirmed answers, concerned that we not hurt our loved ones who believed that our confession would seal the deal. Also, we still hoped for a miracle, for news that the doctors' suspicions were wrong.

Looking Up When Life Looks Down

8

THE MIRACLE

The first few days of ECMO were a blur, ups and downs and alarms and trying to remember to take my medicine and not sneeze or cough (you might not understand this part if you haven't had abdominal surgery, but a sneeze will drop you to your knees). When it became clear that Redmond was one of the most critically ill patients and we'd be there longer than a few days, we were moved to a room at The Ronald McDonald House that's located right outside of the hospital. The house is close, but too far to walk as I recovered from the c-section. Rick drove me over every morning and dropped me off at the front door of the children's hospital. I walked in and sat in one of their wheelchairs, waiting while Rick drove back to The Ronald McDonald House to park, and then ran back to the hospital to push me upstairs to the NICU.

I ate my meals in Redmond's room, listening as one ECMO specialist trained another ECMO specialist until I couldn't take it anymore. I learned from listening to them that there are two main kinds of ECMO – VA, which offers heart and lung support, and VV – which only offers lung support. Redmond needed VA ECMO and his case was great for training new specialists, but listening to the teacher go on and on to his students in a clinical way about my son got to me. I wanted to go for walks, but wasn't up to it yet, so I moved out to the hallway to get away from the strain.

Katie, Mom, and I sat on the orange couches and chairs and talked about all kinds of things to keep our minds off the trouble at hand. I took naps back at The Ronald McDonald House, so while Rick ran to get the car,

Katie or Mom pushed my wheelchair down to the front door. I'd walk to the car and get in carefully, then he'd drive me over and relax a little while I slept. Mom and Katie kept vigil over Redmond while we were gone.

We had a few visitors and they kept handing me journals, suggesting that I write things down to remember these long days of waiting and wondering. My response was always, "I don't want to remember! I want to forget that this ever happened." I still didn't understand that we weren't going home with our baby in a day or two, relieved that he was okay and the NICU was just a bad memory. I didn't understand that my life had made a sharp turn in a direction I hadn't planned and couldn't control. I didn't understand anything about this new road we were on. I also had no idea how vivid my memories would be. There's really no forgetting.

Then, on Tuesday, March 7, 2017, I woke up in the morning at The Ronald McDonald House and felt a horrific sense of alarm. What was wrong? How had my baby done in the night? How could I have left him alone for so long? Swallowing down my fear so I could speak, I called the NICU and spoke to his nurse. She said he'd had a rough night but was doing okay at the time. What I heard was, "He's alive."

The second I hung up, the phone rang in my hand. It was the hospital. Confused, I answered quickly, thinking it was too fast for her to call me back. It was Redmond's Neonatal Nurse Practitioner (NNP), June. With a sense of urgency, she said that Redmond had developed something called a tension pneumothorax overnight. It was interfering with the ECMO circuit. Treatment options were very limited and likely to cause damage from which he couldn't recover. His medical team was about to meet to discuss the options, and I should get over there quickly to be a part of the meeting.

Rick and I scurried to the car. Because of the difficult parking situation, he drove me the short distance to the hospital, abandoned the car in the tangle of vehicles waiting in front of the building, wheeled me up to the NICU, and ran back down before our car got towed away.

The surgical team, ECMO team, and neonatal teams stood in a circle and talked. A part of the circle, I sat in a chair and listened, struggling to understand the medical jargon.

What I saw from the chest x-ray taken that morning was frightening. Where a straight line should have been, dividing his chest into two mirrored chambers, there was a very clear line that went off to the left. A small air pocket had developed on the right side, pushing everything out of line, causing major problems. Typically, they could place a simple chest tube to deflate the air pocket. But Redmond was on blood thinners for

ECMO and the chest tube would cause internal and external bleeding that could not be prevented or treated. The chest tube would most likely cause him to bleed to death. Without the chest tube, they couldn't keep running ECMO, which was keeping him alive. It was a no-win situation.

While the medical team talked about what to do, I stared at their shoes and prayed with all my might. In the hallway in front of Room 38, I prayed prayers that felt to me like I was sweating great drops of blood.

"Lord, please let this cup pass from me. Please don't take my baby boy. Give the team wisdom and creativity to see some other way through this thing. Anoint their minds and their hands with supernatural, miraculous power to do their jobs better than they ever have before. Thank You, God, for every moment I've had with my precious boy."

I didn't have to write in a journal to remember vividly that they were all wearing comfortable shoes. Brightly colored sneakers, Crocs, and Birkenstocks graced the feet of the people who were straining with all their might to save my son's life. These people are on their feet all day, every day. They give so much of their time, their mental energy (even when they are away from the hospital), and their very lives to rescue babies like Redmond. I loved them all fiercely, even the ones whose names I didn't know. I loved the time they'd spent educating themselves to handle situations that were so far beyond my ability to understand. I loved the hearts beating in their chests that drew them to save the lives of the most vulnerable babies.

One man in the group wore a suit and dress shoes. I understood that his biggest value came from the way his mind worked and the finesse in his hands. He spoke with authority. He was the pediatric surgeon who would need to place the chest tube.

With a heavy Indian accent, he asked, "What do we do when we don't know what to do?" No one answered, so he continued, "We wait."

Although I heard later that the other two teams were frustrated with his response, they heeded his voice of reason and decided that they could wait six hours before the ECMO interference started causing major problems. They decided to decrease his blood thinners as much as possible to prepare for the chest tube. At 2:00 p.m. they would repeat his chest x-ray and do what they had to do.

The resident with stunning pale skin and shiny, thick, straight, black hair asked me if I understood what they'd decided. I repeated it back to her, my throat burning, my brain seeking a way out of the pressure as I wondered how long it took her to fix her hair like that every day. I imagined hours with a straightening wand as I blindly stumbled to the couch in the hallway and called Rick, then my parents. Maybe she chemically straightens it? Maybe it's naturally that thick and straight? Such strange thoughts during the worst of the crisis left me shaking my head to stop worrying about her perfect hair.

Rick called his parents, who were caring for Eliana and Charlie that morning. I called our church and asked them to stop what they were doing and pray. After a brief discussion, the pastors decided to drop everything and drive 90 miles to sit with us while we waited. My mom and sister came to the 9th floor to wait with us.

I had been very cautious about what I posted on social media. I didn't want to be overly dramatic or raise unnecessary alarm, but the time had come to ask for help. I posted a prayer request as simple as I could make it:

> *"Please pray for Redmond this morning. He faced a
> setback last night. The doctors are giving him until
> 2:00 to see if it will resolve on its own. If it doesn't,
> they'll have to do a very risky procedure to deal with
> the problem. We're praying for complete healing of
> his lungs and heart, and for the doctors to have
> wisdom and knowledge, creativity and innovation,
> so that the issue is resolved without adding risk."*

People from all over the world responded to the request. The heavens must have shaken from all the hearts here on earth who begged God to intervene. We were so blessed by the love and support we received. I was terribly aware that God was running the universe and in the grand scheme of things, it might not be in His plan to save Redmond's life. I submitted to the horrible possibility that God's purpose might be revealed more deeply through his death than through his healing. "He spared not His own son..."

My body trembled with holy fear. I don't know if I've ever been more aware of the awesome power of God and of His ability to withhold His hand when He deems it necessary. I felt small and insignificant, raw and exposed as I realized how vulnerable and weak I was. Our lives on earth are so fragile, our comfort and happiness so delicate. How my heart ached as I called out to God – *please let my baby live.*

We sat in a tight little circle as we waited, praying, trying to find a way to make it through the hours that dragged by. My pastor told funny stories in an effort to get our minds off the fear, and I appreciated him for it, but dread hovered over me. I had lost so many times; I braced myself for the worst loss of them all. I knew well the sharp sting of disappointment, the feeling of the earth crumbling as everything crashed around me.

I still didn't understand what Down syndrome would mean for our family. I once confidently believed that it was faith to know - without doubt - that I was protected by God from hardship. I believed that someone who submitted their life to God was exempt from disease and heartbreak and poverty. I felt like I was holding shattered pieces of that belief in my bleeding hands. All that remained was blind trust that my holy and powerful God held the world in the palm of His hand. If He did not heal Redmond, then He had a very good reason. He would be with me in my shattered grief, just as He had been with me every other day of my life.

At 2:00, the x-ray tech wheeled a large, portable machine into Redmond's room, which was already crowded with ECMO equipment, over 20 digital screens, lines, pumps, and computers. We waited for news as the medical team studied the x-ray. I couldn't stand it. I walked over to them and peeked over their shoulders at the screen. What I saw looked to my untrained eye as a perfectly straight line down the middle of his chest. I scurried like a guilty child back to the couches to wait before they could catch me. I hadn't yet learned that I was right to go look at that x-ray and my appropriate place was right next to the medical team.

They pointed and talked, nodded at one another, and slowly disbursed. June, our NNP, walked up to us and smiled. "The pneumothorax is gone."

"What?" I needed her to say it again. I needed her to say more words like that.

"It's gone. His heart and lungs have realigned and are in the right place. No chest tube is needed." Her tone was firm and assuring.

"It's gone?" I asked again, making sure I understood correctly.

"Yes." She reaffirmed her answer.

And then I saw it. Tears of disbelief and joy threatened to spill out of her eyes. Her scientific mind, so accustomed to delivering bad news to parents, was also overwhelmed with the good news she shared. She probably needed this miracle almost as much as we needed it.

Something inside me felt like it cracked right open – a shell I'd tried to place around my heart as I waited to mourn for the rest of my life.

It was the closest I ever came to fainting right off the chair the entire time we were there. As relief flooded over me in almost violent waves, the sobs I'd been holding back broke loose. Sobs of relief wracked my body as I thanked God over and over again for saying YES.

My mom had stepped away to take a phone call and came running back at the sound, horror on her face. My mind told me to pull it together and not be so dramatic (in front of my pastors, for Pete's sake), but my body had other things to do. I don't remember anyone else's response. I don't even remember if anyone hugged me. Where was Rick? I don't remember.

I only remember asking June if she'd ever seen anything like that before.

She replied, "I've been working in the NICU since 1995 and I've never seen anything like this before. A tension pneumothorax does NOT go away on its own."

My mom clarified, "Would you call this a miracle?"

Tears spilled down June's cheeks, obviously against her will. "What just happened is an undeniable miracle. Only God could do it."

She went on to give us more good news. According to the x-ray, it appeared his heart was healing. Those are words I wish I'd written down, but my only memory of that conversation is from my Facebook post.

> *"We have our miracle! The nurse practitioner just told us that in 22 years of working here, she has never seen what happened today. In six hours, his body realigned and the risky procedure will not need to be done. We are so grateful for all your prayers - and to our great God for healing him. We also received good news that his heart is healing. I'm crying tears of JOY. He's able to continue ECMO, which we pray will allow his heart and lungs to fully heal."*

One of my pastors who wasn't with us tells me that he and the rest of the staff were sitting in the conference room praying for Redmond when the call came in. God had answered their prayers. He said faith rose up in him like never before, so moved that our prayers had been answered. He'd been waiting to make plans for a funeral, but instead he received a call to joy.

My sister headed home that day. She'd been away from her family and job for a week and it was time for her to get back to her responsibilities. It was so hard to see her go, but the worst of the crisis was over and she'd held my hand through it. I will be grateful to her for the rest of my life. Mom always told us when we were young that when everyone else leaves you, you always have your sister. She was right. No one had "left" me, but she had shown up at a critical time and helped us all.

We spent the rest of the day in grateful celebration and praise. Mom, Rick, and I left the hospital for the first time that night, driving to a nearby restaurant where we giggled at how guilty we felt for leaving, but gratefully ate soup and sandwiches before we rushed back to Redmond's room. I remember standing in that line to order and realizing how normal we looked. No one could tell that we were in the middle of a war, that our souls were scarred and bleeding, but we had won a major battle. It felt like we should have had signs over our heads that read: Escaped NICU Parents/Grandparents. Reality struck me as I looked at those around me, wondering if they'd escaped from the shadow of death or if they were blissfully complaining about problems at work.

Blissfully complaining about problems at work? What a weird thought. But at that moment the idea that the worst thing in my life might be problems at work was blissful. The idea that the worst thing in my life might be sleepless nights from a colicky baby seemed glorious. I wanted to shout from the rooftops – "Be thankful! Hold your babies and glory in their normal problems! Fight with your spouse and be glad that you can! Drag yourself out of bed after another sleepless night with a toddler kicking you in the face and giggle!"

I restrained myself.

What began as the worst day of my life ended with great joy. Death was defeated and our son was saved. God whispered healing words into my heart. Satan had been using Scripture to lie to me, and in my muddled state I had believed his lies.

The verse that had echoed through my mind, "He spared not His own son..." is from Romans 8:31-32 and actually goes like this:

> "What, then, shall we say in response to these things? If God is for us, who can be against us? He who did not spare His own Son but gave Him up for us all - how will He not also, along with Him, freely give us all things?" (NIV).

God didn't spare His own son but gave him up freely - so that He could **save** us. He isn't heartless and cold; He is generous and self-sacrificing. He didn't need for us to give up our son to save anyone or anything. It had already been done by Jesus for the purpose of saving us! It was His great pleasure to redeem the life of my tiny boy.

Our salvation rests in the capable and gracious hands of a loving and generous Father.

Triumphant and at peace, we slept soundly that night and awoke refreshed and full of hope. When we arrived back at the NICU the next morning, June approached us with a worried expression.

She said, "It looks like the pneumothorax is back."

We stared at her in shock. Would God really do that? Would He really answer our prayers, only to take our miracle away?

She explained that the radiologist was reading the x-ray and would let us know for sure in a few minutes. Those minutes were long as we waited and I struggled to comprehend the possibility. My mind repeated like a staccato drum, "No, no, no, no, no, no, no."

I don't know how long we waited, but when June returned, she was smiling. It was not back. Radiology had better screens than they did and could see the picture much more clearly. Nothing was pushed off to the side that morning. No air pocket threatened him. Redmond was fine.

That was the day I realized that the NICU was a place full of wildly different reports, depending on who you spoke with, and I did my best from that point forward to hold my emotions in check and wait to see what the outcome would be. That decision got me through the next month without losing my mind.

9

MOUNTAINS TO MOVE

Before the day of the pneumothorax, they called Redmond a touchy baby. The nurses had to move him every four hours, changing his diaper and caring for the outside of his body. When they did, I sensed their dread as alarms went off and levels inside his body had to be adjusted. After that day, he started tolerating movement. Alarms went off less often. His body began responding to ECMO in the way it should. In my mind, I see Jesus reaching out to touch him that morning and healing more than the pneumothorax. It was a dramatic turning point.

Different specialists came in to see him every day, running tests and cultures and checking his blood gas levels. It seemed like several times a day they told me that he might have this infection or that problem, but I held my peace. We felt like they were so shocked by his healing that the specialists were all looking for something to be wrong. We knew he was healed though.

Every test came back negative for further complications. When he had been on ECMO for five days, they decided to try to turn off the circuit and see how he tolerated it. The clock on the wall in the room was noted and the team decided to turn it off for five minutes. We all waited breathlessly, watching the screens carefully for any signs of distress. Minutes ticked by as he surprised everyone by responding well. Suddenly, one of the nurses said in an alarmed voice, "It's been 20 minutes!"

We all looked at the clock on the wall, then at the clocks on our phones and computers, and realized she was right. The battery had run out on the wall clock at the exact moment they turned off ECMO. He did so well that no one noticed how long it had been.

They turned ECMO back on, discussed what had happened and what adjustments needed to be made. Then they made plans to trial him off ECMO completely the next day. Rick and I just stared at one another, breathing deeply and quietly thanking God. Mom grinned from ear to ear. We'd been told to expect him to be on ECMO up to 14 days.

On the sixth day, they turned off ECMO completely. Many people gathered in his room and watched closely, waiting to see how he did. After a half-hour, most of the people left. After a few hours, they decided it was time to cut the tubes that attached him to the machine. Although the end of the large tubes remained in his neck, a few hours later they moved the machine into the hall outside his room.

On March 9, 2017, Redmond no longer needed ECMO. Our hearts were dancing in grateful praise.

I took a picture of the specialist moving the machine into the hall as evidence of our miracle.

A few days later, the machine disappeared from the hall. Redmond's heart and lungs were working.

The nurse told me that the next priority was to let me hold him, and I almost burst with anticipation. The very next day, when he was 10 days old, I actually got to cradle my baby in my arms for the first time. He had so many things attached to him that two nurses and a respiratory therapist worked together to put him in my lap.

It was scary because I didn't want to mess up any of the things attached to him. They pinned his ventilator to my shirt and I held him the best I could. I couldn't get close enough to his face to kiss it, but I knew that would come. Tears of gratitude spilled down my cheeks. After I talked and sang to him for a while, I fell asleep. He was still heavily sedated, so we slept like that for an hour, so relieved to be together.

We hadn't been home to see our older kids since the brief stop to pack a few clothes on the day after Redmond was born. They'd been up to see us twice, but both visits had been brief. We were all hurting to be together again, so Rick and I made the very difficult decision to leave Redmond overnight and go home. Mom agreed to stay with Redmond so he wasn't alone.

Tearing myself away from him when he was 12 days old was crazy-hard, but I had to see Eliana and Charlie. Knowing Mom was there really helped. We left late that afternoon, drove the 90 minutes home, and hugged and kissed and hugged and kissed those precious two- and four-year-old children who we love so dearly.

One of our hospital visitors had given us a Play Dough kit, so while Rick did some farm chores, the kids and I sat on the floor in the kitchen and played. I remember thinking that we should sit at the kitchen table, but I had such a sense of urgency that I didn't want to waste any precious time moving to the table. I played with them right where we'd hugged it out. Instead of trying to keep the colors separate and not make a mess, I let them mix it all together. We created Play Dough hamburgers and French fries, donuts, and whatever else their hearts desired. We took silly pictures of them "eating" our creations as I gave them every ounce of my attention.

When Rick came in, his obsessive desire for neatness kicked in hard. He immediately started cleaning up our giant mess, chastising me for not going to the table. Would Play Dough be in our grout forever? I laughed and told him it would all be fine. If Play Dough stained our grout, I'd always have a visual memory of that day and all the love we shared. We put our creations up on the counter and frivolously let them dry. (Normally, we'd never waste good Play Dough.)

The members of our church, our family, and our friends had stuffed our freezer, deep freeze, and Rick's parents' deep freeze full of meals for us, so we chose from the amazing selection and ate dinner together. Rick's parents' Sunday school class provided meals for them while they cared for the children in our absence. I thought my heart might burst, so touched by the thoughtfulness of our community.

After dinner, I did laundry and repacked our bags, adding things we'd been missing. Rick typically bathes the kids, so he happily gave them baths that night. It was wonderful to be home and somewhat back into our normal routine. Our babysitter, Kristina, went home for the night, but it was clear that she'd been running our home like a pro. There was food in the refrigerator, the house was clean, and the mail was neatly stacked and waiting for us. I wondered where she'd gotten money to buy groceries. It had never occurred to us to give her any.

That night the kids slept in our bed with us, which was soothing balm for our souls. We were happy for little legs kicking us and children plastered to our sides. We got up in the morning and ate breakfast together, did a few more things around the house, then brought the kids over to their grandparents' house so we could go back to the hospital.

As we drove away, I felt like my heart was tearing down the middle. I wanted to stay with them, to get back to normal, to feel their precious arms around my neck every single day. My newborn was in the hospital though, and that's where I needed to be. I marveled at how well Eliana and Charlie handled it when we left, happy to go back to the fun at Grandma and Grandpa's house again and anticipating Kristina's return later that day. My heart squeezed tight as I thought of the providence of God to let us have them so close together so that they had each other.

My mom hung out in Redmond's room all evening while we were gone. She read to him, sang him songs, and drilled the nurses with questions. She made friends with our neighbors in room 34, learning about baby Amber and telling them about Redmond. The Ronald McDonald House had given us a room large enough to share with her, so she had a night to herself there, letting a security officer drive her back after dark.

While we were in the NICU, it was still winter and a slow time for farmers. That was such a blessing for us because Rick and I could be at the hospital together. We were thankful to Rick's parents and a few of our neighbors, who took care of the daily farm chores while we were gone.

Rick's parents and Kristina kept the kids on their regular schedule, going to preschool, gymnastics, story time at the library, and church – which gave us the freedom to be together with Redmond. My heart ached for the babies around Redmond whose parents couldn't be with them because of lost wages if they missed work, transportation problems, and a lack of childcare for their children at home.

In the days that followed our visit home, we established a NICU routine. Rick learned his way around the giant hospital complex and found the best places to go for meals. He went for long walks, ate in the cafeteria, and discovered that even though the hospital only had sugar-free drinks and low-fat food, they allowed for M&M ice cream sandwiches. The irony of eating two soft sugar cookies with M&M candies sandwiching vanilla ice cream while drinking Diet Coke was not lost on him. He despised their dietary restrictions.

We often returned to The Ronald McDonald House for a late afternoon nap and supper. They had vending machines with regular Coke for a quarter, and Rick made a point of stocking up every day. Different civic organizations and church groups came in every night and provided supper for us. They spoke warmly to us while they served the often-homemade meals, which were not subject to the hospital's rules about sugar and fat. Leftovers went into the large refrigerators to be reheated by anyone who hadn't made it for the hot meal.

Before she left, my sister found a book in the NICU library called, *Babies with Down Syndrome: A New Parents' Guide*. While I napped in the afternoons, she glanced through it and told me what not to read. I'd picked it up a few times but put it back down again because I couldn't quite accept the diagnosis yet. The book was waiting for me when we got back, so I made myself read a few pages at a time. It was time to learn something about this possible diagnosis.

I was surprised to find out that people with Down syndrome have low muscle tone, which affects every muscle in their bodies. Since muscles run our bodies – including the heart, lungs, eyes, mouth, digestive system, etc. – it affects everything. While sharing cute stories of children with Down syndrome, the book details the problems that can come with low muscle tone. It also explains that there are three kinds of Down syndrome: Mosaic, Trisomy 21, and Translocation.

There are three kinds of Down syndrome:

Mosaic: Only affects part of the chromosomes, and depending on which ones it affects, can be fairly minor or hard to detect.

Trisomy 21: The most common type that affects every chromosome.

Translocation: A very rare kind that can be passed down through a genetic mutation in one of the parents

Rick and I agreed that if he had anything, it was surely Mosaic. We could see none of the telltale features on his face, only the single Palmar crease in each of his hands. His ears aren't low set. His eyes were always closed, but we didn't see an almond shape. We couldn't tell about his muscle tone because he was sedated and unable to pull his body into the fetal position. His nasal bridge didn't appear flat to us. His hands aren't square and his toes are kind of crazy, but don't have the telltale gap between the first and second toes. When we looked at him, we saw a beautiful baby boy with too many tubes and wires attached to him.

When he was around two weeks old, I was sitting alone in his room when his doctor came in. She quietly told me that they'd received the results of his chromosome test and it was positive. He had Trisomy 21, or Down syndrome.

I nodded my head, trying not to over-react to the news. It didn't occur to me that she should've waited until Rick was there. I merely wondered why she hadn't asked my beloved NNP, June, to tell me. Since it had been suspected since the night he was born, I understood that she didn't feel like she was delivering shocking news.

I'd let June know that if he did have it, I wanted to know what kind – Mosaic, Trisomy 21, or Translocation. The doctor told me that she understood that I had some questions. She said I could ask her anything. I hadn't yet learned that it's important to write down questions for doctors when I'm thinking clearly so that I don't freeze up in the moment and forget.

I stumbled over my words, trying to remember what I'd wanted to ask. Finally, I remembered and squeaked out the words, "What kind?"

She looked at me kind of funny and repeated, "What kind?"

"Yes, what kind of Down syndrome is it? There are three kinds," I explained like she didn't know.

She was probably trying not to laugh at me as she repeated, "He has Trisomy 21."

"Yes, but *what kind?* Is it Moasic?" I didn't understand that Down syndrome has three types, one of which is Trisomy 21. There are not three types of Trisomy 21.

"It's not Mosaic. It's regular Trisomy 21," she replied, finally understanding my question.

"Oh," I responded, feeling like I'd had the wind knocked out of me.

After a pause, I choked out the question, "How bad is it?"

She looked at me quizzically, "How bad?"

Unsure of myself, I clarified. "How severe is it? Does he have a mild case or a severe case?"

I fully expected her to say it was mild, but she explained that only time would tell us that. There is no test to measure the severity of it. A person either has it or they don't. She explained that everyone has varying levels of intelligence and athletic abilities, and people with Down syndrome are the same - with varying levels of intelligence and physical capability.

She explained that our state has an early intervention program that would work with us to help Redmond be the best Redmond possible. They would come out and assess him when he got home, and they would work with him to provide physical, occupational, and speech therapy from a very early age. It had been determined in recent years that the earlier the therapies began, the better chance he had to succeed in life.

I nodded, and then I stopped asking questions. I wanted her to leave so I could absorb the diagnosis without anyone staring at me. I sat for a long time that afternoon, quietly allowing my heart and mind to adjust to the knowledge that he really did have Down syndrome. When Rick returned to the room, I told him. Together we decided that our prayer would be for him to have the least possible negative effects of it, and we committed to do everything in our power to help him become the best he could be.

He might have Down syndrome, but it wouldn't define his life. He was Redmond Samuel Wyse, our miracle baby, and we would fight fiercely for him and give him every opportunity to succeed.

We let our parents and siblings know the confirmed diagnosis. My parents didn't know if it was necessary for us to share the diagnosis publicly. He didn't appear any different to us, so it might be better if we kept the news to ourselves. Why put a label on him that would follow him for the rest of his life? Why not wait and see what he could do and only tell people if we felt it was necessary? Their wisdom made sense to us, so we considered and prayed about that option.

Pastor Brad came to see us and we shared the news with him. He knew the struggle we felt about making a "negative confession" and causing dear loved ones to feel we'd made a big mistake. He understood our feelings about giving him every opportunity to succeed in life without a label hanging over his head. Very carefully and graciously, he said what we needed to hear.

Pastor Brad has a way with words that is a great gift. I could never hope to capture his exact phrasing here, but in his calm and quiet manner he spoke cautiously and wisely something like this: "We live in a very small community and people are interested in one another's lives. Do you want them to wonder about Redmond's diagnosis and discuss it behind your back? You have the opportunity to let them know right up front by putting it into your own words and setting the tone for what they think and believe about him."

Rick and I figured that given our unique circumstances, we were already the subject of enough speculation in our small town. It would be better to share the news in our way. We also decided that if God ever chose to heal him of Down syndrome and no one even knew he had been diagnosed with it, the miracle couldn't be celebrated as fully as it could be.

We made a few phone calls to our closest friends, making sure that they knew first. It took me several days and many edits, but I carefully crafted a blog post introducing Redmond to the world. It was similar to the ones I had done for Eliana and Charlie. With Rick's blessing, I published the new blog post. I went through the basic details of the rough start he'd had, and then ended the post with these words.

> *Redmond has some things that will continue to challenge us as he grows. We've been told he has a ventricular septal defect (VSD), or a hole between the lower chambers of his heart. It's possible that it could close on its own, be something he's able to live with, or need to be repaired surgically in the future. We are praying earnestly for God to close that hole without the need for surgery. The hole is a complication of Down syndrome, or Trisomy 21. This diagnosis came as a surprise to us, as none of the tests we had done before he was born suggested it. It took a while for the chromosome test to be completed, but we were told it was a possibility within an hour of his birth.*
>
> ***Redmond*** *(wise protector)* ***Samuel*** *(God has heard)* ***Wyse*** *will not be defined by this diagnosis. Named in honor of his paternal grandfather, Samuel Wenger, his name means "God has heard and blessed us with a wise protector." We chose this name before we knew anything about him and believe God has a purpose and a mission for his life. He will be a mighty man of God, given every opportunity to succeed, and supported through*

every possible path he may take. We have prayed for him since before he was born, asking God to give us another child, and have believed that he would bring "life and health, joy and peace." He is our great blessing and we praise God for answering our prayers. He has already exceeded the expectations of our doctors, and we look forward to seeing all the ways he exceeds the expectations of the rest of the world.

My hands shook as I pressed the "Publish" button, my heart racing as the news went out into the world. I updated my Facebook status to let my friends know I'd written a new post, and then I waited for the responses. I knew that if people didn't read the post, or didn't read all the way to the end, they wouldn't know. That felt good to me, knowing that only the people who were truly interested in our lives would have the information in the beginning. To me, it was a slower way to roll out the news since my heart still felt like it was bleeding and sensitive.

The comments I received were incredibly gracious and encouraging. Not one person said anything hurtful. My friend Pamela, who I lived with for many years in Nashville, wrote the words that reached into the deep places inside me and brought such life.

"I sit here with tears in my eyes for all you have gone through as a family. I look forward to the day I am sitting here with tears in my eyes as you share about Redmond's first day of school and his first date and his prom too. I know the future is far away, but I believe with you, Rick, and all your family, for great things in the near future and the distant future as well. Love all of you, praying for all of you. Kiss that baby on the head for me."

At that point, I couldn't imagine him having a first day of school, a date, or any of that. Pamela's faith in all that Redmond could accomplish in life lit up my soul.

Redmond proved himself to be a fighter in the NICU, getting better faster than anyone expected. We'd been told he might need to be there for months, but when he was 15 days old, he no longer needed the ventilator. When he was 16 days old, they weaned him off sedation enough that I heard the amazing sound of his cry for the first time. I never expected to be so happy to hear a baby cry, but I hadn't heard a sound from him since those first cries immediately after he was born. He'd been medically paralyzed and had a tube down his throat for so long that those first kitten-like cries were incredible.

Day after day I watched as they stopped one medicine after the other. I'd sit by his bed and sing to him, looking up at a double IV pole full of medication. My friend Janessa had texted me at the beginning of the whole ordeal with a song suggestion. She said she'd been praying for us when "It Is Well", sung by Kristene DiMarco of Bethel Music, came on. She'd really listened to the lyrics and prayed this song over us. When I listened to it, I felt God's presence fall on me in such a meaningful way that the song became the theme of my time there. At any point in that long month, those nearby could hear the lyrics flowing out of me. I was determined to praise the Lord through the storm.

I'd think about how everything was well with my soul - despite all we were going through – as long as I remembered to keep my eyes on Jesus. I'd imagine that IV pole - my mountain – thrown into the middle of the sea. I'd imagine him leaving the hospital on no medications at all. I'd remind myself to keep my eyes on Jesus no matter how big the waves that surrounded me. It truly was well with my soul.

When his stomach was finally able to tolerate food for the first time, he received it through a feeding tube. They defrosted the tiniest bit of the colostrum I had pumped on that first day in the NICU and put it into a little syringe. It then dripped slowly into his belly through a long tube. We held our breaths as we waited to see what would happen and rejoiced when he tolerated it well. We were relieved that he was finally healthy enough to have food.

When he was 22 days old, things got even better. The mountain moved and he was taken off *all* the medications that had been pumping into his little body. His PICC line was taken out, he got his Foley catheter out, and I was able to pick him up by myself to hold him. The need for nurses and respiratory therapists to help me hold him was gone. I felt a little naughty picking him up by myself, but there was absolutely no reason not to do so. I looked around for permission, but the nurse was taking care of the other baby she was now responsible for in addition to Redmond. Instead of two nurses watching him at all times, he shared one nurse with another baby.

When he was 23 days old, they switched him from a c-pap breathing machine that forced air into his lungs to supplemental oxygen, which is one step away from breathing on his own. They call it "room air" and it was made available to him through clear, thin, plastic tubing that flows naturally, allowing him to breathe it in on his own. His lungs had to be able to do the work by themselves for room air. They were getting stronger!

The nurses taught us how to tube feed him but encouraged me to try to nurse him. I couldn't believe it. I could try to nurse him! I was so joyful when I got to try and he responded a little bit. The medical team didn't want to send him home until he could breathe without supplemental oxygen, which meant that his oxygen level had to stay above 92% most of the time. They also wanted him to take at least 75% of his food by mouth, which would assure them that we were well on our way to freedom from the feeding tube.

I tried so hard to nurse him, but he couldn't latch on for more than a few minutes, and milk poured out of the side of his mouth and down my belly. We had no way to measure how much he actually swallowed, so we tried to count swallows. It was tedious. Knowing he couldn't go home until he ate 75% by mouth, I decided to switch to bottle-feeding because that was measurable. My heart ached to nurse him, but I needed to consider the needs of our whole family. Eliana and Charlie needed us to get home. So, every three hours I pumped, collecting the liquid gold to be frozen and stored until needed. Then we defrosted the oldest bottle of pumped breast milk and tried to bottle feed him, carefully counting every milliliter he drank. Then the rest went into the feeding tube.

It melted my heart to see my calloused farmer husband carefully holding that tiny boy, struggling to follow the special instructions for how to position Redmond while attempting to give him a bottle. We had to contort ourselves into special poses and sort of pinch his cheeks into a pucker while holding the bottle. It did not feel natural or normal at all.

While Rick and I were together in the NICU, we didn't argue. We were a team, surviving together. He took care of me, I took care of the medical things, and we comforted one another as we grew increasingly anxious to be with Eliana and Charlie. For the first week, Rick drove me back and forth from The Ronald McDonald House. Parking at the large university hospital was awful due to the massive amount of traffic, limited spaces, and cost. Rick decided that he was going to push me in the wheelchair back and forth instead.

It was March in the Midwest, so it was cold and windy. Plus, all the banging around in the hospital hadn't exactly led to a great sense of security in me. Now he wanted to cross actual roads with cars on them? I was not excited about his plan, but he insisted. He was tired of driving and running. I've learned with him that while he typically goes with the flow and does what I want, when he insists on doing something his own way, there's no point in arguing.

That night, he bundled me up and we went into the freezing, extremely windy night air. He carefully pushed me through the hospital, avoiding door jams and obstacles. He wheeled me smoothly through the main doors, down the sidewalk into the wind, to the crossing where he pushed the button and we waited for the light to change. I shivered, cold and scared that he might accidentally dump me out of the chair and reopen my incision.

When the light changed, he pushed me across the street, then up on a sidewalk, across a large open area next to a student dorm, puffing as he fought the wind in our faces on the uphill sidewalk. He hadn't thought through the way the incline and strong wind would affect his ability to push my wheelchair. As he puffed and groaned, struggling with the wheelchair and his fragile wife, nerves got the better of me and I started giggling. I could imagine us reminiscing about "that one time he thought it'd be a good idea to push my wheelchair uphill, facing high winds, to The Ronald McDonald House." That is, if he didn't dump me out of the chair and reopen my incision.

When we got to the end of that sidewalk, we had to cross another road – this one without a crosswalk. Of course, that one went fairly steeply downhill. Why not? Focused on pushing me up the hill, Rick used too much force on the downhill section and nearly lost control of my wheelchair. As he struggled to get it back under control before I rolled away, I screamed in fear. But he's strong and he held on tightly, then smoothly guided me into the parking lot, up on the sidewalk, and to the front door. As we went into the building, my laughter returned uncontrollably and tears ran down my face. We made it! "Relieved" isn't a strong enough word to express how I felt.

I thought he'd for sure drive me from then on, but not my husband! His confidence was built when he got me there successfully, so he pushed me from that point forward. He stopped banging into things and I was able to relax and trust him to get me there safely. We had a good laugh that night, which we needed more than we even knew. No matter what happened in that hospital, we had each other and I clung to him.

When Redmond was a month old, the medical team let us know that he wasn't terribly interesting to them anymore. He didn't need any medication at all. He was taking about 40% of his feedings orally, and he only needed a whiff of supplemental oxygen. They told us that they planned to send him home after the weekend, given that nothing changed and he remained stable until then. We'd been told the day before to expect to be there for at least another few weeks, so we were ecstatic. We were to spend the weekend taking care of him ourselves, under the watchful eyes of the nurses. We needed to learn how to manage the feeding tube, how to run the oxygen tank he would need, and how to handle problems that might come up.

That Thursday evening, the hall we usually walked down was blocked, so Rick and I walked out a different way. Four babies on our hall had been on ECMO. As we walked by the last baby to still be on ECMO, the room was dark except for the lights from the machines. A couple we'd never met sat in the dark on a small couch at the back of the room, holding hands. Rick and I waved and smiled, hoping to make a connection with them, but they looked down. We couldn't understand why they weren't friendlier. They had to know that our baby had been on ECMO.

When we came back the next morning, we immediately noticed that the last room on our hall was empty. Rick exclaimed happily, "They must've gotten to go home!"

Dread washed over me. "Honey, there's no way that baby got released from the hospital when he was on ECMO last night."

Rick realized his mistake right away. Of course, he didn't go home. It hit us both pretty hard. We didn't know the family at all, but we were getting ready to take our baby home while they were planning a funeral.

It was a hard lesson for us. We thought they were being kind of rude because they wouldn't acknowledge us, but they'd been saying goodbye to their precious baby. They weren't one bit concerned with what we thought of them. They probably hadn't even noticed us, or they were hurting because they knew our baby was off ECMO while theirs didn't get better.

How often had we assumed someone was being rude or inconsiderate when they were desperately trying to survive their own crisis? How often had people thought that we were being rude during Redmond's crisis when we were just trying to keep our heads above water? Our ability to be gracious to others grew exponentially that day. Rather than assume the worst, we now try to ask ourselves what they may be going through that's incredibly hard that day. We try to stop and pray for that person, rather than take up an offense.

That same day we had to take a class in infant CPR, which was really a class to teach parents how to handle an emergency with the baby. We held a life-like doll and learned to press HARD on it to force breath into its lungs. The instructor walked through a crisis with us, explained what to say when you called 911, and then had us do it ourselves. After hearing, "if your baby's not breathing" repeatedly for an hour, we left shaken. The responsibility we undertook as we left the competent care of the NICU team was heavy.

After that, we returned to Redmond's room and his nurse told us that it was time to learn how to insert a neo-gastric (NG) feeding tube. We watched as she opened new tube packaging, explained how to measure him for correct placement in his stomach (not lungs, which could cause him to aspirate and die), removed the guide wire, lubricated the tip, and guided it up our baby's nostril, back into his throat, and down his esophagus, until it reached his stomach.

There were numbers printed on the tube, so we pushed the tube deeper into his nose until the correct number was outside his nostril. Then we had to hold it in place with one hand while we put a prepared syringe of air into the port, placed a stethoscope on his belly, and listened as we pushed air into the tube. If it was in the right place, we heard a "whoosh" sound. Then we sucked the air back out and closed the port. Placement confirmed, we then used thin, breathable tape to fasten it to the side of his face. Since he already had oxygen tubing taped to his face, we were to run the tube right next to the oxygen tube and tape them together.

Who wants to be on either end of that process? Ugh. Of course, Redmond screamed like we were shoving a tube up his nose, making it incredibly hard. When he screamed, the tube sometimes coiled up in the back of his throat or came out his mouth instead of going straight down. Sometimes the tube got stuck at the top of his nose and didn't want to round the corner down his esophagus. One of his nostrils is tighter than the other, so that side takes a forceful push to get it over the hill.

I backed away from the nurse, shaking my head "NO." I have absolutely zero medical training and had no intention of being in charge of the feeding tube. The nurse reminded me that we couldn't take him home until we not only learned how to do it but were comfortable with it.

Shaking and sweating, I swallowed hard and gave myself a little pep talk. "You can do hard things. You can do ALL things through Christ who gives you strength. Come on, girl! Let's get this baby home."

> "I can do all things through Christ who strengthens me" -Philippians 4:19 (NKJV).

I took the tube from her. Tears stung my eyes and I had to stop and wipe them so I could see what I was doing. Rick was a little irritated with me for overreacting, but I could not apologize. Although Redmond and I both cried, I found some reserve of strength deeper than I knew I had and got that tube in place and taped it down.

For the rest of the day, I was undone. I couldn't stop crying and trembling. It was too much. Rick tried to help me to calm down, but I couldn't. I missed my kids. That other baby had died. We'd learned about how to respond if our baby stopped breathing, shoving our fingers as hard as we could into a doll's chest while trying to imagine it was our fragile son. Then I'd actually had to force a tube into his nose, down his throat, and into his stomach so he could eat. These things weren't going away either. We weren't going home with him like the NICU had been a bad dream. We were going home with a medically fragile baby who needed things I didn't think I could give him.

I grieved for the loss of my dream. I wanted to go home and sit in my chair and nurse my baby. I didn't want to deal with oxygen tubes and feeding tubes. I didn't want to know that Down syndrome was more complicated than intellectual disabilities. I couldn't comprehend specialists and therapists and special needs. I was a wreck.

Rick had no idea what to do with me. When we went back to The Ronald McDonald House that night, he went to the family room to watch TV. He understood me well enough to realize how much I needed to be alone.

God met me there in my puddle of frustration and tears and disbelief, drowning in it all and He knew what to do. He prompted my cousin Shelly to call me that night. I wasn't up for talking. I didn't trust my mouth. I couldn't subject anyone to my unfiltered self that night, but knowing that someone recognized my aching and was willing to climb down in the hole and sit with me a while was comforting. I texted her and told her as much. She texted back that she was praying for me. She was shaking the gates of heaven on my behalf. Rick was surely praying for me too. Rick's parents were praying for me.

At the end of myself, I ate a snack and went to bed. Sometimes when we are so shaken and out of sorts, like Elijah in I Kings 19, a little food and sleep are exactly what we need to reset. I woke up the next morning feeling like I could face another day. I took a long shower, fixed my hair and makeup, put on clean clothes, and walked over to the NICU with my coffee and my husband. We held hands; fingers laced together in unspoken support. Together, we were going to make it through this challenge.

That day Rick had to insert the feeding tube. It didn't go well. Redmond screamed and fought, something we weren't used to because we'd only been able to hear his voice for a few days. We'd barely been able to bond with our sweet baby and we had to hurt him. He didn't understand and our hearts broke in places we didn't know we had. It took several tries, but he finally got it in. After that, Rick left to take care of things at home in preparation for our return. I don't know that Rick would ever admit it, but I think he cried too. Alone in the car, totally shaken up – he cried. At home, he told his parents about it, feeling bad for not being more understanding with me. The nurse told us we'd each need to practice putting the tube in several more times before we could leave. The idea of hurting Redmond over and over horrified us both.

Rick's Aunt Jo is a retired nurse practitioner who only lives a few miles from our home. When she heard about it, she came to the rescue. She told Rick what to say to the NICU team and assured us that we'd never have to do it ourselves again. We could call her or even Rick's cousin who lives right down the road and is also a nurse. They would make sure we didn't have to insert that feeding tube again.

Rick called me with very specific instructions, "The next time they try to make you insert the feeding tube, you tell them no. Say you've already done it once and you're comfortable with it. You have a good support system of nurses in your family at home and if you have any problems, they will help you."

Rick is not the kind of person who tells someone in authority "No." I tried to back pedal a bit, but he was adamant. We are not going to do that to Redmond. He repeated several times, "YOU TELL THEM NO," until I promised that I would do it.

So, I told the nurse no. She acted a little surprised and had the nurse practitioner come in to talk to me about it, but I held my ground. Aunt Jo was right. They left us alone about it after that. It was the first time we ever exerted our parental authority over medical practitioners, and it was past time for us to learn that our voices were the most important ones in his medical care.

On our last Sunday morning there, Rick and I left the hospital and found a little café in town for brunch. They served us fancy coffee and amazing food. It was like a little oasis for us. The farmer who rarely left his fields to go to the nearest city sat comfortably with me as a host with a man-bun seated customers and a tattooed waitress in a red bustier served us. He had learned how to get around the bustling university campus, with students launching themselves into oncoming traffic without so much as a glance to see if a car was coming, narrow one-way streets, and impossible parking lots. Living at the hospital in such a large city for a month had changed him, forging in him new confidence and capability.

On Monday morning, the nurse practitioner came by to let us know we were going home. Medical supplies were waiting for us in boxes on our front porch. Redmond passed his car seat test. Our prayers that he'd be free from his feeding tube and oxygen before we left weren't answered like we'd hoped, but we decided we could handle those things if we could be together as a family. Rick packed our things and cleaned our room at The Ronald McDonald House while I signed papers and received final instructions from the NICU nurses.

In the last week that we were there, hospital staff members had been sneaking into our room and quietly marveling over Redmond. Many of them whispered that they were Christians and had been praying for Redmond. One nurse told me that she regularly came into his room at night and held him, praying over him. I was told several times a day by someone different each time that Redmond was a miracle and they had to stop in and see for themselves. We were deeply touched by their care and compassion. What a gift!

The nurse practitioner who released us that day wasn't June, but we'd grown to appreciate him. He's married with lots of children. They were Christians and giving me that information made him very nervous. It didn't take long at all for me to realize the big state university hospital did not encourage their staff to discuss their faith. I'd had to ask him very pointed, direct questions to find that out, and he had squirmed as he cautiously revealed his faith. He acted like he was waiting for me to mock him or disagree. I happily told him that we believed the same way.

I'd also discovered that NICU nurses and doctors fell into three main categories: the optimist, the realist, and the pessimist. Depending on the nature of the person speaking with us that day, we'd receive vastly different interpretations of the same information. We learned to take it all in stride and not accept anything as truth until it actually happened. This nurse practitioner is a very realistic, practical man. Any time I showed excitment about Redmond's progress, he'd make sure to let me know that things could still go wrong and bring me back to "reality."

He surprised me by coming to Redmond's room and staying for a while that morning, just talking to me. He was concerned about the large hole in Redmond's heart (VSD). The pediatric cardiologist had stopped by on Thursday to let us know that Redmond would definitely need open heart surgery within four to six months to repair the large hole. He gave us the signs of heart failure to watch for and explained that if we saw any of them, we were to call him immediately. The nurse practitioner told me what to expect with the surgery and how to prepare for it. I stopped listening as he went on and on, refusing to accept the news of open-heart surgery. I finally spoke up, interrupting him.

"I understand why you're telling me this stuff, but I want you to know that Rick and I are optimists. We believe God has healed Redmond's heart and he won't need open heart surgery. He's going to be fine."

Then I held my breath, wondering how in the world this man of science who saw babies go into heart surgery on a regular basis would handle my bold statement.

"Well," he said, "With all the miracles that we've already seen in Redmond, I can totally understand why you feel that way. You're right. God has healed him miraculously and I think you're right to have faith that he won't need surgery."

Then he smiled brightly at me. No more depressing talk about another long stay in the hospital, his breast bone sawn in two, his body frozen, etc. I was the best kind of surprised. Even the hospital staff had to admit that there was no way Redmond Samuel Wyse should be alive, much less leaving the NICU after only 34 days. He gave me some papers to sign, explained about all the appointments we had coming up that week, and wished us luck.

When we finally had permission to leave, it felt like someone should have thrown us a parade. Everything in the NICU continued on, business-as-usual, as we left Room 38 for the last time. Rick had loaded all our things from The Ronald McDonald House in the car, brought down the cooler full of frozen breast milk that I'd pumped, and it was time. I pushed Redmond down to the lobby in his stroller and car seat. Rick walked behind us, pushing a large oxygen tank on wheels.

We went out into the crazy traffic in front of the hospital and carefully locked our son's car seat into place, gingerly placing the oxygen tank beside him, and then we got in the car and drove away. The whole way to the car I kept expecting someone to stop us and say, "Just kidding. You can't leave." But we were free. As we drove home, Redmond slept. He was so cute with his pudgy cheeks in the car seat. I took a picture of him and posted it on Facebook with the caption, "We get to keep him."

Redmond slept for the first 24 hours at home, opening his eyes only occasionally to glance around at his unfamiliar surroundings and go back to sleep. Eliana and Charlie were so happy to have us home. We were all together at home for the first time on April 4, 2017.

We hadn't noticed any effects from the long separation in the kids before that day, but I braced myself for the storm that I figured would come once we were home. I watched like a hawk, searching for signs that they weren't doing quite as well as they appeared.

We saw it in Charlie first. He wasn't quite three years old yet, and he had always been a daddy's boy. I got myself comfortable in the recliner in the living room, surrounded by everything I needed – breast pump and supplies, feeding tubes, syringes, bottles, phone and charger, and TV remote. He knew where I was. But whenever Rick left the room, Charlie couldn't stand it. He needed to be able to see us both at the same time. If Rick was in the house but not in the living room, he couldn't handle it. If Charlie came in the living room and saw my chair empty, he'd call my name loudly until I let him know where I was. We learned to let our little guy know where we were going before we left, which helped his anxiety a little.

Charlie also regressed in some areas that he had previously had no problem with, so we had to be patient with him. He became very clingy outside of home too. We couldn't leave him with his grandparents, in Sunday school, or at his normal classes like Little Ninjas. If we pushed him and left anyway, he spent weeks stuttering and out of control. He wasn't purposefully acting out. He was very shaken up.

Encouraged to leave him anyway and force him to toughen up, we decided instead to withdraw him from all activities, took him with us to our Sunday school class, and stopped leaving him with anyone for a while. If we HAD to leave, we told him where we were going and when we'd be back. We let him sleep in our bed with us every night. We were very concerned about what would happen when he started preschool the next year, but by then he had mostly recovered and was a lot better. There were a few really tough and concerning months though.

Eliana showed her anxiety differently. She chewed her nails until they bled. It upset me so much because I was a nail biter and worked hard to stop. I didn't want her to go through that. I didn't want my four-year-old to be anxious! I started researching how to be a great parent when I was in high school, wanting to make sure our family was doing the best we could for my little brother. In my 20's, I went through six years of counseling with a marriage and family therapist, determined to make sure I didn't have any blind spots when it came to emotional health. I wanted to be the best wife and mom possible. And now my daughter had anxiety and it had nothing to do with poor parenting. All the best parenting choices in the world couldn't have prevented it.

As we prayed over them while we were in the NICU, God reminded us that control had always been an illusion. Our children belong to God first, and He entrusted them to us. He loves them more than we ever possibly could, and He isn't going to abandon them. *He* took care of them – through the hands of their grandparents and babysitter - while we were gone. What better caregiver than God Himself? So while my heart hurt that they had ever been separated from us at all, that they had been forced to learn at such a young age about near-death sickness and the fragility of life - even in newborn babies - I had no choice but to trust that God was also using this challenge for our good and His glory.

Later, I read a fellow special needs mom's blog, about something similar. She called it "resilience training."[1] Those people in your life who are so resilient and seem to take everything in stride? There's a reason. The reason is highly likely to be that they have a family member with special needs or dealt with some other challenge in childhood. Like Eliana and Charlie, the siblings of children with special needs or medical complexities don't have the luxury of knowing Mom and Dad will always be available no matter what, and there is something good coming from that reality.

As I write these words today, Redmond is two years and four months old and Eliana no longer bites her nails. Charlie goes to White Ninjas (the class above Little Ninjas), Sunday school, and is looking forward to kindergarten. He's still a little unsure of himself in new situations, and sometimes we have to get a little tough with him and require that he give it a try, and he handles it. They simply needed some extra care after such a hard time in our lives and it worked.

When we got home from the NICU, not only did we bring home a new baby brother, but we also modified our home to accommodate that baby. A large oxygen concentrator was set up in our living room. It took the oxygen from the air and concentrated it, forcing it through 21 feet of tubing into Redmond's nostrils. That tiny whiff of 1/8 liter of oxygen kept his

---

[1] http://www.jillianbenfield.com/special-needs-siblings-resilient/

saturation level in the high 90's, but without it he quickly dropped down into the high 70's or low 80's. We worried that the kids would trip over the tube and pull the tape on his face, but they never did. They made a game of jumping over it.

In our little house, we could take Redmond into all the main living spaces and his bedroom. His tubing also reached into the first few feet of our bedroom, so we set up a small crib right next to our bed, right inside the door. We also had a baby swing in the living room that he liked as long as we didn't swing him or turn on the music or vibration. After not being able to hold him much for the first month of his life, I gloried in the opportunity to sit in my chair and hold him.

At night, I put him in the crib and slept beside him, jumping at his every noise. I was terrified to sleep deeply, thinking of the NICU nurses who had hovered over him for his entire life. He'd always been hooked up to monitors, numbers flashing reassuringly over his bed with his heart rate and oxygen saturation level. We'd not been given a pulse-oxygen monitor when we left the hospital because the doctors thought it would cause anxiety. The only way I knew his levels was to ask the home health nurse to come over with her portable monitor to spot check him. Alarms didn't beep at me all night long, but my fear screamed louder than any monitor.

Pastor Brad asked me how I was doing one day. I told him how hard it was to sleep. He prayed a simple prayer over me, reminding me that Psalm 127:2 says, "He gives His beloved rest."

> "It is *vain for you to rise up early,*
> *To sit up late,*
> *To eat the bread of sorrows;*
> For *so He gives His beloved sleep.*" (NKJV)

That night as I laid my tiny boy in his bed beside me, arranging his tubes so they wouldn't get tangled, I prayed that ministering angels would watch over him. I asked God to let me sleep peacefully and wake me if Redmond needed me. I slept soundly. I heard Redmond's noises, but I was also aware of two beings wearing white and hovering over him. When I woke for his next feeding, I had a deep sense of peace. God allowed me to sense the presence of the powerful angels that watched over us.

Since that time, I've often thought of other new mothers and the anxious thoughts we so often have. I had difficulty sleeping when I first brought home my other babies. Wild thoughts crashed through my mind, dark fears, and unspeakable horrors. I panicked with every sniffle or cough, so afraid that they'd catch a cold. A cold seemed like one of the worst things possible. Germs loomed in my mind, threatening our peace. I obsessed over small decisions, ran at every cry, and struggled to allow myself to fully give in to love, so afraid that it would be taken from me.

I imagine I'm not alone in my fears. Anytime I tried to say the words out loud, I was silenced. No one wanted to hear my out of control thoughts, or if I said them anyway, they wanted to medicate me. There's a time and place for medication, but what I needed at that time was a way to cope with the fear in a meaningful way. I cried out to God to help me, aware that Scripture repeatedly tells us not to be afraid, but to trust God fully. He graciously answered my prayers and helped me develop a way to relax into love and fully embrace my children.

I learned to handle my fear through these four steps:

1. Redirect your thoughts. Whenever I caught myself having dark thoughts, I'd immediately call a friend or turn on some good music, anything to redirect my thoughts. I refused to indulge in those fantasies any longer.

2. Don't let fear rob you of love. I decided to love my children with all my heart, holding nothing back for fear that I might lose them. There is no more room in my heart for regrets. If I ever lose them, I will know that I gave them everything I have.

3. Speak your fears out loud. I asked my husband to listen to all my fears one time. I apologized in advance, warning him, but then I told him everything. When I said them out loud, I heard how ridiculous and dark they were and that took away their power. After that, all I needed to say was "the dark thoughts are back". He understood and he stopped what he was doing to pray for me.

4. Pray. I learned to pray for God's ministering angels to protect them. Our children belong to God and He loves them more than we ever could. His protection is so much greater than our own.

At the time of this writing, the song *Fear is a Liar* by Zach Williams is popular. It's true, and you can replace the word *fear* with *Satan* and get the same results. Satan is a liar and the father of lies. There is no truth in him (John 8:44). I don't like to give much credit to the devil, but Satan would like nothing more than to steal our joy in our children. Satan would love to destroy our families. He plants fear in our hearts to lie to us and keep us from living abundant lives. It often helps me to put that song (and others like it) on repeat and listen to it until the anxious thoughts have no place in my heart and mind. I refuse to give the devil one more minute of the space in my mind.

I encourage others to take the time to pray over your home, anoint the doors with oil, and ask God to protect your family. You don't even have to be at home to pray over your home. God's presence isn't bound to a building. Ask God to put a hedge of protection around your home and your family, to send His angels to keep you safe, and then rest in the knowledge that He hears your prayers and delights to honor those requests.

When I pray for my children before bed at night, I ask God to cover them up with a blanket of His peace, to give them sweet dreams, and to help them sleep well and wake up refreshed and ready for their day. I ask God to send angels to stand guard over them to protect them in all their ways for all their days. I claim that they are full of the fruit of the Spirit – love, joy, peace, patience, kindness, goodness, gentleness, faithfulness, and self-control.

And then, I sleep deeply.

10

HOME AT LAST

On the day we brought Redmond home from the hospital, Rick started sneezing. When we got home, we discovered that Eliana and Charlie had colds. Despite all my efforts to keep Redmond healthy, within a few days, he got congested. My 34-day old baby who had survived so much got a cold. It was not good.

Because of Down syndrome, Redmond's immune system isn't naturally strong. People with Down syndrome have an over-abundance of interferon, which is a protein released by our cells when a virus is present. Its job is to interfere with the virus and prevent it from replicating. In healthy individuals, interferon is what keeps them from getting every virus that comes their way. People with Down syndrome have way too much interferon, which disrupts their immune system, causing their bodies to be full of inflammation and making them more vulnerable to viruses. So of course, Redmond got the virus they all had.

On top of Rick, Eliana, Charlie, and Redmond all fighting off a nasty cold, on the last week that we'd been in the NICU, I developed a strange pain along my bra line. At first, I thought an underwire in my bra had broken through the fabric and was poking me, but I wasn't wearing an underwire. After feeling slightly uncomfortable for a day, I investigated. The pain came from a small, red spot right under my breast. A pimple? I thought it was odd but wasn't too concerned.

The next day, it really started to bother me. Because it had anything to do with my breast, Rick was adamant that I not let it go. My family's history of breast cancer weighs on his mind, especially since his brother's wife had breast cancer at a young age. Her mother and sister also had breast cancer, and it took her mother's life prematurely. It's not something he messes around with at all.

Unsure of what to do without my own doctor nearby, I mentioned it to Redmond's nurse, Courtney, who we'd gotten to know pretty well. She told me to go to triage to have it checked out. Because of the location and pain, we thought it might be mastitis. Rick and I went right away. Concerned that it might be serious, the midwife instructed me to keep it dry and apply warm compresses. I was to go back the next day if it wasn't better. I couldn't figure out how to keep it dry while applying warm compresses. The only warm thing I had to apply was a wet washcloth.

The next day it was significantly worse, bothering me so badly that I couldn't wear a bra, which was particularly uncomfortable because I was pumping and leaking. I wore the tightest tank top I had under a baggy top and went back to the midwife. The spot had grown again, so they swabbed it to check for MRSA – an antibiotic-resistant staph infection common in hospitals. I got an antibiotic prescription and instructions to go to the pharmacy immediately to start the antibiotic. Rick and I followed her instructions, relieved that no one thought it was cancer and it wasn't mastitis. It didn't get better though.

It really hurt, but I got to bring my baby home, so it wasn't as much of a priority as something like that would typically be. A few days after we got home, my mom and dad came to visit for a week. They brought our niece Alexis with them. Alexis was nine years old and her cousins adore her. She was excited about the new baby and happy to be with us. Mom was determined to get Redmond to take his bottle, so she helped that first week with daytime feedings. He had to eat every three hours. Each feeding took 90 minutes.

First, we attempted oral feedings, then we tube-fed the rest. After he ate, we'd hold him upright for 20-30 minutes to help his food settle. Then I'd put him down and pump for 20 minutes. Rick washed all the supplies and brought new ones back to me. I had about 45 minutes in-between feedings to sleep, eat, and pay attention to the older kids. We repeated the feeding routine eight times a day. It didn't occur to me to only tube-feed him at night so I could sleep a little longer.

But while I cared for Redmond and tried to adjust to life at home, I was in a lot of pain. Redmond was assigned a home health nurse who came by within 24 hours of his release. She came to our house twice a week to check Redmond's vital signs, weigh him, and answer my questions. I liked Nurse Jane immediately. She's experienced and practical, also a Christian, and familiar with ECMO.

I showed her the spot and the antibiotic. She didn't understand why they had given me that prescription. She said it wouldn't do anything to clear it up. She suggested that I call my midwife, tell her what was going on, and let her know that the nurse had suggested a different medication. In the meantime, she gave me a large, sponge-like bandage treated with medicine to help to pull out infection. She also suggested warm compresses, but with the bandage I didn't want to put a wet washcloth on it. I couldn't think of any other way to handle it, and I didn't have much energy for anything other than Redmond. It got really bad.

I called the midwife, but she wanted to see me before she prescribed anything. I neglected to convey the seriousness of the situation, so I couldn't get on her schedule for five days. Frustrated and in misery, I finally realized I could tuck a heating pad under my shirt while I sat in the recliner and fed Redmond. That did the trick and the boil-like spot, which was by then the size of a quarter with a hard, white center, drained.

I'll spare you the details, but when it finally stopped draining, I could not believe what I saw. A large hole had formed where the raised spot had been. Horrified and overwhelmed, I put some Neosporin on it and covered it with a new bandage. My entire body trembled with pain and disgust. I had a gaping hole in my body and the memory of it still makes me tremble as I type.

The next day was my appointment with the midwife. The pain was excruciating. When she removed the bandage, she covered her mouth and stepped back a bit, motioning for her nurse to look at it. The nurse's eyes widened kind of wildly. I'd finished the first course of antibiotics and my midwife agreed that I'd been given the wrong kind, telling the nurse what to order for me instead. Then she asked for a gown, mask, gloves, and goggles. She felt concerned that the infection might shoot out and hit her in the face.

When she tried to touch the wound, I screamed in pain. She told me that she'd barely touched me, but my whole body shook uncontrollably. She called in the OB who had forced me to know Redmond's gender and asked him what he thought. He glanced at me and stomped out of the room, yelling at her as he went, "It's MRSA. Give her Bactrim."

She called after him, "Should I pack it?"

"No," was the only response he'd give.

She came back in the room, apologetic, and asked the nurse for lidocaine. I tried so hard to be strong, but I had no ability to keep my voice down as she administered the little shots of numbing medicine around the wound. Her sympathetic nurse let me squeeze her hand, but I'm sure the entire practice heard my screams.

Once I was numb, she cleaned out the wound, which I was surprised to learn hadn't fully emptied. When she'd gotten out all that she could, she measured the hole. It was 2.5 inches long by 1.5 inches deep. She put on a new dressing and told me to come back after the weekend. MRSA is highly-contagious and resistant to most antibiotics. She told me that she hoped the antibiotic would make a big difference by Monday, otherwise we'd have to consider sending me to the wound care clinic.

My parents planned to leave the next day so they could be home for their church's Easter service. I knew there was no way I should be alone while I was in so much pain and everyone else was sick, so I swallowed every bit of pride and my independent spirit. I begged my mom not to leave. It would be hard for her to stay, especially since she had a major part in the Easter service. Alexis was with her and my brother and sister and the rest of her family planned to drive from South Carolina to Virginia to be with them for Easter weekend. She also had real estate business to do at home. But I was terrified. How was I going to handle four sick family members, one on a feeding tube and oxygen, when I was in so much pain? I admitted to her that I was in more pain than I'd felt in the entire time I was recovering from the c-section.

Our parents raised us to be fiercely independent, capable people. As a young child, my dad made a point to give us jobs that were very hard for us to do. He taught us to use our brains to figure out a way to do things that our bodies weren't big or strong enough to handle. We learned to work hard, helping with household chores and the garden. When I was just 11 years old, I was thrilled to become my siblings' babysitter while my parents went out without cell phones and no way to contact them. At that age, I was also in charge of ironing all the family's clothes, doing the dishes, and helping my parents with whatever tasks needed to be done on a given day. I had time to play also, but we worked hard. I have no doubt that this careful training had a huge impact on how I handled this whole situation. It was not in my training to ask for help, but I was desperate.

Although Mom has dropped everything in the past to come to my side when I needed her for much lesser things, this time I was fully grown with a husband, a home, supportive in-laws, and financial resources that I hadn't had back then. She couldn't see past all the arranging it would take to stay on with me another week. The Easter service is incredibly important, and I knew it would be hard to do it the way they'd planned without her. I also thought everyone in our family and their church would understand if she explained how badly I needed her. She was in tears when she left, but my family was my responsibility. She had her own responsibilities. I wasn't resentful, but I was disappointed.

This would have been a good time to have an in-home nurse assigned to us for several hours a day. I asked around, but my energy was limited and my brain foggy. I didn't know how to arrange for anything like that, didn't realize that our health insurance would have covered such an expense and helped us arrange it. I was in a dark hole of shock, ignorance, and terror.

I was right to be afraid. The days that followed stretched me beyond anything I've ever known before.

Because I'd been told that my infection was MRSA, fear became like a thin piece of red cellophane over my eyes. Everywhere I looked, I saw the gaping red wound, teeming with infection. I was pumping breast milk for my newborn, caring for him around the clock, and the last thing he needed was to get a highly contagious infection from me. Nurse Jane said I didn't need to stop pumping, but I shouldn't try to nurse him. She said to wash my hands frequently. I washed my hands so much that my skin became raw. I was afraid to touch his skin, so I dressed him in footie pajamas and put socks on his hands. Rick wore a mask and changed his diapers.

Redmond had always breathed kind of funny, which the NICU staff attributed to Down syndrome. His nasal bridge is flat (despite our earlier inability to see it), causing his nasal passages to be extremely small, which makes it hard for him to breathe through them. When he gets congested, it sounds terrible. His chest pulls in sharply and he makes a staccato-like noise with each breath. That day, his nostrils flared and turned white with each breath and he threw his head back wildly. He sounded like he might stop breathing at any point, and when he cried it got worse. Then I'd cry and beg Rick to tell me what to do. He didn't cry much unless I laid him down, so we decided that I'd hold him until the congestion cleared up.

Easter weekend, 2017, I only got up from the recliner if I absolutely had to get up. Rick wore a mask and washed his hands constantly, hand sanitizer bottles were all over our house, and I held the baby. Rick brought me everything I needed, and if I had to put the baby down, he held him as far away from his face as possible. I slept for no more than 45 minutes at a time, averaging about 2.5 hours a day total.

While I held Redmond, I scrolled through Facebook and felt very, very sorry for myself. My friends posted photos of their beautifully dressed, healthy children at Easter egg hunts, playing outside with friends, and living their carefree lives. My husband's parents took care of Eliana and Charlie during the day, and even kept them overnight during the worst of the sickness. I missed them so much, but I couldn't take care of them. I literally couldn't remember the last time I'd had a shower.

Beautiful clothes hung in our closets in anticipation of being together at church on Easter Sunday, but we were too sick to go anywhere. I didn't care that my friends had probably threatened their children with their lives if they didn't stand still in their pretty clothes and smile for the pictures. I didn't care that they might have all been fighting or stressed about money or running late or mad at their mom. None of that stuff touched the fight I was in for my son's life.

In the middle of the night I woke from a light sleep, panicked by the way Redmond was breathing. I didn't know if I should call an ambulance or go back to sleep. My lack of medical training mocked me. I couldn't tell if I was over-reacting or what needed to be done. I knew that the level of exhaustion I had reached made my judgment unreliable. Rick was asleep on the couch, but he wouldn't know any better than me.

In those early weeks of his life, I tried so hard to pray, but it often felt like my prayers landed flat at my feet. I only felt God's presence when I sang. I'd heard of people who walked through hard times like they were in a cloud of peace, literally feeling the arms of Jesus around them. I felt no such thing. I was afraid, terribly aware of my ignorance of his medical issues, and so alone. That night, I cried out to God in complete desperation, "What do I do, Lord? I need you to tell me what to do!"

It was one of the few times that I felt God's presence in a tangible way as a wave of peace washed over me. The answer was as clear as anything I've ever heard.

"You're doing exactly what you need to do."

I had a deep sense of calm then. God had given Redmond to me and Rick, and He also gave us everything we need to take care of him. We needed to do the next right thing and we would be okay. Too tired to keep my eyes open if I didn't stand up, I went back to sleep until the alarm sounded for his next feeding.

On Sunday afternoon, in a fog of exhaustion, I texted Nurse Jane and asked if I could give Redmond some Tylenol. He was restless and wiggly, and he woke up every time I tried to put him down. I was so tired that I was afraid I'd drop him. I thought if he was in pain, Tylenol would give his body a chance to rest peacefully.

She said it was fine, so I looked at the bottle for dosing instructions. It said to ask a doctor, so I texted her back to ask for the correct dosage. She texted back a photo of the dosage chart. I found his weight, looked across the row to the next column and saw 5 mL. I got out the Tylenol syringe and filled it to 5 mL, then pushed it through his feeding tube into his stomach. Within minutes he completely relaxed. I felt terrible because he'd obviously been in pain. Relieved that he felt better, I slept deeply until the alarm sounded next to feed him. When he became restless again, I gave him another 5 mL dose and it worked like a charm. His body relaxed, I laid him down right next to me and slept soundly until the next alarm. Those two uninterrupted times of sleeping for one solid hour were enough to give me the strength I needed for the next day.

On Monday morning, Kristina arrived, and I turned Redmond over to her with great relief. I took a fast shower, dressed, and ate a little breakfast. Kristina asked me what was going on with Redmond's breathing. She looked scared. Her response let me know that it wasn't my imagination or over-reaction. There was a problem.

I gave her brief instructions, then left to go back to the midwife to have my wound checked. It was hard to leave, but I knew if I didn't take care of myself, I wouldn't be able to take care of Redmond.

Thankfully, the wound turned out not to be MRSA, but a regular staph infection, and the antibiotic worked. She was able to touch the wound without much of a reaction from me at all. She told me that she'd thought about it all weekend, so concerned for me. We laughed together because what she actually said was, "I thought about your breast all weekend!" Then when she tried to say it a better way, she only ended up repeating herself. It felt good to laugh for a moment. We were both so relieved!

When she asked how I was doing, I swiped at tears as I told her what I'd been doing all weekend. She suggested I call the pediatrician and tell her what was going on. It wouldn't hurt anything for me to have a little peace of mind. With Eliana and Charlie, I'd been the paranoid mother calling the doctor for every little thing. I didn't want to bother anyone with unnecessary concerns, so her suggestion gave me the permission I felt I needed.

I called the pediatrician from the car on my way home. When I told her nurse what was going on, she told me to bring him in to the office at 1:00. Rick and I spent a little time with Eliana and Charlie while Kristina handled Redmond. We ate a quick lunch and took him in. The pediatrician checked him over, then calmly told us that she'd feel more comfortable if we took him to the hospital to get him checked out. She didn't think we needed an ambulance, but we should head over there that afternoon. She said that since he hadn't been a patient there before, she couldn't admit him. We needed to go through the ER. That didn't make any sense to me, since he was there for three days right after birth, but I was too exhausted to argue.

We went home and packed an overnight bag. We kissed the kids goodbye, leaving them in Kristina's capable hands, and drove the hour to the children's hospital ER. Rick dropped me and Redmond off at the door, then went to park. I got us registered at the front desk, which included taking off Redmond's clothes to weigh him. As soon as the clerk saw how Redmond's chest sucked in and nostrils flared, he stopped trying to weigh him and sounded some silent alarm. We were rushed back to a room while he yelled some stuff about "retractions" and people came running from every direction.

Doctors and nurses hovered around us in a small room. A scrappy little nurse barked at a large, unidentified man who wanted to come in, telling him they didn't need him and shoving him out the door as she closed it on him. People poked Redmond, stuck needles in him, and irritated him – which made his breathing much worse. The pediatrician hadn't seen this level of labored breathing in her office. The doctor's eyes were wide, and she quickly turned his supplemental oxygen up from 1/8 liter to two liters. People hovered around us, worried looks on their faces. They were in full-on freak-out mode and we knew it.

The doctor came back after a while and said she wanted to send him by ambulance back to the larger hospital. We were stunned. Our pediatrician had seemed so calm, like the hospital was a precaution. If we went back there, the doctors knew Redmond and wouldn't likely freak out like these doctors were, but the doctors in our local hospital needed to get to know him. We couldn't be hauling it off to that hospital (a two-hour drive with traffic and parking) every time he breathed funny. This hospital was a good one. Initially, we agreed to the transfer, but it took forever for them to get an ambulance and an empty bed there.

While we waited, Redmond calmed down and so did his breathing. When our nurse came in to check on him, I pointed out how much better he was doing and asked her if it was necessary to leave. She got the doctor and we discussed it again. She agreed to let us stay and got us a room.

As soon as he got into his room, the new nurse came in and checked him over. He again became irritated and his breathing got worse. She called a respiratory code on him and people came running. His bed was suddenly surrounded by doctors, nurses, respiratory therapists, and who knows who else. Rick and I sat by, stunned, because nothing he did was different than what we'd been handling at home for days. When they arrived, the nurse yelled, "Why did they send him up here!? I can't handle this!"

The code got him moved into the pediatric intensive care unit (PICU). He was placed on a c-pap breathing machine. Unlike supplemental oxygen, which flows softly from the nasal cannulas, the c-pap forces air into the lungs. It's an ugly thing, almost completely obstructing the baby's face with all the straps needed to keep it on. The nurse explained to us that if his oxygen dropped like that every time she came to his room to assess him, it would be more than she could handle. He needed to be in a place where they could give him more oxygen if he needed it.

Ten days after he got out of the NICU, he was admitted to the PICU. I was distraught because I knew what it meant for Eliana and Charlie, but I was also relieved. I had no idea that I'd been providing him with his own personal ICU - untrained and apparently not frightened enough. I was so tired that I sat down in the only chair that could fit in the tiny room and cried. His nurse assessed the situation quickly, got me a room at The Ronald McDonald House, and commanded me to get a good night's sleep. Rick and I left Redmond in the care of another set of doctors and nurses feeling simultaneously defeated and relieved.

We collapsed into bed that night and slept soundly until we woke up the next morning. No alarms. I don't even remember if I got up to pump. One of the first things the ICU doctor did was order him "NPO", which means nothing by mouth. We had no feeding schedule to maintain. Praise.the.Lord.

We were thankful that this time around we weren't in fear for his life, but we hated leaving him overnight. Those rooms are so small in the ICU that there's very little space for anyone to spend the night. Truthfully, I was relieved to be able to leave. He was asleep and had no idea I wasn't there, so it worked for us all.

They had run a battery of tests overnight and diagnosed him with rhino entero virus – the common cold. To be safe, they were doing blood and urine cultures, which take three days to complete, but he needed extra support until the worst of the virus was over. His little lungs weren't strong enough to handle a cold alone.

Rick went home to be with the kids and pack a few more things while I sat in the room with Redmond. A few days earlier, I'd been given a copy of the book, "The Lucky Few", by Heather Avis. My friend Sarra had stopped by the house with her daughters that week. They dropped off the book and a cute matching t-shirt. Sarra is the head of our local mom's group that I've been going to since Eliana was born. I'd joined the leadership team that year but had been able to do embarrassingly little to help. I was sick with my pregnancy, then in the hospital. She and some of the others on the steering team had come to the NICU one evening and prayed over Redmond, then taken me, Rick, and my mom out for dinner. It felt so weird to sit around a table with friends and eat dinner like nothing was wrong, but it was very comforting too. They left us with goodies – gift cards, cash, kids' activity books for when the kids visited the hospital, and healthy snacks. I was blown away.

I had quickly thrown the book in my bag before I left, so I passed the long hours in the PICU reading it. *The Lucky Few* is a book about the theology of surrender. The Avis family couldn't have biological children, so they chose to adopt a baby girl with Down syndrome. Macyn was very sick, like Redmond, and needed supplemental oxygen and heart surgery. Reading what Avis wrote about it all calmed me down and even taught me a few tricks for dealing with all the tubes. I admired her for surrendering to the call to love a child that few would accept. **I loved her for reminding me that in the hardest moments of life, we find our strength in the Lord. Through suffering, we learn to know God in a way we never could before, which makes us truly lucky and blessed.**

As I read, I underlined and wept, then did it again. I took pictures of key passages and posted them on social media. I quoted her, "Oh, how I wish I could've known God back then like I do now. But would it even have been possible without these difficult, unwanted, scary circumstances?"

I hoped that something good would come out of all our difficult, unwanted, scary circumstances. I wanted so badly to know God better, to understand His heart, and to understand how He could let these terrible things happen to us. I wanted to understand how God could allow an innocent baby to suffer. I wanted to understand how God could give such hardship to someone who loved Him so much.

2 Chronicles 16:9 says,

> *"For the eyes of the Lord run to and fro throughout the whole earth, to show Himself strong on behalf of those whose heart is loyal to Him...." (NKJV).*

I'd always taken that to mean that I would be protected from hard times like this one. I hadn't realized that what it actually meant was that *in the middle of hard times*, God would show Himself strong by helping us through it. We aren't exempt. We are merely able to lean on the Lord and receive His strength. It is a tremendous thing to receive the strength of the Lord.

The PICU doctor had a memorable talk with Rick and I after a couple days. I'll never forget how he introduced himself by his first name and sat down for a chat like he was an old friend. It took us a few minutes to realize he was the doctor.

"This isn't ECMO. Redmond's going to be okay. The situation isn't as concerning as we originally thought it was. One thing we've discovered is that he has a pectis excavatum. That's a divot in his chest that makes it appear like he's severely retracting when he's actually breathing normally. Did you know that he had that? His lungs look pretty bad on his chest x-ray, but I think that's because of his early lung issues. He's never going to have a pretty chest x-ray. Scar tissue will always make it look a lot worse than it actually is."

No one in the NICU had ever mentioned that to us. I'd sat through rounds (the time when all the medical providers assigned to him got together at the beginning of each day to discuss and agree to his care plan) most days and never heard it mentioned there either. The doctor went on to explain that it's just a cosmetic issue and poses no health risk, but it makes his work of breathing appear to be more difficult than it is.

We were relieved to hear that they were getting to know him on their own terms. No one really wants a hospital to know their child well because that means he or she is sick. I'm thrilled that no hospital has a clue about Eliana and Charlie. But when you have a child with complex medical issues, it's a great comfort to know that there's a group of gifted medical providers who understand your child's history and unique circumstances.

I had been beating myself up for not bringing him in sooner but felt much better after the doctor explained what they'd discovered. In hindsight, I also realize what a defeat it felt like to us to return to the hospital with him after we'd just been sent home. The NICU staff planned to keep him longer, but I was so eager to get home to Eliana and Charlie that I fought my way out of there with all my might. Rick disagreed with me, feeling like we should stay as long as we could so he could get as strong as possible. I did not want to be wrong.

Getting him readmitted to the hospital after such a short time at home felt like admitting that I had been terribly wrong. It also meant further separation from our children, although this time around we were closer to home and took turns going home to be with them.

One day Sarra, who had given me the book, showed up with lattes and stayed to talk for a while. Nurse Jane came by later with a big salad and commanded me to eat. She helped me process through all the things the doctors told us and listened while I shared the things I was learning from my new book crush. I was deeply touched by their visits. It's hard to ask people to come visit you an hour from home while your child is fighting a contagious virus, even if it is just a cold. It means so much though. The hours sitting alone in a tiny hospital room surrounded by the sound of alarms going off and machines whirring and beeping can get to a person.

When the blood and urine cultures came back clean, it was a great relief. Redmond was able to go back on regular oxygen after a few days. The pulmonologist (lung specialist) on call in the PICU agreed with me that a patient with Redmond's history should have a monitor at home that told us his oxygen saturation level. He told me that he would write a prescription for the pulse-ox monitor, but he didn't want me to keep him hooked up to it all the time. He explained that Redmond's oxygen might dip down at times, then pop right back up, but the alarm going off all the time would be hard on us. He said that we should only use it for spot checks. If Redmond didn't appear to be breathing like he should, we could find out right away how he was doing. I was so relieved that we finally had access to that machine at home.

He was moved out of the PICU and into a room on "the floor" (hospital lingo for a regular room). In his new room, a new doctor came in to examine him. As he pressed on Redmond's belly, he muttered. After a while, he looked at me and asked, "Why is his liver enlarged?"

I stared at him blankly. How was I supposed to know?

"Did you give him any medication before you brought him in?" he asked.

"Just a little Tylenol," I answered.

He never asked me how much. He only muttered to himself and asked me again why his liver was enlarged. I thought he was really strange. Nothing else was ever mentioned about it.

Seven long days after he was admitted, we finally got to bring him home. Every night we were in the hospital, I'd gone back to The Ronald McDonald House and slept deeply. My infection continued to heal. Redmond still breathed funny, but it wasn't so terrible. I had renewed strength for the days to come.

Once we got settled in back at home, I was disturbed to find that Redmond acted like he was dying after every feeding. He screamed and threw his head back, breathed funny for a while, and writhed in pain. We took him to the pediatric cardiologist who we'd met while we were in the PICU, concerned about his heart. The doctor listened to our concerns and suggested that he might have reflux. Reflux? I felt so silly for not thinking of that. It was the first time of many that I'd consider a fairly normal problem to be something serious and life-threatening.

I spent the next several weeks focused on feeding him. We still got up every three hours to give him his bottle, then tube-fed what he didn't take. It was extremely important for him to gain weight at the proper rate so that he could grow healthy new heart and lung tissue. He writhed in pain after every feeding, so we tried reflux medicine with little luck. But once Rick's cold was better, we took turns with night feedings. We were both better rested and able to think more clearly.

About two weeks after the hospital, I decided to give Redmond some Tylenol to see if that helped with the pain. As I put 5 mL of the medicine in the syringe, it occurred to me that I was giving him as much as I gave our four-year-old. That struck me as odd, so I went back to the message I'd gotten from Nurse Jane about dosing Tylenol. I sat down hard as I read it. The proper dose for Redmond was 1.875 mL. I'd read the chart incorrectly. 5 mL was the suspension, but the dose was 1.875 mL. I'd given him over two and a half times the correct amount.

I had to work hard to steady my breathing and not hyperventilate. I closed my eyes and let the shock sink in. I had overdosed my medically fragile newborn on Tylenol – not once, but twice. Was it more than that? I couldn't remember. A Tylenol overdose can be deadly. It depletes the body of glutathione, an essential antioxidant that affects our immune system function, along with many other functions of the body. It can cause the body to go into liver failure. His liver had been enlarged because of the Tylenol overdose. Somehow the PICU doctors missed it, and I think the regular doctor was afraid to mention it because the specialists hadn't noticed. If he'd only asked me *how much* Tylenol I'd given Redmond, he would've known immediately.

I quickly researched Tylenol overdose and discovered that there's little that can be done if it isn't treated within the first 24-hours. God had again protected Redmond and somehow he'd survived the massive overdose I'd given him in my exhausted, muddled state of mind.

Sobbing, I called Rick and told him what happened. We talked about it more that night, trying to decide what, if anything, we should do. We agreed to tell Nurse Jane when she came to see us. For days I trembled, crying off and on, so upset about what I'd done. I feared that when I told Nurse Jane, she'd report me to child welfare and they'd take him from me. I wondered if maybe they should. Who was I to care for this baby? How was I in charge of supplemental oxygen, a feeding tube, and figuring out Down syndrome? I've never felt more unqualified or ignorant in my life.

When Nurse Jane came the next time, I quietly told her what I'd done. I could barely squeak out the words, but I needed to tell one of his medical providers. If anything could be done now, if anything needed to be done, I didn't want to risk his health to protect myself. Jane told me that there was nothing to be done at this point, and that she believed me that I'd never purposefully hurt my child. She even went so far as to blame herself for not just texting me his dose. She said she knew how little sleep I was getting, and she shouldn't have sent me a chart. It certainly wasn't her fault that I couldn't read a chart clearly, but I appreciated her even more for her graciousness to me.

Much later, I discovered that glutathione can be supplemented through diet. Anyone who takes Tylenol regularly can benefit from it. If I ever need to give him Tylenol now, I start with half a dose to see if that will help. I also increase his supplemental Glutathione for several days afterwards. That was one of the many things I learned as I sat in my chair, tube-feeding Redmond, researching Down syndrome like it was my job.

11

REDMOND'S HEART
AND MINE

Rick and I took Redmond back a few weeks later for a follow up appointment with his cardiologist. We were feeling hopeful. Six days after Redmond had been released from the NICU, we'd had our first follow-up appointment with this doctor. We liked her immediately. She greeted us after his heart echocardiogram with a big smile. She gleefully explained that the hole in Redmond's heart was no longer classified as large, but medium, with partial obstruction. The other hole, an ASD, was completely gone. She was cautiously optimistic that it would continue to close on its own. I felt like I'd wiggle out of my skin with joy and gratitude.

In the PICU, on April 18, 2017, just 14 days after he'd been released from the NICU with a large VSD, and just eight days after we were told it was medium-sized, we were given this news: **the hole in his heart is small, with obstruction. SMALL!** Something they couldn't identify appeared to block the hole at times, then not at others. She wondered if a small flap of tissue had formed close to the hole, but she couldn't tell from the echocardiogram.

During this visit, eight weeks after he was released from the NICU, the cardiologist practically danced with joy. There didn't appear to be any need for open heart surgery. The hole in his heart was small and partially obstructed by something. We talked to her about our recent PICU stay and how we'd been introduced to a local pediatric cardiologist. As much as we liked her, we were wondering if we should transfer care to him. She agreed immediately, telling us that it would be really good for us to have a local doctor who knew him in case of another hospitalization.

By the time Redmond was three months old, the threat of open-heart surgery was gone. God miraculously healed his heart.

I couldn't help but remember the prayer Pastor Brad prayed over him that day in the NICU when I felt something in my spirit jump and I knew that God had healed his heart. It wasn't immediate, like I thought it should be, and the hole didn't disappear completely, but it was real.

At Redmond's one-year appointment with his cardiologist, he had another heart echo. The doctor explained to us that the hole was still there, but it was very, very small. Only two millimeters. The odd thing is that the obstruction they'd once seen and couldn't identify was definitely a flap of tissue that had no business being there. That flap had attached on the other side of the hole. *It looked to him like a hand was closing over the hole.* There's still a small amount of blood flow through that area, but it's negligible. He can live his whole life without any negative side effects of the hole. In my mind's eye, I see the hand of God cupped over that hole, healing it in exactly the right timeframe, fully and completely whole. When I think of Redmond, I think of a young man who has God's hand on his heart. What can a young man who has God's hand on his heart do? There is NO limit.

We recently returned to the cardiologist for Redmond's two-year appointment. A very active and opinionated toddler made the heart echo and EKG extremely difficult for the radiologist to do, but she got it. (Thank you, *Baby Shark* and YouTube.) Another mother sat in a nearby room crying softly. I noticed the nurses and office staff's attentive concern as they huddled around the room and spoke very quietly in the hallway. I understood that the doctor hadn't been able to give her the news she desperately wanted to hear. I didn't see a child anywhere, so I knew the staff must have been entertaining him in another area so they could speak with his mother alone. I wanted to go in and hug her tight, pray for her, beg God to heal her child. Instead, I whispered quiet prayers as I waited, praying that I wouldn't leave this office in tears as well.

The cardiologist took a long time to come in and see us and Redmond didn't make the wait easy. He flopped around in Rick's arms, throwing his body back and forth in an effort to get down and crawl on the floor. Germs mean nothing to a two-year old. I let him down on a doctor's office floor once, and the first thing he did was bend over and lick the floor! LICK! Ugh! So, we took turns holding him, trying everything we knew to distract him while my mind raced with the fearful possibilities of what might cause the doctor's delay. When he finally came in, we wiped our sweaty brows (literally, he was so wild that we were both sweating) and waited for the news.

The doctor examined Redmond, listened to his heart with the fanciest stethoscope ever known to man, and commented on how amazing it was to see him active and opinionated. We agreed that it was amazing, and a great way to burn calories! He leaned back in his chair, relaxed and laughing, and told us the news I'd been breathless to hear. The hole in Redmond's heart is now even smaller, barely noticeable, and we have nothing to fear.

I very badly wanted to hear that the hole had closed completely. Instead, I reminded myself that the son of our good friends was about to go into open-heart surgery to repair other issues with his heart. I chose to shut down the petulant child inside who hadn't quite gotten her way and come before the Lord with thanksgiving and praise. Redmond's healed heart is a miracle of the highest level and my heart is nothing but grateful.

I don't understand God's timing or His ways. I don't understand why He chooses to heal one child and allows another child to suffer through heart failure, leaking valves, and other problems. I don't understand why one child whose parents pray as hard as we do needs open heart surgery while Redmond escapes it. But I am a grateful receiver of this miracle. The doctor says that the body has a wonderful, mysterious way of healing itself. I say that God is a miracle-worker. We give Him all the glory.

The tension we live with as we befriend other families of children with Down syndrome (and other complex medical issues) is seeing them progress in areas where Redmond falls behind or seeing Redmond surge ahead while they suffer frustration and battle despair. One good friend learns to eat on his own while Redmond goes from a temporary feeding tube to a more permanent one. One friend's daughter appears to have no developmental delays at all. She walks and talks right on schedule with her typical peers while Redmond is behind in some areas by a whole year. A loved one makes it through extensive surgery to repair her heart after a massive heart attack, then comes off ECMO a few days later, only to crash within moments and pass away. Her devastated family and friends are left to wonder why. Everyone I mention here is from a family who loves Jesus with all their hearts and prays, believing for miracles.

As I repeatedly learn to trust my God, who doesn't make mistakes, I can't help but wonder how He makes decisions. However, I remember the Scripture and the over-arching theme of the Bible that can be summarized this way: No good comes from arguing with your Maker. Who is the created vessel to say to the Creator, "What are You making?" and who are we to say to the Lord, "You have no skill?" (Isaiah 45 and 64, Jeremiah 18-19, Romans 9).

I choose not to argue with my Maker. I choose to lean into the mystery of the God I do not understand, thankful that I can fully trust that He does understand - and He is working out all things for our good and His glory. I refuse to argue with God any longer.

There was a time in my younger years when my heart had become somewhat hardened and I desperately wanted something that wasn't God's will for my life. I sensed that He was blocking my rebellious plan, so I lay with my face buried in the carpet for hours, sobbing the deepest of cries as I begged God to change His mind. I refused to get up or eat until I felt released in my spirit that God had heard my cries and answered me the way I thought He should. I manipulated every promise in the Bible that I thought might apply to the situation as I made my case, and I begged Him to keep His word. God did what I asked of Him that night, but I knew in my soul that it wasn't His best plan.

Because He loved me so much, because He understood the desperation of my cries, because He valued me enough to teach me a hard lesson while I was still young - He relented from His perfect plan to satisfy my demands. I got my way, but it was a terrible thing. I have always wondered how my life might have been different if I hadn't demanded from God what He knew I didn't need.

I received a reluctant gift that turned to dust in my hands. I learned my lesson. I no longer argue with my Maker. Even when I cannot understand, I humbly receive from His hands what He chooses to give me, believing with every fiber of my being that His ways are higher than mine (Isaiah 55:8-9).

Jesus addressed this very issue in Matthew 19. The Pharisees defended the practice of divorce and Jesus told them that the law was only written because of the hardness of their hearts. It wasn't God's intention at all. It wasn't His best plan, but because their hearts had become so far from Him, He allowed it.

How I wish that in my earlier years I had chosen to keep my heart soft and tender toward God, rather than fighting Him so often. As I look back on those years now, I'm thankful for the prayers of my parents and grandparents. I couldn't fight my way past them. As hard as I tried to sin, I believe that their prayers blocked my efforts. I'd try to drive to a place where I knew I shouldn't be, and I'd get so lost that it became comical. I knew where to go, where to turn, but I kept turning the wrong way. I'd finally capitulate and head for home. Miraculously, I'd make all the correct turns as I headed away from temptation and sin. I'd get so mad as a teenager, knowing that my parents' prayers for protection kept me from getting too far from the straight and narrow path. God only ever allowed me to go so far. I knew. I'm so grateful now.

Perhaps that's why I'm able to trust God so fully? My efforts to rebel against Him, to do things my own way, never worked out well. Things that seemed, at the time, to devastate and ruin everything worked out for my good in the long run. So, I have to believe that feeding tubes and oxygen monitors and hospitalizations and genetic anomalies are something God is using for our good. They are something God is using for the good of the whole world. Who am I to argue?

12

BACK TO THE HOSPITAL

Redmond improved a little at a time at home. He still didn't breathe easily, but I didn't feel the need to hold him around the clock to keep him from crying. Because of the feeding schedule, we had a little set up in the living room. I spent most of my time in the big recliner with him right in front of me in his glider. It kept him at enough of an angle to help him breathe better, and I could keep an eye on him.

I found a new song on YouTube to encourage me as I dealt with Down syndrome, oxygen tubing, and the feeding tube. It's called *Old Church Choir* by Zach Williams. I'd turn it up loud and sing along with the chorus about the joy of my restored heart and how nothing was going to take my joy away. After a while, I changed the words to "He's got a heart that's healing and he's been restored/No feeding tube or oxygen will steal our joy!" I couldn't get up and dance, but I did my best to boogie it down in the recliner.

Eliana fell in love with the song too. Together we would belt it out, especially when I got extra tired or frustrated, and she would dance a jig in the living room. Soon she started demanding that song every time we got into the car. It's pretty hard to stay discouraged when you're singing an upbeat and fun song about joy with your four-year-old daughter. She and I learned every word and it made me giggle when I looked in the rearview mirror and saw her bobbing her head along to the beat, just like me. I ended up downloading the entire album and learned every word to every song on it. What else was I going to do while I was stuck in that chair?

A year later, my sister moved to Nashville (can you believe the gall of her, moving there *after* I left?) and found out that her neighbor was Zach Williams! Eliana and I nearly lost our minds. We wanted so badly to camp out on the sidewalk in front of his house and serenade him, but we restrained ourselves. In Nashville, that is especially *not cool*. Instead, my sister went to a party at his house and hung out with him. She casually mentioned that her sister is a fan. Eliana and I still may serenade him one of these days!

On the way to Redmond's three-month check up with the pediatrician, we probably had that song on repeat the entire time we were in the car. The pediatrician asked me about our sleeping arrangements. I explained that Redmond made terrible noises while he slept, causing me to fear that he'd stop breathing. I called it "janky breathing". I had to get up to feed him every three hours anyway, so I slept in the recliner with him in the glider beside me. The scary truth was that I probably spent about 20 hours a day in that recliner during that time of my life. I tried to wear my FitBit for a while, but it was depressing to see my step count at the end of the day – 1600 steps, maybe 2000 if I went to the grocery store, so I stopped wearing it.

The pediatrician told us that most babies breathe funny while they sleep, so we should put him in his crib every night and close the door. She said that he'd let us know if he needed us. I shook my head at her, thinking THERE IS NO WAY I'M DOING THAT. But I thought about it all day, and that night I decided to give it a try. I prayed over him, reminding God of the ministering angels whom He'd sent to watch over Redmond while he slept soon after we got home from the NICU. I put him in his crib and closed the door. I went to my own bed and slept until the alarm went off to feed him. The quality of sleep I got was significantly better than in the recliner. Plus, my butt didn't feel so completely flat!

When Redmond was three and a half months old, he still struggled after feedings. One night was particularly bad with him writhing in pain that never seemed to stop. Rick and I took turns holding him for hours, but at 5:00 a.m., absolutely exhausted and frustrated because nothing worked to settle him down, I laid him in his bed. He didn't close his eyes, but he didn't cry either. My heart broke to see him blankly staring into space, but no one benefitted from what I'd been doing. Reminding myself of the angels I'd seen watching over him, I closed his door and went to my bed.

As I lay down, the familiar thought crossed my mind, "While you were sleeping, he was dying." I cried myself to sleep, too worn to go back and get him. I awoke two hours later with a start and jumped out of bed.

Guilt washed over me as I realized I had slept deeply, not even listening for him. I ran to his room and opened the door, stunned to find him in the exact position I'd left him in, eyes wide open staring straight ahead. The oxygen concentrator was very loud, so we'd moved it into his room the day before. We figured it would make good white noise for him in there. His tiny room was unusually warm and as I scooped him out of bed, I couldn't believe how hot he was. Quickly, I unwrapped his swaddle and unzipped his footie pajamas. I stripped it all off him and blotted his skin with a wet wipe. Unsatisfied, I ran to the bathroom and wetted several washcloths. I laid them on his forehead, chest, and belly.

Then I changed his diaper and took his temperature. It was 104.9° F. In a panic, I cried out for Rick to come. He jumped out of bed and ran in, shaking off sleep.

"What's wrong?"

"His temperature is 104.9! We have to get him to the ER right away."

While I gave him the correct dose of Tylenol, Rick got on the phone with his parents, who rushed right over to watch Eliana and Charlie. I called Nurse Jane, wondering if I should call an ambulance. She explained that an ambulance would only take him to the nearby health center, but we needed to get to the children's hospital (an hour away). We packed another overnight bag, trying to think through the fog of worry, and rushed to the car. I held him in the back seat as we drove, unwilling to strap him into the car seat for what I feared might be the last moments of his life.

We hadn't had time to feed him before we left, so I tried to nurse him. Much to my surprise, he latched on and suckled off and on for the entire hour. I was crying from fear and happiness. If he could nurse, then maybe he would be okay?

When we got to the hospital, his fever felt to me like it was completely gone. I was surprised when it registered 102.5° F. They catheterized him for a urine culture, put in an IV, and took blood for a culture. Giving him an IV is not a fun experience. His veins are hard to find, blow easily, and rarely cooperate. The nurse had to stick him several times before it worked. While she was trying to get the IV in, I had to go for a walk. It was too hard to hear him scream.

Doctors and nurses fired all kinds of questions at me. They wanted to know if he'd had his three-month immunizations. He had. They wanted to know how long it had been. It had been about five days. They praised my decision to vaccinate him, stating that if he hadn't been vaccinated, they would have had to test him for all kinds of other infections. I was so relieved that I'd gotten them done on time.

He was admitted and sent to the general floor. The room was awful – small and awkwardly shaped, in the older section of the hospital, with a wallpaper border that showed healthy, happy children playing on a beach. I was furious. All I wanted to do was go sit on a beach in Hawaii and enjoy happy, healthy children. Instead this wallpaper mocked me, a constant reminder that I could not sit on a beach and enjoy my children.

The floor was busy, with one nurse caring for 6-8 patients at a time. I sent Rick home immediately to be with the kids. I felt like I could handle the situation on my own. I called The Ronald McDonald House to arrange for a room. The woman at the desk was an old friend by now, and she offered her condolences that we were back in the hospital again, but that night they didn't have any availability. I delivered frozen breast milk to the nurse and explained his strict feeding schedule, then settled in for the night on the uncomfortable hospital furniture.

A glance in the tiny bathroom mirror stunned me. I had deep, dark circles under my eyes, despite swiping on a little concealer, and I looked like I'd aged ten years. I'd always thought I looked a little younger than my actual age, but that day I saw an old woman staring back at me. I was too tired to be upset about it though.

The night nurse was kind, telling me to sleep and she'd deal with him as quietly as she could. I put a pillow over my head, turned on some white noise, and barely woke as she came in to care for him every few hours. The next morning, the doctor told me that nothing had grown on the cultures overnight. They'd tested his blood for viruses and bacteria. However, a number I'd never heard of before – procalcitonin – was very high.

A quick Google search informed me that a number greater than two indicates sepsis and septic shock. A number greater than 10 indicates severe sepsis and septic shock. Sepsis is a potentially life-threatening condition caused by the body's response to an infection. The body normally releases chemicals into the bloodstream to fight an infection. Sepsis occurs when the body's response to these chemicals is out of balance, triggering changes that can damage multiple organ systems. Septic shock is a potentially fatal medical condition that occurs when sepsis, which is organ injury or damage in response to infection, leads to dangerously low blood pressure and abnormalities in cellular metabolism. I read further that only

30% of patients who go into sepsis or septic shock after an ICU hospitalization survive the first year after hospital admission. Basically, it's really, really bad.[2]

Redmond's procalcitonin number was 18.

I'm not sure how close he actually came to death that night, but I tremble at the knowledge that the angel of death was again blowing hot breath down our necks. **But those ministering angels that God sent were much more powerful than any attack of Satan and they woke me up when he needed me.**

Doctors scurried in and out, considering every option, and finally decided that they wanted to do a spinal tap.

The crazy thing was that despite his extremely high procalcitonin, Redmond had been fine all night. He'd slept soundly, his fever had broken, and he was in good spirits. He wasn't even writhing in pain after his feedings. I had no idea what procalcitonin was, and none of the doctors mentioned sepsis or septic shock to me, so I was not going to submit him to a painful test that seemed completely unnecessary. I knew the signs of bacterial and spinal meningitis and he didn't have it. It didn't take a medical degree to see that. (Every medical practitioner reading this now is likely cringing. I realize that I'm not the easiest mother to deal with. I'm also not sorry.)

While the doctor argued with me, trying to make me feel the alarm she was feeling but still never mentioning sepsis, Rick walked in the room. He'd spent the night at home and had some things I needed with him. He'd been planning to have his parents bring the kids up later that day, but the doctor forbade it, saying that what Redmond had was likely contagious and we shouldn't have any visitors.

She turned on Rick quickly, surprising him by explaining what was going on with Redmond's procalcitonin, asking *him* for permission to do a spinal tap. Rick and I had talked on the phone earlier and he knew how Redmond was doing that day.

Without a moment of hesitation, Rick said, "No. No spinal tap."

I fell in love with him all over again in that moment.

Disgusted with us, she said she was going to send over the infectious disease doctor to look at him. We were fine with that. Within moments that very doctor walked in the room and spoke pleasantly with us for a few

---

[2] https://en.wikipedia.org/wiki/Procalcitonin

minutes. The pediatrician spoke with her in the hall, then left. The infectious disease doctor came back in and looked Redmond over.

"This baby does NOT have meningitis." The words were emphatic and clear.

We both blew out sighs of relief as we said, "That's what we thought!"

Someone in that place had looked past the numbers to see the baby lying there and used common sense. She told us that he looked healthy to her and she wasn't going to order any more tests for him. She explained that any other baby who came in with his symptoms and presentation would have been sent home by now, but because of his medical history they needed to be extra cautious. I was sorely tempted to leave against medical advice at that point but felt a little concerned that social workers would show up at my house and take my child away.

Rick and I went to lunch in the cafeteria, then he went back home. I contacted the people who had wanted to visit to let them know that they couldn't come, then I went back to his room. This time I was reading the book, "Bloom," by Kelle Hampton. Kelle was a young, pretty, fun mom with lots of friends when her second child was born with Down syndrome. She mourned the diagnosis deeply, surrounded by friends and family, and then decided that they certainly didn't choose this journey, but since it was the one they were on, they were going to rock it.

It wasn't any theological treatise and I struggled through it. I still felt like my friends who could handle the depth of emotions I was dealing with were in Nashville. My mom and sister were dealing with their own lives, hours away. With our rural farm, there was nothing easy about the commute, so they couldn't simply come visit me for a day or two. Reading about the wealth of her friendships highlighted the lonely ache in my heart.

Also, Hampton's daughter was healthy. Her intense mourning was over Down syndrome alone. I knew that my feelings weren't gracious and if Redmond had been perfectly healthy, I might have faced the same emotions, but at that time in my life I felt annoyed. I realized that I hadn't had much of an opportunity to process Down syndrome because I was dealing with medical crisis. That had taken up most of the space in my head.

A young man was admitted to the room across the hall. Our door was open and where I sat gave me a direct view to his door. His mother closed his door tightly and I saw his head pop into the window, then down, then back up again. He repeatedly jumped up to look at me through the window. The expression on his face was disturbing. I closed our door. The commotion in the room across the hall left me feeling concerned. I had a room for the night at The Ronald McDonald House, but I was concerned about leaving Redmond alone. Would the child attempt to injure himself or someone else? How severe was his condition?

When the nurse came to check on Redmond, I told her that he was overdue for his feeding. I couldn't feed him because I had to wait for a nurse to bring the milk from a locked freezer, heat it in a lukewarm cup of water, and try to feed it to him cold. When she finally returned, over an hour later, I told her that I was very concerned about the situation across the hall. I asked her if Redmond was safe there without me and if she had the resources to handle the other patient, Redmond, and the other patients on that floor.

She confirmed that my concern was legitimate, but she couldn't give me any details. Later, she came by my room, asked if I needed anything, then left the door wide open. I was able to overhear her talking loudly to a colleague right outside my room. The child was having a bad reaction to medication, causing mania, but they'd gotten it under control. He was sleeping for the night and his mother would stay with him. I appreciated her thoughtfulness.

We decided that it was possible that the feeding tube might be causing an infection in his stomach. A foreign object in the body is always concerning. I decided to pull it out and have it tested for infection. No one was there to put it back in when it was time to feed him next, so I only bottle fed him. It took an hour, but I got him to drink 75% of his feeding. I was thrilled and thought the irritation from the tube might cause him to drink less. I decided to leave the tube out and try to bottle feed him for the next feeding to see what he would do.

Redmond's IV blew then and they couldn't get in a new one, so they had to call in a team from the NICU. The only place they could get it in was on the top of his little head. He had something like 14 pokes on his arms, legs, hands, and feet where they'd tried over and over to get a vein – while he was awake. I was furious with them for that, but I'd walked away during the procedure because I couldn't stand his screams, so I had no say in it. (Lesson learned.)

They gave him a strong antibiotic through that IV. I looked it up and saw that if the IV blew it could cause the skin around it to turn black and die. Right next to his brain? It was an awful day.

I couldn't pick him up because I was terrified to damage the IV and he was content, so I made plans to leave for the night. Both our nerves were totally rattled. He cried hard during the whole IV procedure, so I told the nurse not to wake him up for his next feeding. He'd never missed a feeding in his life, but I thought that night rest might be more important than keeping a strict schedule.

"Just let him sleep. He's been through enough." I gathered my things and headed over to my oasis for a good night's sleep – my consolation prize in the trials of our third hospitalization in three months.

When I got back the next morning at 9:00 a.m., they were returning him to his bed. He was screaming loudly and I saw a bag of frozen breast milk sitting in a cup on the table. I soon discovered that the feeding tube was back in and he'd recently returned from having a chest x-ray to check its placement. No one asked me if it was okay to expose him to more radiation or to put the tube back in. He's already been exposed to so much in his little life that I try to avoid it as much as possible.

At home we didn't have one and our method seemed to work well, but the nurse wasn't comfortable with it. I was struck by the knowledge that trained medical professionals who worked with sick children for a living were nervous to do the things I was expected to do for him at home.

When I asked how he'd eaten overnight, the nurse told me that he'd slept through the night and woken up at 7am. She had reinserted the feeding tube, gotten the x-ray, and was about to feed him. He was only three months old and it had been over nine hours since he'd eaten last. Never in his life had he gone more than three hours without eating. I had never missed one feeding, no matter how exhausted I was. And this nurse hadn't tried to feed him once all night.

I was livid. He's a heart patient! He HAS to eat! Not only was I furious with her for not feeding him, but I was indignant that she hadn't even tried to give him a bottle before she shoved the feeding tube back up his nose. Biting back tears of frustration, I did something I'd never done before. I opened my mouth and spoke up.

"He hasn't eaten in over nine hours? How could you do that? He's a three-month-old heart patient."

She responded by saying, "You said not to wake him up. He slept the whole time."

White hot fury seethed through me. "You're a pediatric nurse. You should know that you can't let a newborn go that long without food. I meant that you didn't need to wake him for the next feeding. I didn't mean for you not to feed him until he wakes up. I had no idea he'd sleep that long. I always wake him up to feed him every three hours. I thought you might wait four or five hours. And you didn't even try to give him a bottle!"

She quickly rushed from the room, quite possibly in tears. She was very young. We'd gotten along fine the night before, but I couldn't believe what she'd done.

I spoke to every person who came into his room about it that day until the hospital finally sent someone official to speak to me. I lodged a formal complaint. Later that night, the pediatrician who was on duty talked to me. She apologized and explained that it had been a failure on multiple levels. Not only should the nurse have known better, but the doctor on duty and the nurse manager were also responsible. The pediatrician requested their best nurse for Redmond that night. She assured me that I could leave and rest, knowing he was in good hands.

Redmond was well-cared for that night. But the next day, sitting alone for hours in that room with the mocking children playing at the beach, I became overwhelmed with the responsibility of not only caring for him, but making sure medical providers didn't injure him. I had to watch doctors and nurses like hawks to make sure they didn't stick him with the same needle 14 times in an effort to get in an IV, to make sure they didn't do unnecessary and painful tests on him, to make sure they didn't neglect or starve him, and to make sure other patients didn't hurt him.

Although Redmond had been on the regular floor in that hospital once before, it was the first time I really noticed how different the care was from the intensive care unit. I was accustomed to ICU-level care. The nurse who failed us that night was responsible for more complicated patients than was reasonable. I have a feeling she probably didn't get a meal or bathroom break all night and was thankful that Redmond kept sleeping. She didn't have time to sit and bottle feed him, then tube feed him, and then hold him upright for 20 minutes to make sure he didn't have reflux. Those are things that ICU nurses and mothers do. I felt traumatized by what happened but had to remind myself that he was okay. It didn't actually cause him any long-term harm to miss a feeding – or two. He was growing appropriately, gaining weight, and maybe he benefited from a night of uninterrupted sleep too. But at that time, I could not see that side of it for anything. I was a mess.

We'd been in the hospital for eight of the thirteen weeks that he'd been alive. I called Rick several times a day to have him add new things to the list of what he should bring when he came back to the hospital. I couldn't believe I forgot my phone charger, again. I went on Amazon Prime and ordered a second set of my favorite travel-sized toiletries, an extra phone charger, and a few comfort items so that I could always have a hospital bag packed and ready to go. It was hard to think about packing a bag when he was in medical crisis. I needed to be prepared for next time.

My mind worked in circles that day. Most of my thoughts centered around kicking myself for not praying harder about having a third baby and making sure we had God's blessing before we made such a big decision. I thoroughly wore myself out, calling myself names like *Greedy, Selfish, Reckless, Stupid, Proud, and Sinful.* I tried to remember if Rick had been 100% on board or if he'd just gone along with me. I tried to pray, but I couldn't feel God's presence anywhere. It was like every prayer I prayed hit the ceiling and fell flat. I had ruined our perfect life and I was sure that God was mad at me.

I looked at the wallpaper images of children playing on the beach and allowed my mind to drift away. I was sitting on a beach in Hawaii, drinking a frozen fruity drink, tan and relaxed. Waiters served me drinks and fanned me. I had no responsibilities at all. No one expected anything from me. Children played, carefree and happy, but they weren't mine. I enjoyed watching them but didn't have to do anything for them. I fought back the tremendous urge to walk out of the hospital, get on a plane, and fly far, far away. I couldn't work out what to do about Eliana and Charlie, because I knew I'd eventually want them around. In fact, I'd want Redmond around too, but my fantasy didn't include them or Rick. No one in Hawaii needed anything from me at all.

My body hurt, still not completely healed from birth and the infection. I hadn't brought the right medicine and Rick had gone home for the day. Stress made it worse and I winced in pain every time I moved. One of the nurse aides came in to check on Redmond, then looked at me with compassion and asked, "Are you alright?"

Tears sprung to my eyes. I'd been trying to keep it together, but it wasn't working. I explained my embarrassing and very personal physical pain to her. She nodded and said, "Of course! You just had a baby. Give me a minute."

I didn't know what she was doing, but she went to the labor and delivery floor and got some kind of magic potion I'd never seen before for me. She brought it right back and handed it to me with a soft smile. More tears, this time of gratitude. God sent an angel, even in the middle of that lonely hospital rooms where I wondered if He'd forgotten us.

Then a young woman with a big smile came in to see me. She introduced herself as Aimee, explaining that she worked in the area and was on a break. She placed a large basket on my table and said, "Congratulations on your baby! He's beautiful."

She explained that she's from a small group of families in our area who have children ages three and under with Down syndrome. A mutual friend had put me in touch with another one of the moms who I'd tentatively texted a week before, nervous as could be. I'd already been given several phone numbers to call other moms of children with Down syndrome, but the idea of calling them totally weirded me out. What was I supposed to say? Would I be able to talk or would I just cry? I don't know what I thought would happen, but I wasn't sure I wanted to be a part of a Down syndrome group either. Texting worked for me, and the woman on the other end of the phone had been more kind and comforting than I imagined possible. She invited me to join a Facebook group and when I saw her photo, I was stunned that she was young and very pretty. I don't know what I thought she or the other moms would be like, but she seemed so... normal.

My perception of families of children with Down syndrome wasn't exactly defined, but it didn't naturally include young, trendy, personable moms. If I'd drawn on my experience with the mothers I did know who had children with Down syndrome, I would have had a very realistic view. One of the mothers was quite young when her son was born. Her son is an adult now and she is stylish and fit, active in church and our community, and has been helpful to me. The other mother is someone I've known since I was a little girl. She's a beautiful, talented, and savvy business owner in our area. These amazing women are great examples for me.

I realized that my fear had blinded and confused me.

The basket Aimee delivered was to let me to know that I wasn't alone. It had gift cards, pampering items, board books, adorable baby outfits, and a little toy for Redmond. It was really good stuff. I was deeply touched by the graciousness of those who'd obviously gone to a lot of cost and effort to put it together.

Aimee explained that she had a young daughter with Down syndrome. They'd found out when she was born. Their extensive testing had all been negative for Down syndrome, making it a huge shock. Both she and her husband had worked with children for years and they knew a lot about Down syndrome. She shared some of her experience and feelings with me, which was so encouraging. I don't remember what I told her, but it probably had to do with all the guilt I felt that day. She encouraged me to come to their next get together and meet the other families. I told her that as long as Redmond wasn't in the hospital or sick, I'd try to make it.

Even with those two bright spots in my day, I still struggled. Darkness felt like a shadow over me. I tried to use my life coach training to coach myself out of my funk, but it didn't work. The name of a woman I knew in Nashville popped into my head. Karen's a godly woman with a fun and spunky personality. I chuckled, thinking of how they'd made me the new women's minister when they could've had her do the job. Man, she would've been so good at it. I'd heard that in the time since I left, she'd gone to work as the women's minister at a different church. I had no doubt that she did a fantastic job there.

I sent her a message that simply said I was struggling with some things and her name came to mind. I asked if she might have some time to talk. She wrote me back quickly and said she'd be happy to talk. We set up a phone appointment for that night.

When I spoke to her, I laid it all out. I'd been having some thoughts that had no basis in reality, but to me they felt very real. Karen quickly saw where I was headed with my narrative and cut me off. She didn't need to hear the rest. She knew exactly why God had placed her name on my heart. She relayed a personal story that mimicked my own distorted thoughts. It had taken her years to straighten out her thoughts about it, and she didn't want me to suffer any longer than I already had.

Karen ministered to me that night in deep places where my heart desperately needed to be touched. It wasn't that she said anything different than what my mom and a few friends had said when I hinted at what was in my mind, but there was an anointing over that conversation that broke the lies of Satan that I had believed. Her unique life experience had prepared her for that conversation, and it was a blessing to talk to her.

I was able to receive the freedom she offered to me. When she prayed, she said that I was never to speak the words aloud again. She said I would never again believe those lies for a moment. God answered her prayer. I can no longer even write about the specifics of the lie that I believed. I've never spoken about it in any detail since that day. And the lie has had absolutely no hold on me since then. It was completely untrue and I can now see that clearly. Praise the Lord.

That same night, I opened my messages to find one from an old friend from seminary who I've stayed in contact with over the years. She has a daughter with some special needs and had seen a Facebook post I'd made about being in the hospital with Redmond again. Among other things, she wrote the following:

"Over a very short period of time, you are going to begin seeing that God has developed within you a ferocity that you had no idea you were capable of feeling. Your first inclination when reflecting on it may be to self-correct, thinking your responses are coming from a place of being hungry, tired, angry, etc. But, although it is still very raw, that response is the work of the Holy Spirit awakening you to see & hear exactly what Redmond (and Rick) needs and to advocate for those things. Rather than change or harness it, allow the Holy Spirit to refine it and empower you to walk this new path. You are absolutely correct when you say to yourself (and God) that you cannot do this in your strength, but He has already equipped you with all you need to care for your family.

As I prayed, I kept seeing an image of you doubled over at the waist, your torso, arms, neck and head hanging limp, as if there is no energy or life in them. But a small light penetrated and began to shine in your belly, and as the light grows and becomes brighter, every part of you is strengthened, until you are standing upright in a "Wonder Woman" pose. As He fills you, you will experience a newfound sense of self-confidence, awareness, and courage to take appropriate action... As His light fills you, may you rise up in confidence and with great courage!"

My friend had no idea of what I'd faced in the hospital with Redmond the day before, or what I'd told God on the morning that we left for the hospital. In total desperation as a response to something I'd read earlier about being a Jesus girl, I'd rashly prayed, "Whatever You're doing in me, I'm not your girl, God. I can't handle this. I'll stay small. Please, pick someone else and heal my baby now."

God knew that I couldn't mean I wasn't His girl. He knew that I was weary from all the stress and worry. He knew that every other day of my life I'd told Him, "I'm Your girl. Do what you want in me and through me. I'll tell the story of Your work in my life to anyone who will listen."

My friend's words reminded me that I was already God's girl, and that He'd already given me all I needed to handle what was happening in my life through Redmond. And she was right. Fierceness that had always been there, but that I had tried to stifle because it felt wrong, rose up in me through the things I'd experienced. A sleeping giant awoke. All the training I'd had to soften, quiet, and gentle my imperative personality was shaken off in a moment and inside I felt a roar rising. For once, I didn't stifle it. I began to shake with the power of it, and inside I began to roar.

I shook off the guilt and shame, and I picked up the sword that I had tried to ignore. I would fight for my son without a moment's hesitation. God gave this child to me at this time in my life and I wasn't going to be limp and ineffective any longer. I felt the light shining out of my belly and I embraced it. I'd heard the phrase "mama bear" before and I embraced that too.

The next day, Redmond's cultures were completed. He had a tiny bit of bacteria that indicated he might have a urinary tract infection. He'd already been getting IV antibiotics, so they did one more dose and sent us home with oral antibiotics to finish out the treatment. He'd never had one more fever and his belly hadn't bothered him at all since we'd been admitted. I felt like I was going home from war, triumphant.

When we got home, I started to make his bottle. At that time, I was pumping four times a day, which was half as much as he needed. I supplemented the other half with high-calorie formula. We'd been given sterile water at the hospital, which comes in a pack of small bottles. We'd started a new pack, so they'd given us the rest to take home. I decided to use the rest of the sterile water to make his bottle, since we had it. As I poured the water in, the thought crossed my mind that the water we used in the hospital was the only thing different from what we did at home. At home, we used tap water from our well.

Thunderstruck, I hollered for Rick. I frantically explained that the water must have been causing Redmond's stomach upset! It was the only difference! Rick looked at me sideways, suspicious of what this might mean to his wallet. I couldn't have cared less what it cost. Redmond's bottles from that point on would only be made with sterile water.

I got a gallon of distilled water for $.82, and it worked like a charm. Redmond has never had a stomach ache like that since. When I told his doctors about it, they didn't believe that something as simple as water would cause such an issue. I know what made the difference though.

13

BECOMING A ROCKIN' MOM™

Thankfully, I didn't have to use that "go bag". My extra toiletries and supplies ended up being used for travel, rather than emergency hospitalizations. Redmond did not go back to the hospital again for the rest of the first year of his life. We got down to the business of raising our baby, feeding him, weaning him off supplemental oxygen, and learning as much as we could about Down syndrome.

The cardiologist didn't want Redmond on supplemental oxygen at all and told us he didn't need it. He could live a good life with oxygen saturation levels in the high 80's.

The pulmonologist said he absolutely needed oxygen and we could not turn it off. She said oxygen is medicine. It gave him energy and allowed his body to heal. She said his saturation level needed to be a minimum of 93.

I had no idea what to do. When I asked them to talk to one another to make the decision, they refused. I asked Nurse Jane what she thought. She said to ask the pulmonologist if we could start weaning him off oxygen a little at a time.

When Redmond was about four months old, we got that permission to start weaning him off the supplemental oxygen. We were supposed to turn it off for one hour every day for a week and watch him. If he didn't seem overly tired and his oxygen level didn't drop below 92, we could do it for one hour in the morning and one hour in the afternoon. If that went well, we'd slowly increase the amount of time he was off the oxygen until he only needed it at night.

It was hard to relax, but I slowly gave him breaks from oxygen, watching closely. We noticed that he did very well as long as he wasn't sleeping. I followed directions, increasing the time off in increments. Redmond maintained his normal energy level and was alert and happy when the oxygen was off.

Then, when he was five months old, he turned all his energy on removing the oxygen tube. He yanked on them all day long. Where they'd once hovered right under his nostrils, providing they tiny whiff he needed, he now pulled the tube into his mouth and chewed on it. His little cheeks were raw from constantly yanking on the tape.

One day he ripped the tape off his face and tore off the top layer of skin on both cheeks. There was no space remaining to attach the tubes where the skin was still intact. I decided to give him the day off. I hooked up the oxygen monitor and paid close attention. His oxygen level was in the high 90's and stayed there.

He was alert and relaxed, rolling around on the floor happily without anything to slow him down. When he fell asleep at nap time, his saturation level remained in the 90's. It remained high all afternoon and evening. That night I sat in his bedroom and watched the monitor while he slept. It stayed right around 92-94. The alarm was set to go off if it got below 88. I fell asleep in the chair and the alarm didn't sound.

The next day was more of the same. After 48 hours, I relaxed. Redmond wasn't showing signs of fatigue. His oxygen level remained high. I called the pulmonologist to report the happy news. She was not impressed. She said we should still have the oxygen on at night. I told her about his rebellion against the tubes. She suggested mittens or socks on his hands. When I told her that he had them and could do it anyway, she didn't have any other suggestions. She just wanted oxygen on him at night.

I tried everything I could think of, but he pulled it off. Given what the cardiologist said, I gave up the fight. I continued to spot check, and he continued to do great. His energy level remained the same. He didn't turn blue or appear to have any problems breathing. Any time I was around a nurse at church or in the community, I was *that* mom, asking her to check him for signs of oxygen deprivation. He was pink and healthy.

Since there was no good reason to stay home, we went to a social gathering of our local Down syndrome group. After I met them, I couldn't remember why we'd been so hesitant to join. We met wonderful families –

all of us in the same situation, learning a new normal, cheering for one another as our kids grow and learn.

Our farm is fairly rural, so many of the other families live about an hour from us, closer to the city. But one family lives nearby and has kids the same ages as our kids, including a son with Down syndrome who is close to Redmond's age. Their son also had a feeding tube, they are Christians, and our personalities have meshed well together. We've come to consider them some of our closest friends.

Through this group, we learned of the Down Syndrome Diagnosis Network (DSDN), which is an online group of over 10,000 families across the world who have children with Down syndrome. It's aimed at families with young children who've recently received the diagnosis. I joined the group with hesitation, remembering the hyperemesis gravidarum (extreme morning sickness) and gestational diabetes groups I'd been in before that had depressed me. This group was nothing like those groups.

My "birth group" is for moms of babies born between January and June of 2017. We're called Rockin' Moms™ because if we're going to deal with a Down syndrome diagnosis, we're going to rock it! We're going to do Down syndrome better than anyone has ever done it before. Our kids rock their extra chromosome! We share resources, offer support, and even share the burden. We celebrate when each other's children reach milestones that we know have been so hard. We vent to one another about stupid things other people say. We ask questions about physical therapy, age-appropriate toys, and whatever else comes to mind.

I'm also a part of the larger group of moms of kids of all ages. Moms who've been doing this longer help the newer ones and we figure things out together. I joined the group in 2017 and discovered that they were having a retreat that fall in Chicago, which was a convenient location for me. Several of our local group moms went together, and I wanted to go, but there was no way I could leave Redmond. He'd just turned six months old and still needed my full attention.

By September, 2018, Redmond was doing so much better that I was finally able to go! The location wasn't convenient, but I felt compelled to make it happen. That year, I attended my first DSDN Rockin' Mom's™ Retreat in Phoenix, AZ.

A couple months before the retreat, the DSDN leaders let us know that they planned to expand their Medical Outreach Team in 2018. They invited retreat attendees to apply to be a part of the team. Members had to be willing to travel to at least one medical convention in 2019, and they had to be able to attend training the day before the retreat started. Team members would learn to talk to medical providers about the best way to give a Down syndrome diagnosis to a new family. Because the diagnosis experience sets the tone on how they accept their new baby, it's a very important time.

I'd been looking for a way to volunteer with DSDN and hadn't seen an opportunity that worked for me, but I knew this was something I could do. Traveling is in my blood and talking to medical providers felt like a great way to make an impact. I didn't discuss it with anyone, didn't even pray about it. I quickly filled out the application and hit send.

A few weeks later, an email popped up in my inbox from the group leader – Jen Jacob. I was pleasantly surprised to find that it was an invitation to join the DSDN Medical Outreach Team. I decided that they'd probably invited everyone who applied. Nevertheless, my grin was from ear to ear.

A few minutes later, Jen Jacob posted about it on Facebook. She thanked everyone who'd applied and said that they'd been surprised by the number of applications they'd received. They could only accept a small group this year but would look into expanding it in the future.

There were only about 15 of us. One of the group members is a blogger I discovered while Redmond was still in the NICU and have been following ever since. I was a little star struck and embarrassingly eager to be in this small training with people I had learned so much from.

DSDN sends representatives to medical conventions and events throughout the country to talk to medical providers about the best way to give a Down syndrome diagnosis to a new parent. We want to change the dialog from what is highly likely to happen now: "I'm sorry to say that your 10-week old fetus has Down syndrome. When would you like to schedule your termination?"

Or if the parent receives a birth diagnosis, "I'm sorry to tell you that it appears that your baby has Trisomy 21/Down syndrome. Look at his low muscle tone, almond-shaped eyes, low-set ears, fat pad on the back of his neck, sandal toes, Palmar crease, and square fingers. He will be short in stature, mentally disabled, and unlikely to talk or take care of himself. You have options. There are organizations that take Downs babies for adoption."

The diagnosis is often followed by nurses and doctors who act awkwardly around the parents, offer no information, or give out-of-date information. Very few doctors are as awesome as my OB was, congratulating the parents on their new baby! They don't share encouraging news about all the wonderful things people with Down syndrome can do, how loving and accepting they are, or how they will bring joy to the life of their family. They're uneducated about how much things have changed. It's actually very likely that their child will talk, go to school with their typical peers, and be able to work and live with a lot of independence.

The DSDN has printed beautiful, current materials for doctors to give to parents when they receive the diagnosis. They have resources for doctors on the best way to share the news, what new parents wish they'd been told, and so forth. They want to send new parents a welcome gift and get them connected to the support that can make such a difference for their family.

While the DSDN is a pro-information group, choosing to stay out of the abortion debate and instead focusing on the importance of embracing our differences and loving everyone, I quietly pray for a revolution in the hearts of everyone involved. From my perspective, God has sent children with Down syndrome to teach those of us who are so capable and accomplished and acceptable to the world to slow down, see the value in what's truly important, and to make sacrifices that we'd never typically think to make. Those sacrifices are what will change the world. Our children with Down syndrome are messengers from heaven, if only we will allow them to live and embrace their differences.

I hope to give new parents a different experience than the ones I've heard so much about. If we can change the conversation at the diagnosis level, we change the world.

I got to Phoenix the day before and spent the night with Rick's aunts in the suburbs. That night, I got really sick. I was sick every fifteen minutes, all night long. I finally got a little relief and slept for about an hour before the alarm went off.

Rick's aunts had an early morning appointment and were out the door before I woke up, but they let me use their car that weekend. I dragged myself out of bed, got ready the best I could, repacked my heavy suitcase, pulled it up the stairs, somehow mustered the energy to lift it into the car, and drove to a drug store. There I bought every bit of over the counter medication I thought might help, sat in my car with a bottle of water and took it all, then prayed something would work. Shaking and clammy, I found the retreat resort and tried to figure out where to park. I left my luggage in the car and located the training room – nowhere near where I parked. I fluffed myself up the best I could in the bathroom, then walked in a minute before it officially started.

There was an optional breakfast an hour before, so most of the other attendees had a chance to get to know one another a little already. I was afraid to touch anyone or get close, but there was *no way* I was going to miss that training. Jen Jacob met me at the door with the warmest smile. She was a celebrity to me but acted like my next-door neighbor. Her friendliness helped lift my spirits. I quietly explained to her that I'd been sick all night, but I was there and ready to get to work. I found a seat and tried to focus on the presentation.

I felt like I had been made for that team. It's amazing to feel so at ease and excited about a job I feel privileged to do. When training ended, I made my way to the other end of the sprawling resort to a restaurant where other women from my birth group had gathered for lunch. I was late because of training and I was moving very slowly, so again everyone had a chance to get to know one another a little before I showed up. Normally, I'd mingle around with the group until I caught up, but it was everything I could do to be upright and smiling. I didn't have the energy to mingle.

After lunch, one of my new friends helped me get my luggage from the car to the hotel registration desk. I somehow made it to my room and collapsed on the bed. While everyone else socialized, I slept. When my alarm went off, I got up and showered. I did my hair and makeup while sitting on the side of the bathtub. There was a first-timers reception before the other events of the night, so I found the event registration table - on the other side of the hotel - and made my way to the reception. Our birth group administrators acted as hostesses, welcoming us warmly. Pink flamingos and special pink cocktails specially developed for this event were everywhere.

Instead of mingling through the crowd and meeting as many of my online friends in person as I could find, I found a seat and settled in. I smiled at everyone who came near me and got up to introduce myself to one person who I saw nearby and wanted to be sure to connect with that night, but that was about all I could manage. Frustration that I could barely enjoy the event I'd anticipated all year plagued me.

That was the story for the entire event. A group of my fellow birth group moms really got to know one another well that weekend and I was sad to not be a part of their bonding time. During down times, I slept so I had energy for the meetings. It seemed like everyone had made at least one good friend to hang out with and I was alone.

Because I wasn't totally comfortable in one group of friends, I ended up talking to the author of that book I had so connected with in the hospital – Heather Avis. She had a booth at the retreat where she signed her books and sold t-shirts that said "The Lucky Few" in bold letters on the front. During a short break, I stood in line to meet her. I felt a little silly, coming from Nashville where we *do not* make a big deal about celebrities when we see them out and about. It is the height of not cool. But she was at her booth to meet fans and sign books, so I shut down that voice in my head and boldly told her what her book meant to me. I bought a t-shirt and got a photo with her and a fellow writer-friend from my birth group. Every time I wear my t-shirt, I can't help but smile.

I was high on that experience. I called my friends and family, talking in my squeaky, passionate voice about how I got to meet *the Heather Avis!* They had no idea who she is, but they know about me. I'd rather meet an author whose book I've connected with deeply than Thor any day. I mean, if you know Thor and want to introduce me, I won't turn you down. But I've met enough celebrities in real life to know that it's a little disappointing to see the real deal. Reading a book that lets me inside the mind of someone who looks like a regular person, but is actually full of supernatural grace and wisdom that I might never know if not for the words they write is what lights a fire in my bones.

On the last night of the retreat we had a "mom's night out" that included a comedian, karaoke, and dancing. The group I inserted myself into got on stage together to sing a '90's song that I barely knew. I recognized the chorus but had never paid attention to the words. We got on stage and started scream-singing the song. I stood at the edge because I didn't know the lyrics. As the words came across the screen, I was mortified. I don't know if it's because I'm a singer and have made a habit of standing on stages singing songs with meaningful lyrics, or if I'm a fuddy-duddy, but I couldn't stay up there.

I casually backed off stage and stood off to the side for a minute, cheering the other girls on while they finished the song. On the floor in front of the stage, I laughed with Heather Avis about how I'm too old for those shenanigans and danced with her and her friends for a while. Yup. I danced with Heather Avis. I have now achieved most of the celebrity dreams of my life and my bucket list is happy. Unless Heather wants to become BFFs with a midwestern farmer's wife? That would be even more awesome.

Later that night, I connected with another mom from the medical outreach team. She was expecting, so neither of us were letting loose like some of the other moms who had waited all year long for this one night to safely have fun. We found a table and talked for quite a while. We were both pleased about the opportunity to be on the medical outreach team and a little nervous about going to our first event.

I had to laugh a little as we walked her to our rooms together that night. Despite my sickness and disappointment, I connected with some amazing people that I might have missed if I'd been able to do all the fun things I'd expected to do. It wasn't what I'd expected from the retreat, but it was good. And I did connect with the awesome moms in my birth group, just not in the deep way I'd hoped. I could see very clearly how God uses all things for my good. I'm anticipating how the new connections I made might also bring Him glory.

14

LETTING GO, AGAIN

The 2018 Rockin' Mom's™ Retreat in Phoenix was a long way from the big, brown recliner in our living room. Even though I'd been sick, Redmond was healthy enough to be without me for long enough that I could attend. Those long, tedious months at home until Redmond was about six months old had been ruled by medical equipment and a regimented schedule – and I was in a totally different place.

During those early months, a large syringe hung from the hall tree that Rick's cousin Jon made for us as a wedding gift. A long, thin, clear plastic tube attached to the bottom of it and connected it to Redmond's feeding tube. Day after day, hour after hour, I sat in that recliner feeding him. I tried to bottle feed him, riding the waves of emotion as he struggled. One day he took almost the entire feeding by mouth, and the next day he took hardly anything. Back and forth, up and down, my emotions were attached to how well he ate. I didn't want to be like that, but I didn't know how to be different.

Eliana and Charlie spent a lot of time with their grandparents. I hated sending them away, but I was grateful that they had a safe, warm, and loving place to go. They were excited to go and have fun over there. I was no fun in my chair.

I always dreamed about the mother I wanted to be. I spent my life watching other mothers, collecting information and gaining skills, making plans for how I wanted to treat my children. I planned to be the kind of mother who savored every day with them, not wishing away the long hours of diaper changes and needy cries. I soaked up every moment with Eliana like the driest sponge, staring at her precious face for hours, laughing at her tiniest expressions and glorying in her accomplishments. It broke my heart when I found myself too sick during my pregnancy with Charlie to meet her every need myself. Before I knew I was pregnant, my mother-in-law had agreed to watch her two days a week so I could work on writing. I couldn't write, and Eliana ended up spending a lot more than two days a week with her.

When Charlie was born, I had two babies. I was thrilled to have a son. TWO BABIES! I repeated those words to myself often. What a blessing. The woman who had none now had TWO BABIES! But how does someone who's basically been on bed rest for the last 25 months have the energy and strength to care for two babies? I had to accept help so I could heal and be the kind of mom I wanted to be. When Charlie was a year old and things settled down, I stirred them back up with the job application process and then – when they were two and three years old, another baby.

Raising children with another person who has their own ideas about how it should be done can be interesting. It never occurred to me during all my dreaming and planning years that their father would have an opinion about this parenting thing, much less their grandparents. I was pretty much on my own as an adult and I did what I wanted. Marriage and co-parenting were a surprise to me. Oh, Rick thinks we should do things a different way?

For me, motherhood has been a series of exercises in letting go of my plans and learning to relax into reality. It's been a long time since I expected to be in complete control and I've learned that I have very little control at all. I make plans and someone always laughs.

I had a choice to make. It would have been easy to allow bitterness to creep in while I watched my two healthy, fun, energetic children have fun with their babysitter and go off to their grandparents' house day after day because I had to tube-feed a baby who couldn't do the basic things a baby is supposed to do – breathe and eat. It would have been easy to sit there and demand to know how God could allow me to miss out on such an important time in their lives while I struggled to help the new baby survive. Hadn't I been through enough? Was God cruel?

Or I could choose to be thankful for a wonderful babysitter who loves them and takes excellent care of them, one who God provided for us before the storm hit so she could help keep the boat afloat. I could choose to be thankful for grandparents who live so close and are basically retired. They had the time and energy to help when we most needed it. I could be bitter that I had to tube-feed a baby on supplemental oxygen, or I could be thankful that I got to take the time to bond with this new baby.

I can see the circumstances in my life as a curse or a blessing. I decide if I allow the trials to steal my joy, or if I find the joy in my circumstances. It's a choice I make daily and sometimes I don't decide well. Some days I let the bitterness creep in. That's when I turn on praise and worship music and get my attitude back on track. That's when I remind myself, you're going to be okay. You're going to make it through this hard time. When you get to the other side of this storm, while your muscles are deteriorating and your butt is turning into something you don't recognize, *you are growing other muscles that no one can see yet.* **There's something coming up inside of you that nothing else could grow.** Don't get discouraged. God is doing something new in you and it's going to be good.

After my little pep talks with myself, after those hours of singing positive lyrics to refocus my mind, my good attitude returns and I have the energy to make it through another day. Sometimes the energy we receive is only enough to make it through the current day. Then sometimes God gives us a burst of strength that lasts for quite a while.

When Redmond was not quite four months old, the burst of energy I had for those crisis moments ran out. I'd been running on pure adrenaline and fatigue set in hard. As much as I wanted to give my baby the very best, I decided that it was time to stop pumping. My milk supply was good, but every time I hooked up to that pump I disappointed someone in the family. Once I started pumping, I didn't want to stop because it takes a while to get things moving, so I'd sit there for 20 minutes, four times a day, unable to pick up the baby or leave my seat, and it was hard for my family to understand.

A medically complex child brings with him people who come and go from your house in a pretty steady stream, plus two curious little ones had questions that I didn't have the energy to answer, so I always had a shirt and cover on. If I'd been nursing, no one would've expected anything of me during that time, but I wasn't holding the baby and they couldn't see the mechanics of it, so it appeared like I was doing nothing.

The last straw was the day Rick walked into the living room after work and I asked him to change Redmond's diaper. I was sitting in my chair with the breast pump in my lap, suction cups loudly making their annoying sound (like a cow being milked), and I had a book on the arm of the chair. I wanted to make the most of the time I was stuck in the chair.

Rick glared at me as he muttered, "You can't get up and do it?"

To Rick's credit, I spent a lot of time in that chair and I'm sure he was as tired of it as I was. I looked at him quizzically and said, "I'm pumping. If I wait until I'm done, he'll have a sore butt."

Rick picked him up and carried him to the changing table in the nursery. Soon I heard him hollering for me. "This is a mess! Kimberly, I need a little help. Can you please get in here?"

I called back in frustration, "I'm pumping!"

"GET IN HERE! I NEED YOU!"

Breathing deeply through my nose, I disconnected the pump, pulled my clothes into place, put down the pump and book, got up, and walked into the nursery.

"What?" I asked, really annoyed.

"He made a huge mess! I need your help." Rick was clearly annoyed with me.

I changed huge messes by myself daily and he'd changed plenty of dirty diapers, so I wasn't very compassionate about this one. I walked over to the changing table and tried to figure out what he wanted me to. I ended up taking over and finishing it myself while he went to wash his hands. When he came back, I grumbled at him.

"You're the one who doesn't want me to stop pumping because Redmond needs the best chance he can get after all his problems, but you don't even have the decency to let me finish pumping. You act like I'm being selfish when I pump, but it's not like I can do anything else. You could've cleaned up this mess yourself. You didn't actually need me."

Rick stopped in surprise and stared at me, wide-eyed. "You were *pumping?*"

Apparently, the open book had totally thrown him off. What he heard me say was, "I'm reading." He was really frustrated that after working all day, he had to change a dirty diaper while I sat there and read. I shook my head in frustration.

"Since when do I ever refuse to do something for my baby because *I'm reading?* That doesn't make any sense."

He agreed, but we were sleep-deprived, scared, and just surviving. While I cared for the baby, he did all his regular work, plus everything for the older kids when they were home, dishes, laundry, and anything else that came up. We were pretty close to a breaking point. That day I decided to stop pumping for the health of my entire family. I didn't tell Rick because he hadn't been open to the idea the other times I'd brought it up. I quietly cut back to three times a day, then two, and then one.

The last time I pumped I knew it was the last time and I ugly-cried. I hated pumping, but I loved the ability to provide milk for Redmond. I knew that by giving up pumping, I was giving up the possibility of ever nursing him if he eventually grew strong enough to suckle. I also knew that when I pumped or nursed, it gave my body a super power that nothing else ever has. When I breast-fed my children, I could eat *anything I wanted to* and lose weight! It was astounding to me. Even still, it was time to stop.

When I had gone without pumping for three days, I told Rick. He hadn't noticed. When he started to question my decision, I held up my hand and stopped him. I let him know that the case was closed. We packed up all the pump supplies and gave them away.

I had enough frozen milk to last for a while but knew it would run out way before Redmond was a year old. Much to my surprise, a friend who knew nothing of the situation asked me if I could use some extra breast milk. She had more than she needed for her son who was a few weeks older than Redmond. The idea of giving him someone else's breast milk seemed really weird to me, but I knew it had been done. Women used to hire wet nurses to feed their babies. I asked my friend Michelle, who was with me when Redmond was born and happens to be a lactation consultant, about it.

Michelle said that although he wouldn't be getting my immunities, which is a great reason to breast feed, he'd be getting immunities from the other mom. She wondered if it might boost his immune system to have immunities from another mother. It might actually keep him healthier? That was all I needed to hear. I let my friend know that I'd be glad to receive her extra breast milk. I had to handle it a few times before I got over the weirded out feeling, but soon I felt very comfortable with it.

After that, I was incredibly blessed to receive donated breast milk from two other friends. I like to think that Redmond was lucky to receive a wide spectrum of immunities – and he sure needed it. The milk lasted for a long time and I never had to ask for it. Every time it showed up for him when it needed to.

15

FEEDING FRENZY

When we left the NICU, the team there felt confident that we could get Redmond off the feeding-tube without their help. Babies who are born prematurely are often kept in the NICU until they're able to eat by mouth. But Redmond's crisis was over, and we had spent enough time there to learn what we needed to do. We needed to get home to Eliana and Charlie more than we needed help with feeding, and we had a lot of support at home. I had big plans to get home into my comfortable chair and spend a week or so teaching Redmond how to nurse and getting the stupid feeding tube out. I knew we could do it.

On her first visit to us, Nurse Jane encouraged me not to resent the feeding tube. She said that babies need good nutrition for their brains to grow as their bodies grow. They grow so quickly when they're this young that a lack of food can really affect them later in life. I was so scared of the cognitive delays that are a part of Down syndrome that I relaxed a little about the tube. I didn't want to cause any further delays from malnutrition.

Although no one told us this news until he was over a year old, because Redmond was on a ventilator for the first two weeks of his life, the soft roof of his mouth as a newborn was pushed up very high. That made it impossible for him to get the correct seal around the nipple, and quite a bit of the milk he was able to suck in dribbled out the side of his mouth. We always tucked a burp cloth in the crease of his neck to catch the leak, but we attributed it to low muscle tone and kept working to get those muscles stronger.

During those first few months of life, Redmond slept A LOT. We woke him every three hours to eat, but he went right back to sleep as soon as we let him. His heart and lungs had to work so hard to maintain his basic bodily functions that he didn't have energy for much else. When he was awake, we often put him on his play mat where toys dangled overhead. Eliana and Charlie loved to sit and play with him. I sang him songs and talked to him, but I couldn't carry him around the house like I'd been able to do with the older ones. Not only was he attached to the oxygen tube (21 feet of clear, plastic tubing attached to the oxygen concentrator that we eventually located right outside his bedroom door), but he often arched his back and threw his head backwards. I joked that it took three hands to carry him.

With Eliana, I always put her head on my shoulder and tucked my arm under her bottom. She curled her body into mine and hung on. If I needed to bend down, I tucked my chin over her shoulder and everything was fine. Charlie didn't do anything to help me hold him, so I called him "my little tank." But even with him, I could use the same method, the other hand ready to place on his back if he got a little wiggly. This method did NOT work with Redmond. I either had to tuck him into the crook of my arm and hold him in a cradle position, keeping him steady with the other arm so he didn't arch and throw himself backwards, or I had to put him up on my shoulder, tuck my chin over his shoulder, and use both hands to hang onto him.

The entire time I held him like that, he actively threw himself back. Everyone who held him commented in concern that they'd drop him because of how much force he used to throw himself backwards. "Low muscle tone" did not apply to his back muscles.

We learned later that he arches like that because it helps him open his airway and breathe easier. People with Down syndrome tend to have narrow nasal passages and enlarged tonsils and/or adenoids, making it harder for air to flow through easily. However, they also have so much flexibility that they can bend their necks back far enough to help open the airways. Occasionally, he still does that when he's sleeping. If we're holding him, we know it's time to put him in his crib so he can get into a position that's comfortable for him.

We also learned that nursing or taking a bottle is an aerobic activity for babies. It takes a lot of energy and strength to coordinate the necessary pattern of suck-swallow-breathe. It's an innate urge that babies have immediately when they're born, but during the time that Redmond should have been doing that, he was struggling to breathe. As he fought for his life, the thing that should've been second nature to him was lost.

When he did take the bottle, it took him a long time to get a few ounces. Because we didn't want to completely wear him out, we only tried to nurse or bottle feed him for about 20 minutes at a time. He rarely ever took more than a couple ounces, and much of that dribbled out of his mouth. I prayed every time (and continue to do so) that God would give him the strength to eat, begging God to intervene on our behalf and help him do what should be so natural. To this day, I continue to thank God in advance that Redmond is an excellent eater and has the strength he needs to sustain his own life through eating and drinking.

A speech therapist came to our home every week to help us work on feeding issues. The Early Intervention team through our county started coming. We were introduced to Danielle, our service coordinator, and Teresa, Redmond's physical therapist. Teresa has a lot of experience with feeding issues, so she was a great resource beyond physical therapy.

Feeding Redmond was my life. I tried everything I knew to do, joined online support groups and talked to local moms to learn about tube-weaning and tube-feeding support. While I fed Redmond, I researched. The FBI has nothing on a mother who's afraid for her child. While no one's handing out degrees in Down syndrome or feeding issues, if they were I would surely have earned one by now.

When Redmond was five months old, we introduced him to baby food. He did surprisingly well with it. I started spoon feeding him several times a day, introducing him to different tastes and textures. Rick and I were determined to avoid a g-tube, which is a feeding tube that's surgically implanted directly into the stomach for long-term use.

Redmond decided to declare WAR on his feeding-tube. He spent nearly every ounce of his energy, awake or sleeping, trying to pull out his tube. The tape that was always on his face from the oxygen cannulas and feeding tube irritated his skin and left it red and angry. He screamed whenever I changed it, no matter how carefully I tried to remove it. Despite all of that, he pulled mercilessly at it, tearing his skin until it bled. I tried all kinds of tricks, but the bottom line was that it was a huge challenge to keep the tape in place.

Redmond became an expert at pulling it out. Our child with delayed motor skills could hook his finger into the tiny gap between his nostril and the tape and rip it out so fast that I rarely had a chance to stop him once he got started. We put mittens and socks on his hands, doubling them up, and it didn't matter.

When I put it back in, he screamed and twisted his body away from me, desperate to escape. We hated it. I'd sob every time, unable to remain emotionally distant while he fought and screamed. Afterward, I'd hold him and sing to him, trying to calm both of us. Even when Rick did it though, Redmond seemed to be mad at me for it. People said a baby couldn't be mad at me, but he's smarter than anyone gives him credit for.

He was mad. At me. And it was awful.

In addition to the discomfort of putting the tube back in, there was this overwhelming fear that he would pull it out during a feeding. If that happened, milk could go into his lungs rather than his stomach, causing him to aspirate. Aspiration could lead to pneumonia and death, especially for a baby with Redmond's lungs. While many people I met online walked away from their baby during an ng-tube feeding, I could not. If I put him down, the first thing he did was go for his tube. He could get that thing out so fast that I just held him, holding his hands down, so it stayed in.

Nurse Jane and his physical therapist suggested that we seriously consider getting the g-tube. It would get the tape off his face and he would have a much harder time pulling it out. If he did get it out, it would be much easier to put back in. The online support groups I was in had really scared me about the g-tube. I'd seen photos of infected sites and read about terrible things that could happen. At least I knew how to use the ng-tube. At that point in my life, I was so overwhelmed with all the new things I needed to know, I couldn't handle one more thing.

We waited until Redmond was seven months old before we finally accepted that a more permanent solution was necessary. Then we took him to a new specialist – Gastroenterology (GI) – where he went through a series of tests to be sure the g-tube was what he needed. We spoke with more speech language pathologists, talked to other parents who were happy with the g-tube, and finally rested in the knowledge that those online support groups where we'd seen the weird stuff were showing things highly unlikely to happen. They were weird, which is why people posted questions about them. Typically, g-tubes behave themselves.

Redmond got his new tube in November. The surgeon told us to expect an outpatient surgery with a "23-hour observation." He would get to go home less than 24 hours after surgery! We arranged for the older kids to stay overnight with their grandparents, and then drove to a new hospital

90 minutes from home so that we could have the surgeon we wanted on the date we wanted. Two of our pastors met us in the hallway as we tried to figure out where to go. We were honored by their willingness to drive so far to be with us. We took Redmond into the room to prepare for surgery and he charmed everyone with his happy smile.

They put him in a bright yellow gown and he laughed and flirted with the nurses. I documented it all on Instagram, where I'd decided to do what I could to raise awareness of Down syndrome by sharing Redmond's cuteness with the world. Our wise protector, my little Wyse, was already showing the world that wisdom isn't all about meeting typical standards of success.

During the surgery, we sat with our pastors in the waiting area. I figured they'd pray with us and then head back home, but instead they suggested breakfast in the cafeteria. We hadn't thought to eat that morning before we left, so we agreed. Talking to them kept our minds off the surgery, and soon it was over. Redmond was transferred to a room on the general floor, which surprised me because I thought we'd stay in the recovery room with him for 23 hours. A nurse instructed us to go back down to registration and get different arm bands indicating that he was admitted as a patient. We were confused, but we went with it.

Redmond was back on oxygen when we got to his room. The nurse said that it was normal for a surgical patient to be on oxygen for a while as they recover. I got nervous because his oxygen saturation level was in the 70s. Once the morphine wore off, it went back up, but then it became clear that he was in pain - so they gave him more morphine. His oxygen went back down again, this time into the 60s. Scared, I called the unimpressed nurse and asked her if we could turn up the flow. She said she'd check, then returned a while later to fiddle with the tubing that connected to a metal outlet on the wall.

She pulled the tube off the front outlet and attached it to one directly behind it. When she did so, the room suddenly got very quiet. I hadn't realized that we'd been listening to a "whoosh" sound the entire time we'd been in the room. His saturation level shot up to 100%.

The oxygen tube had been attached to the wrong flowmeter.

The nurse didn't apologize. She switched them like it was no big deal and tried to leave the room without acknowledging what had happened. I stopped her.

"Was the tube attached to the wrong flowmeter?" Obviously, it was, but I wanted her to tell me.

"Yes," she admitted slowly. "Sometimes that happens. It's hard to tell which one is on."

I knew it wasn't hard to tell, but I just listened. I considered launching an official complaint, but I decided it wasn't worth it. Redmond was okay. He hadn't had low oxygen for days and days, and she had made a genuine mistake. But her lack of apology nearly had me calling for a supervisor. I realized that she probably wasn't allowed to open the hospital up to a lawsuit by apologizing, so I dropped it. I made a new mental note to check the flowmeter if something like that ever happened again. File that under, "Things I shouldn't have to know."

As soon as the morphine wore off, they switched him to Motrin and his oxygen level stayed up. We spent the night and I began preparing to go home. I asked the nurse when we could expect to be discharged and she looked at me strangely.

We discovered that patients typically stay in the hospital for three days following g-tube surgery. No one seemed in a hurry to send us home, but we were anxious because of the impact it would have on Eliana and Charlie. I shared my frustration with the surgeon, reminding him that he'd told me to expect an outpatient surgery. I reminded him that we had older children who were already traumatized by their parents' unexpected absences for their brother's medical needs. Although we could call on Rick's parents to care for their physical needs, their emotional needs could not be met by them.

Since the separation anxiety became so pronounced, we make a point to tell the kids exactly what to expect. If we say we'll be home by a certain time, we are. If we plan to be gone when they wake up from their nap, they know. It took work to rebuild their sense of safety and security. We didn't mind staying in the hospital to recover, but we told them we'd be home by the next afternoon. We were very upset by the discrepancy. How had the surgeon understood recovery to be outpatient while the hospital staff expected three days?

The surgeon understood our concern and discharged us early that afternoon. He had us hook up Redmond's feeding tube to the new site and try it out. Although I was extremely anxious about the new tube, everything went well. With no obvious problems, we took our baby home.

I was encouraged that he was sent home without supplemental oxygen. We still had the oxygen concentrator and tubing at our house. The pulmonologist refused to okay him off oxygen 24-hours a day until he passed a two-night sleep study. We tried once, hooking him up to the monitor that recorded everything overnight, but his oxygen level had averaged 92. When we brought him home from the NICU, anything over 88 was considered acceptable. Suddenly the doctor changed it to 93.

The medical supply company took the oxygen monitor after that first two-night study so they could read the results. When he didn't pass, they brought back another one. Six weeks later we hooked him up to the monitor for two nights and had great results. His alarms didn't go off and we were eager to turn it in, knowing he'd averaged around 95-96. When the medical supply company picked it up, we waited for the report from the doctor that we could stop oxygen, but they didn't call.

The company finally admitted that they lost the machine. They brought us another machine, but that one didn't work. It kept shutting off, alarming, and giving us lots of problems. I called the company to report the problem and ask for a new machine, but they never sent us one. I didn't have the energy to keep worrying about it.

Once we were discharged from the hospital without oxygen, I called the pulmonologist again. When I told her that the hospital let Redmond come home without oxygen, that was good enough for her. The medical supply company finally came out and picked up all the oxygen supplies. We were ecstatic to see that stuff leave our house. At eight months old, Redmond was officially off supplemental oxygen.

However, he now had a tube in his belly, and I was supposed to take care of the wound. There were no stitches. A hole had been cut in his abdomen, his stomach had been stitched to the wall of his abdomen, and there was a plastic tube in it. I was a nervous wreck for days, wishing we'd stayed in the hospital for monitoring and wound care by nurses and doctors.

The day after we got home, I laid Redmond on my bed and stacked pillows around him while I did a few things in my bedroom. As I walked around, I leaned down and stroked his cheek, which was free from the bright yellow tube and medical tape for the first time in his life. He laughed and touched his face too. I laughed, relief surging through me for the first time since the surgery. I kissed his cheeks over and over, delighting in the smooth skin that hadn't quite healed from the tape.

Redmond looked into my eyes and giggled. He touched his face too, feeling the absence of the tube. It was one of the most precious, intimate moments of my life. My eight-month-old son who is supposed to have intellectual impairments totally understood that he was free from the tubes and tape. He understood how happy I was about it. He was happy about it.

For about 15 minutes, we stayed like that – laughing, touching his face, kissing those sweet cheeks, and relishing the new freedom. I knew we'd made the right decision.

Within three days of receiving the new tube, his oral feedings tripled. Without the irritation from the tube down his throat, he ate with gusto. His other skills took off also. He'd spent so much of his energy working on getting out the tube that he hadn't developed other skills. It was like he woke up and realized there was a whole new world around him. Within six weeks of surgery, I had completely weaned him off the feeding tube.

I tracked every calorie he ate each day and tube-fed what he still needed for his daily goal overnight at a very slow drip while he slept. Continuous night feeds became intolerable though, causing him to vomit every single night. Cleaning up vomit from a crib with bumper pads, which we used because he slept so restlessly that he constantly whacked his head on the slats otherwise, is no fun. Especially in the middle of the night. We decided to turn off his night feeding when he vomited, which lessened the amount he received. The result was that his daytime hunger increased so his daytime calories increased to the point where he no longer needed extra calories from the tube.

For two months, he ate every one of his calories by mouth. I wrote everything down, added it all up, and gave him the freedom to eat less one day and more the next, like other babies. The only concern we had was that he wasn't gaining weight. He didn't lose weight, but at his age he needed to gain an ounce a week. He was about half a pound under-weight, but no one was terribly concerned.

When he turned a year old, we had a big party. I triumphantly told our 150 or so guests that our miracle baby was FREE of tubes and healthy! The pulmonologist had recently released our ECMO-baby from care, declaring his lungs to be whole. The speech therapist had stopped coming because he was eating. The cardiologist said the hole in his heart was closing and he wouldn't need surgery. He was alert and aware, talking, active, and happy.

It was worth a big celebration, so we had bouncy houses, an ice cream machine, a face painter, and a balloon artist. We also had a large, farm-themed cake that made me smile all the way to my bones. In honor of our "Little Red", we passed out red handkerchiefs for guests to tie around their necks. My mom created a slide show of how far our miracle had come in one short year, and I carefully chose a play list from the songs that had gotten me through. Grass-green table cloths covered the round tables, and toy John Deere tractors and Fisher Price Little People Barns were the center pieces. We had barn doors on the wall and bales of hay to sit on. It was awesome.

God told the Israelites to celebrate their holy days with feasts, reminders to them that God had brought them through so much, so my offering to the Lord was that party. I wanted to honor God and thank our community for all that had been done for us. That party was my thank offering, and I was beyond happy to celebrate God's goodness to us with our friends.

Here's the hard part of that story though...

One week after our big celebration, Redmond got a cold. It lasted a month. Too congested to eat, his weight dropped quickly. He'd already been a little underweight, but now his bones stuck out garishly. It was alarming. At his one-year check-up our Nurse Practitioner told me that I had to hook up the feeding tube again. She's a friend, so she knew what that meant to me. I was encouraged by other friends to keep trusting God and not go back to the feeding tube, but I couldn't let my baby get any skinnier.

Through broken tears, I hooked the despised feeding tube back up again, thinking I wasn't going to tell anyone about it. It was temporary and only until he got better. I bawled, begging God to give me a clear word that I should stop. Instead, the words that squeezed my heart were *fed is best*. Not breast, not formula, not baby food, not gluten-free, dairy-free, low-sugar, or paleo. FED. I turned on the pump and allowed life-sustaining nourishment to flow into his body in the only way I could get it into him, but it nearly broke me.

He stopped losing weight. He continued to struggle through the cold symptoms, but he slowly regained the weight. His little body was back up to where it had been before he got sick when he suddenly took a turn for the worse.

It was Easter weekend and I was determined that we'd have a better holiday than we'd had the year before. I made a special breakfast, complete with cute little homemade strawberry muffins with bunny decorations. Easter baskets waited for the children when they woke up that morning. We wore the beautiful clothes I'd picked out for everyone and took pictures. I cooked Easter dinner for our extended family and decorated my table with beautiful pastels. Eliana and I handmade place cards with Easter-themed designs. I relished the warmth of being surrounded by family and enjoyed using my creativity to welcome guests into our home. I really needed something normal.

When the baby was handed to my brother-in-law that afternoon, he held him for about 20 seconds before he announced in alarm, "There's something wrong with this baby. He's breathing funny." He handed him back to his wife quickly. The night before I'd been up with him several times and thought we might need to take him in, but I was determined that we weren't going to ruin Easter of 2018. It wasn't as bad as it had been when he was two months old anyway.

On Monday morning, I called Nurse Jane and asked her to come over and check his oxygen saturation level. We couldn't do it since we'd turned the pulse-ox monitor in with the oxygen concentrator. She couldn't get there until early afternoon, so we went to Grandma's house and colored Easter eggs with my niece and her husband. We'd done that for the last several years and decided to wait until they were in town to color our eggs that year. While we colored eggs with Eliana and Charlie, Rick's dad held Redmond.

After about 30 minutes, his dad brought Redmond to me and told me in an alarmed voice that Redmond wasn't breathing right and I needed to call the doctor. I explained that I was waiting for the nurse to check his oxygen and she'd help me decide what to do. We went home and put the kids to bed for their naps, praying that his oxygen level was okay.

It wasn't.

Her pulse-ox monitor showed that his oxygen level was in the low 80s. Nurse Jane called the doctor's office and they told us to go to the ER immediately. I realized that Redmond's skin had a slightly bluish color and my concern rose. Rick and I scrambled to pack our bags for an indefinite hospital stay. The kids woke up because they were sleeping in our room. I tried to tell them very gently that we needed to take Redmond to the hospital; they would be home with Grandma and Grandpa and/or Kristina. I couldn't hide my alarm though. Charlie's brave face was betrayed by his trembling lower lip. I hugged him hard and he let out a wail. Scrambling to comfort him, I promised him that Daddy would come back home that night and stay with him. That helped a little, but we left our kids in tears, our hearts breaking again.

Rick drove us to the hospital. Once again, I sat in the back with Redmond. It was a rainy day, so I kept him in his car seat, afraid of hydroplaning with a baby in my arms. My husband has a deep love for back roads, so he meandered through farms and chattered to me about who was doing what on which farm. While he prattled on, I watched our son turn a more obvious shade of blue.

He was driving about four miles over the speed limit. I didn't want to be a nagging wife, and he hates it when I criticize his driving, so I tried to keep my voice steady as I encouraged him to drive as fast as he felt comfortable. He slowed down to exactly the speed limit.

It was everything I could do to not scream and kick and demand that he pull over so I could drive, but I'd been trying really hard to be respectful because apparently that's important to men. Instead, I took a picture of Redmond and texted it to my Bible study group, begging them to pray. Finally, I decided I could respect him the next day and told him that he had to speed up NOW. Redmond was blue and he needed to get the lead out. I couldn't handle one more comment about road construction or flooded fields. I needed him to shut up and drive like he was trying to save his baby's life.

When we finally pulled into the Emergency Room entrance, I grabbed Redmond's car seat carrier, seething, and ran inside. The front desk attendant immediately called back and a nurse ran out to take him from me. As we raced back to a room, Rick parked the car and brought in the bag. Redmond's color improved as they pulled him out of the car seat and slipped oxygen tubes into his nostrils. I waited quietly, straining to remain calm as they examined him, asked about medical history, and prompted me to confirm Down syndrome. I felt ridiculous. How could I have left out that little detail?

He needed a chest x-ray and I forgot that he had kinetic tape on his back from physical therapy. Kinetic tape is the stuff you see on Olympic athletes. It sticks like super-glue, helping to pull muscles into the desired position. We'd been using it to help strengthen his abdominal muscles, because as good as he was doing, he still couldn't sit up. (I'd begged God to let him sit up before his first birthday, and that request hadn't been granted to me.) To remove the tape, it needs to be covered in something like Vaseline to soften the adhesive, and then very carefully and slowly peeled off. If you don't remove it carefully, it tears the skin.

When the x-ray techs put Redmond into a boot-like contraption to hold him correctly for the chest x-ray, the tape caught and ripped off his back. We didn't know it though. He screamed and screamed, but we just thought he didn't want to be in the boot. It wasn't until we got him back into the room and I adjusted his hospital gown that I realized what had happened.

There are so many ways a mother's heart can ache. I am convinced that one of the worst ways is when her child is hurt by something she could have prevented. I had it on my calendar to remove it on Sunday night, but I was so tired from the Easter celebration that I'd decided to do it the next day. I'd been planning to take it off that night before his bath. Oh, how I ached.

The results of the chest x-ray landed Redmond in the PICU. They hooked him to forced oxygen (rather than the slow flow of "room air") via a c-pap machine. It's a terrible-looking thing. By the time they got us into the room, it was after 9:00 p.m. – well after the kids' bedtime. Rick's mom called to let us know that the kids were getting anxious about their daddy coming home. We debated for a moment but decided that it was important for him to go home that night. He didn't get home until 10:30, but he put them in bed with him and provided the best comfort he knew – his presence.

The next morning, he packed the things I'd forgotten (hello, phone charger?) and drove an hour back to the hospital. I checked back into The Ronald McDonald House since there was no place for me to sleep in the PICU. I knew that Redmond was in good hands and there was nothing more I could do.

When Rick and I finally had a few minutes to talk, he apologized for not driving faster on the way there. Apparently, I hadn't told him that Redmond was turning blue. He said I'd been so nonchalant that he hadn't thought much about it. He didn't realize he was going slower and had no idea that I was so agitated until I blew. He understood that I wanted to be respectful, but he gave me permission to convey a greater sense of urgency in situations like that. I believe his exact words were, "If our baby is turning blue, go ahead and yell at me. I just didn't get it."

Whoops.

In the PICU, they stopped feeding him until they could get him stabilized, so he lost more weight. He didn't mind not eating. Within three days, he was alert and happy again, pulling the oxygen tubes out of his nose and maintaining his levels without it. He was diagnosed with rhino entero virus, again, which they said was more severe than RSV that year. They moved him to the main floor and we saw lots of helpful people. His eating issues were addressed by the hospital dietician, a speech language pathologist, and the pulmonologist. The hospital social worker came by and helped me with some financial forms I'd been too overwhelmed to figure out at home.

When he moved to the main floor of the hospital, a new doctor took over his care. I was anxious to get home to the kids, but the pulmonologist wanted him to go a full 24 hours without supplemental oxygen. Redmond felt so much better that he was furious about confinement in his bed. A 13-month old in the hospital is a totally different thing than a newborn! I was not about to let him roll around on the floor like he wanted to do. The only option was for me to hold him or let him scream in his bed. I carefully navigated the IV in his arm, trying to keep him entertained in my lap, happy that he had so much energy and frustrated that he wasn't sleeping.

When the hospital pediatrician came in, she told me that she understood that I was ready to get home, but she hesitated because he was so severely underweight. She wanted to keep him until he gained weight. I tried to explain, but she wouldn't listen. She shook her head and pulled me into the hall to show me his growth chart.

I almost laughed out loud, near hysterics. Instead, I let her tell me all about her concerns and show me the chart I knew by heart. Once she finished sharing her concerns and I was allowed to speak, I explained. I pointed out where his weight had gone up regularly for several weeks, but hospitalization had caused it to drop again. I was ready to leave against medical advice when she relented.

Redmond left the hospital with a new diagnosis – reactive airways – and new medical equipment. We were introduced to a nebulizer for breathing treatments.

Baby asthma.

Babies on ventilators often develop asthma and I'd been so pleased to have dodged that bullet. But here we were, in the thick of it. The new pulmonologist thought the previous pulmonologist had missed the diagnosis and incorrectly released us from her care a month before. We'd been so happy and had a little mini celebration over losing at least one specialist, only to gain a new one right back. I might have said a few cuss words.

We're a little more cautious with our celebrations these days.

Since then, Redmond's eating continues to mystify us. There are days when he eats with gusto, lunging for the next bite. He's now capable of drinking from a straw cup and will hold the cup himself. He can suck down five ounces in minutes, delighting us as he takes in the necessary calories by mouth. He's gone days at a time without needing a tube feeding, and then there are weeks on end when he completely refuses to take anything by mouth.

What causes him to decide to eat or not eat remains a mystery to us. We have cut his tube-feeds to increase hunger and therefore increase oral feeding, but he doesn't seem to mind hunger. So, we continue to tube-feed him, wondering if he's trying to communicate something to us when he refuses to eat. I still pray for God to heal him and help him have a normal hunger response and ability to eat, but I no longer push it.

I think it's possible that part of why he stopped eating is because my emotions were so tied to how much he ate or didn't eat. He sensed my urgency and – a little like his mommy – isn't about to be controlled by anyone else's desires for him.

In recent months, God has answered my prayers by giving me peace with the feeding tube. Sometimes God answers our prayers with supernatural healing power. Sometimes He gives us strength and peace to continue using medical interventions and tells us to be grateful that He gave humans the innovation to come up with them. Until Redmond decides that it's time to eat on his own, I will feed him in whatever way I can. Thank God for feeding tubes.

16

MANAGING OUR EXPECTATIONS

Redmond doesn't meet anyone else's expectations or milestone schedule. He does it in his own way and in his own time. After such a rough start, we often find ourselves so thankful that he does them at all that we don't get worked up when it doesn't happen when others think it should. Our plans mean nothing to Redmond anyway, so why get all worked up? I wanted him to sit up unassisted by one year, begging God for a little nod in my direction with this small thing, and he continued to flop over every time I tried. After that I thought, "What a random thing to decide he needed to do. So what if he starts sitting up at 11 months and 23 days or 12 months and 7 days? He's not going to be 10 and still rolling around on the floor. Relax!"

Sure enough, Redmond sat up unassisted for the first time when he was 13 months old. When Redmond was 14 months old, he learned how to army-crawl. His upper body wasn't strong enough to support him on his hands and knees, but he used his little elbows very effectively. It looked a little strange, but I got over it. I was happy that he was able to get around. When he was 15 months old, he was able to get himself into a sitting position. When that happened, I cheered so loudly that I scared him and made him cry. I trembled for hours afterwards, so completely overwhelmed with joy. I learned to manage my expectations, realizing that

Redmond will do things when he's ready and there's no reason to get worked up about it.

When Redmond was 16 months old, I walked in his bedroom one afternoon and he was standing up at the rail of his crib. He'd pulled himself into standing. We celebrated so hard!

The summer after he turned one, he got another cold, this time with a cough. Eliana, Charlie, and Rick got it too. Charlie got better quickly, but the other three coughed for three months. It would start to get better, even stop for a day or two, but then it would start right back again.

Eliana often coughed all night, crying out in her sleep. We'd sit her up and give her some water, check to be sure the humidifier was running, and try to comfort her. We took her to the doctor, asking if she might have whooping cough. Her pediatrician and the walk-in clinic doctor both said it was just a nasty cough that lasted a long time. We gave her some of Redmond's breathing treatments, extra homeopathic and natural remedies, and anything else we could think of to help. For a couple of days it got so bad that she turned purple and threw up every time she coughed. It was awful.

As awful as it was for Eliana, it was worse for Redmond. He didn't just turn purple and throw up for a few days. He did it for weeks on end. We gave him breathing treatments every four hours around the clock, trying so hard to keep him out of the hospital. We took him to the pulmonologist, begging for help. They offered to hospitalize him and keep a close eye on him, but they weren't going to do anything different for him than we were doing at home and the hospital is full of much worse things than coughs. We didn't want to expose him to anything else, so we chose to keep him at home. His weight suffered again, and he completely stopped eating. I mean, I wouldn't want to eat if I coughed and threw up everything I ate. Why bother?

In August, I got desperate. I declared war on that cough. My research went deeper, considering every possible problem. Was this an environmental or food allergy? Was there something in our house causing this problem? Was there a nutrient lacking in their diets? What was going on???

The first thing I decided to do was get our home environment as clean as possible. We keep our house very clean, but it was built about 70 years ago and lots of changes have been made to it since then. We washed every bit of bedding, stuffed animals, curtains, and anything else we could think of. We dusted walls, ceilings, curtain rods, fans, lights, etc. I moved houseplants out to the porch because I read that they can have a lot of mold in them.

About 90% of the kids' stuffed animals went into bags in the basement. We left out some of the most sentimental ones and watched to see if they missed any others. Only one has come back upstairs. Those cute little toys collect a lot of dust.

One suggestion in the paperwork from the pulmonologist is to use a humidifier, so we'd been using one around the clock. Then I realized that the next page says not to use a humidifier. What? The nurse told me that both things were true. It depends on the child. My sister-in-law moved to a drier climate in part to help with her asthma, and she encouraged us to get that thing out of our house. We stopped using humidifiers.

We had our air ducts professionally cleaned. We discovered then that our house hadn't been sealed properly when we put in central air conditioning the first year we lived there. The furnace had been pulling insulation in and the fine dust from it had been blowing throughout the house for years. I totally freaked out, imagining the lung damage we all had from fiberglass insulation dust, but then I learned that our insulation is basically paper. There's no fiberglass in it. That had led to a lot of dust, which isn't good, but also isn't dangerous. I'd always wondered why I had to dust so often but hadn't considered that there might be a big problem. We had that problem fixed immediately and everyone in our home has been healthier since then.

We decided to let the air in the house settle and clear out. I got the dusty carpets and upholstery steam cleaned, then put an air purifier in the middle of the living room. With that thing running on high, we left for a week.

We took our family on a last-minute trip to a lake about 45 minutes away. It wasn't a fancy vacation, but we spent a lot of time getting fresh air in our lungs. That house is one of the cleanest places I've ever seen. There wasn't a speck of dust to be found and I nearly cried from gratitude. Vitamin D from sunshine and time together as a family was exactly what we needed. Nurse Jane recommended a coffee shop in the nearby town, set in a gorgeous, historic home, and I spent a little time there by myself. It was then that I was refreshed enough to start writing this book. By the time we left the lake, everyone had stopped coughing.

We did one other thing. In all my research, I discovered targeted nutritional intervention (TNI). Research scientists who are also parents of children with Down syndrome began researching and working on the health problems associated with Down syndrome many years ago. The support they offer doesn't have chemicals or pharmaceuticals, and it works to regulate the genes that are over-active due to that third copy of the 21st chromosome. According to their research, Down syndrome is a neuro-degenerative disease that often leads to things like early-onset Alzheimer's and immune-system disorders. By regulating the genes that are over-expressed in Down syndrome, they believe that our children will live longer, healthier lives.

They call it biohacking. Their effort isn't to cure Down syndrome, but to fight against the negative effects that the extra copy of the 21st chromosome can have. After bringing a list of all the ingredients and research to his doctors, I learned that the things in the supplement wouldn't hurt him. No one could guarantee that they would do any good, but we decided to try them.

I started Redmond on a free sample of the daily supplement when he was eight months old. He got a little sprinkle every day. Within a few days I saw major improvements in health conditions that I'd been told were normal and to be expected. I experimented to see if I could correlate the supplement to the health improvements and found a direct correlation. For ten months, I continued to give Redmond a small dose of the supplement, gradually increasing the amount.

I joined an online support group for parents who also give this supplement to their children and learned a massive amount of scientific information about how their bodies work, what appears to cause Down syndrome, and what we can do to help our children live their best lives. I discovered that an anti-inflammatory diet that restricts gluten and dairy is recommended for them. Not only do they suggest the daily supplement, but there are several others as well. It took me a while to decide to give all those supplements to him because I was exhausted from everything we were already doing.

When Redmond was 18 months old, Rick and I decided that if our doctor prescribed a pharmaceutical drug to give him three times a day, we wouldn't think twice about the effort it would take to give it. We decided to view the supplements in that way. I ordered them, started slowly, and built up his dosage until he got to the recommended dosage.

We saw dramatic changes in Redmond in the months to come. He stopped coughing and started breathing normally. His constant congestion left. When the older kids got a cold, he sometimes got stuffy for a day or two, but then he got better. His fine motor skills improved along with everything else. Even the way he sleeps improved. He has always slept without waking at night, but he got into a backwards "s" position that looked frightening. He started sleeping flat on his back or on his side with his chin tucked in.

The supplements are an investment of our time and resources, but we've decided that they're worth it. I've read research that suggests that parents who give their children these supplements do so because they believe that they're helping their children, when in reality the supplements don't do much of anything to help. I had to laugh. If I can believe something works and see actual results in my child, then that's one powerful belief! I'll take it. I can't make up the changes I've seen or explain them away, so that's all the proof I need.

All of Redmond's therapists, specialists, Nurse Jane, and our entire family have seen the change and agree that we're doing something right. I've even started taking some of the supplements that help with improving memory and cognitive function and have seen a major change in my own ability to think clearly.

The subject of these supplements is controversial in the Down syndrome community. I've read that people think we're trying to cure Down syndrome, and our kids are perfect the way they are. They say that the supplements aren't regulated by the government or studied by the right people. I'm okay with that because the researchers test them out on their own children before they pass them along to us. This group doesn't receive kickbacks or payments from lobbyists. There's no windfall for them if we use the supplements or not. They sell them at cost. As Rick and I have discussed and considered it, we believe that using them is giving our son the best chance he has at a healthy and productive life.

The people in our support group have also pointed out that immunizations have not been studied in people with Down syndrome. The package inserts in immunizations say that people with compromised immune systems should not receive them. Since Down syndrome greatly affects the person's immune system function, it's very important to consider carefully whether immunizations are a good idea for our children. As I looked back over Redmond's little life, I realized that he was hospitalized right after his one-month and three-month immunizations. His little body could not handle the influx of all those inflammatory-response-inducing medications at one time.

If I had it to do over again, if I'd been educated about Down syndrome before he was born, I would have given his body time to get stronger, then prayerfully introduced only the most vital immunizations, one at a time, and watched carefully to see how he responded. I would have had his titers checked eight weeks after each immunization to see if he'd developed any antibodies as a result of the shot.

When we did have his titers checked to see if he'd developed any antibodies as a result of all the immunizations he already had, we were disappointed to see that he had very few. Since they did very little for him, and likely caused his body to react so negatively that he was hospitalized, we have chosen to wait and prayerfully consider further immunizations.

Our decision about immunizations is an unpopular one. There are those who are militantly against them all and are so afraid of them that they tremble to think of their child receiving even one. Our other children have been vaccinated and are healthy, active, and behave appropriately for their ages. We do not believe that all vaccines are detrimental to everyone.

There are those who advocate strongly for all children to be fully vaccinated from everything possible. They see no problem with flooding a child's system with fifteen different vaccinations in one day. We aren't there either. We believe that each child should be considered, that the reality of physician kickbacks, the lack of testing done on newer vaccinations, and the aborted fetal tissue in certain vaccines should all be considered, and wisdom should be applied as parents consider all their options.

These days I keep our home as free from dust as possible. We keep heavily scented items, cigarette smoke, and tobacco products away from Redmond. We open the windows to let in fresh air often (except during days with extra-high pollen counts), always run an air purifier, and feed him a nutrient-rich, high-fat, high-calorie, anti-inflammatory diet of superfoods. We wash our hands every time we come into the house and before we interact with Redmond. We stopped using hand sanitizer regularly, opting for soap and water. We always put Epsom salts in his bath to draw out any impurities and keep his g-tube site healthy. And I have chosen to use the cleanest, healthiest diapers and skin care products on all our children.

The good news is that it's working!

17

REDMOND
SURPRISES US ALL

When Redmond was 18 months old, I couldn't imagine him playing appropriately with toys. He put everything in his mouth and then threw it. His Early Intervention team set that as a goal for him and I struggled to imagine him doing it. Within a week of setting that goal he started playing appropriately with toys. Soon after that he started pulling himself up on furniture and walking around it.

Redmond surprised us all when, at around 19 months old, he started climbing up and down stairs. There are two nice, wide steps at his grandparents' house, and one day Charlie got down on the floor with him and showed him how to climb up and down. Charlie stayed there and spotted him in his four-year-old way until Redmond mastered it. Charlie has so much patience with his little brother, but he acts like a typical big brother when Redmond gets into his things. As I write today, Redmond started crying in another room and I expected Kristina to find out what was wrong and fix it. Before she could get there, Charlie went running to see what happened. I could hear him saying, "Oh Redmond, what's wrong? Are you okay? Do you need some help?" That was it. Redmond stopped crying and I heard the two of them laughing about something together.

Redmond has been speaking very clearly since before he was a year old, but only when he feels like it. On any given week, he has favorite words to say and says them repeatedly. The next week he might concentrate on another set of words or not speak much at all. When I start to get concerned that something's wrong, he'll say something so clearly that I laugh at myself for worrying. One of his favorite things to say consistently is, "Mom, mom, mom! UP!" Of course, then I scramble to pick him up as quickly as I can because who can resist that?

He loves interacting with Eliana. At two years old, Redmond is very close to walking. Eliana loves to hold his hands and walk around with him. She started kindergarten in 2018 and he misses her so much. With riding the bus for an hour each way to our rural farm, she's gone about nine hours a day, five days a week. When she gets home, he lights up. She runs to wash her hands, then she enthusiastically plays with him. She loves to read him simple books, carry him around, and show him new toys. One day she and I were sitting at the table in the kitchen and Redmond was playing happily in the laundry room, babbling away. It sounded like nonsense, but my ears perked up as I heard something very close to "Eliana." I asked her to listen carefully with me, and we both heard it.

"Eliana! Eliana! Eliana!" He wasn't babbling at all.

She jumped up and ran to him. He wanted her to carry him into the kitchen. He was perfectly capable of army-crawling in there, but he wanted her to carry him. He called her name pretty clearly for a boy not yet two years old!

In March of 2019, Redmond was scheduled to have surgery to repair a tube (ureter) between his kidney and bladder. The hydronephrosis he'd had in utero had resolved on one side on its own, but the other side stubbornly continued on. It was major surgery, so we prayed fervently for God to heal him without the need for surgery. I was sad, but resigned, when the pre-op ultrasound showed no change. Surgery would go on as scheduled.

On the day of surgery, the surgical team impressed me with their preparation and care. The anesthesiologist knew his entire medical history and presented me with her plan, including options in case he didn't respond well. My heart was touched by their thoroughness. After he was sedated, the pulmonologist did a bronchial study, checking his airways and lungs for damage or malformation. He called us back to let us know that Redmond's results were fairly normal. Good news!

Next, the urologist circumcised him. We'd planned for that to be done as normal, but since he'd been fighting for his life, it hadn't been done. We had questioned the need for it after so much time passed, unwilling to do anything unnecessary, but several of his specialists encouraged us to take care of it for various reasons. After that, the urologist ran a scope into his bladder to confirm that it was healthy enough for surgery. That is when everything came to a sudden halt.

The surgeon met with us and explained that the circumcision had gone well, but she would not be able to do the next part of the surgery that day. She showed us photos of the inside of Redmond's bladder, which was full of bacteria-filled cysts! If she were to proceed with the surgery, infection could flood his body and he could die. I was horrified. He'd been on two different antibiotics prior to surgery, one for four months, and he still had an infection. The surgeon didn't understand why the antibiotics hadn't worked, but she wanted to try a new one and reschedule the surgery in six weeks.

We were terribly disappointed, not because we wanted him to have surgery, but because we wanted it to be done. Six more weeks of another antibiotic caused alarms to go off in my mind. Redmond had been vomiting daily from the ones he'd already been on, and this one was even stronger. Worry filled me. I was honestly angry with God. How could He allow Redmond to continue to suffer? I was told that his bladder condition was called "cystic cytosis" and it was typically very painful. Redmond had a constant urinary tract infection and never had a fever, never complained, so we didn't know if he had been in pain all of his life and was so used to it that he didn't know any different, or if he has an extremely high pain tolerance.

We brought him home from the hospital that day and immediately noticed a big change in the number of wet diapers he had a day, as well as how wet they were. He'd never soaked a diaper before, but he started waking up each morning totally soaked through everything. We kept having to change his sheets and give him a bath! We switched to night time diapers and made sure he went to bed with a dry diaper. We hadn't considered the number of wet diapers he had before to be odd, but after circumcision, we learned.

Prior to surgery, Redmond would fold over at the waist and whine several times a day. After a minute or two, he'd stop and go on like nothing was wrong. We associated that with digestive distress, but we realized it had stopped entirely. He seemed happier and his development seemed to shoot ahead suddenly.

I mentioned it to the urologist at his next appointment, wondering if circumcision had somehow freed something up. Where had all that pee been going before? The answer seemed to me to be – back into his kidney.

The urologist didn't think so, but she humored me by ordered a new ultrasound. Three weeks after the scheduled surgery, we had a follow up ultrasound and discovered that his ureter was no longer swollen. There was no indication for surgery.

God answered our prayers, not supernaturally, but with a raging infection. I shrugged and thanked Him for whatever means He wanted to use to heal Redmond.

In preparation for that surgery, the pulmonologist ordered a baseline chest x-ray to look at Redmond's lungs when he wasn't sick. As we drove home from that appointment, she called me. She wanted us to know that Redmond's lungs showed little to no scarring or indication of damage. The radiologist had looked at it and deemed it "normal." She was giddy with the news. We were giddy with praise to God.

We discovered several months later that a medication that Redmond had been prescribed for acid reflux (which they said was causing him to not eat well), a problem he was never officially tested for but assumed to have due to Down syndrome, has some severe side effects. Among other things, they include headache, abdominal pain, diarrhea, nausea, vomiting, upper respiratory infection, acid reflux, constipation, rash, cough, loss of appetite, hair loss, chronic inflammation of the stomach, taste changes, liver damage, and inflammation within the kidneys. Not one of his specialists mentioned this possibility to us as we visited one after the other, seeking help for his constant vomiting, digestive issues, lack of appetite, chronic upper respiratory infections, rashes, and kidney issues. We have since taken him off that medication and he has basically stopped having all of the side effects listed above. I have sworn to never give him another medication until I've thoroughly researched all the side effects and am satisfied that he truly needs it.

Life has changed so much in the last six and half years. I went from a single adult who poured herself into her ministry career and friends in a bustling city to a farmer's wife with three children in the rural Midwest. Now I've added the roles of author, speaker, and Down syndrome advocate. It's been quite a journey. I couldn't have made it through without my stable, steady husband who has stood by my side through it all. God has given me an anchor in human form, a man whose love doesn't waver during our trials. Rick provides for our family financially, but he also takes responsibility for much of our daily tasks so I have the freedom to write, travel, and minister to others.

For the first year of Redmond's life, fear tried to steal my joy. I worried about what would happen to him if Rick and I died. I worried about where he'd live and what he'd do when he grew up. Exhaustion and despair led me to times when fear pressed in on me so heavily that unwelcome thoughts plagued me. My dad reminded me that there are times when Satan whispers lies in our ears, then points his finger of accusation at us for having the thoughts to begin with. I decided to give those lies no place in my heart, refusing to accept the dark thoughts as anything more than a combination of fear, exhaustion, and emotional vulnerability.

I remind myself any time fear tries to creep back in that God directs Redmond's steps just as much as He directs my steps. God has a plan for Redmond's life and I don't have to figure it all out today. We take one day at a time, praise God for the opportunity to raise our children, and keep putting one foot in front of the other.

I believed that if we could make it through Redmond's first year of life, we could do anything. I didn't count on the next six months of his life turning into such a challenge, but it was still calm compared with the first 12 months. Months 18-24 brought more improvement, more quickly than we imagined possible.

We're still learning as we go, looking into anything that might improve Redmond's quality of life, trying to help him in the same way we help our other children. Our goal is to help them become exactly who God created them to be – to help them enhance their strengths, to help them overcome or manage their weaknesses, and to be kind to everyone. We highly value fun and a good sense of humor, and although we can't always go out to have fun, we try to make our home FUN.

If you drive by our house, especially in the summer, you'll have no doubt that small children live here. There's a colorful play tower, a trampoline, a play house, a small swing set, a balance beam, and numerous bikes, scooters, and a battery-run John Deere Gator. It's not the nicest, newest, or fanciest by any means, but they don't care! They're as happy to climb the rock wall on a used play tower as a shiny new one. The scenery will change as they grow, but my hope is that it will always be obvious that our home is a place where fun is important.

Redmond is still too small to do much on the outdoor play equipment, but his day is coming. Last summer he was in the kiddie pool with the bigger kids, splashing and laughing right along with them. He got sick that afternoon and spent the rest of the summer coughing, but at least he got to experience it once.

Redmond has struggled with a compromised immune system, which is a part of Down syndrome. Almost all children experience sickness – colds, coughs, broken bones, skinned knees, etc. All parents find themselves up at night, walking the halls in an effort to comfort a teething toddler or a child who is struggling to breathe through congestion. With Redmond, it might last longer and hit harder. We pray for him, we do all we can to protect him, but we understand that this trial is part of the gig. We don't like it one bit, but we take a deep breath and hold his head as he vomits. Or we manage another hospital stay with more grace than we did the last time. We learn as we go and we pray.

I asked the Lord over and over and over to heal Redmond completely. He responded by leading me to Paul's thorn in the flesh.

"And lest I should be exalted above measure by the abundance of the revelations, a thorn in the flesh was given to me, a messenger of Satan to buffet me, lest I be exalted above measure. Concerning this thing I pleaded with the Lord three times that it might depart from me. And He said to me, "My grace is sufficient for you, for My strength is made perfect in weakness." Therefore most gladly I will rather boast in my infirmities, that the power of Christ may rest upon me. Therefore I take pleasure in infirmities, in reproaches, in needs, in persecutions, in distresses, for Christ's sake. For when I am weak, then I am strong" -2 Corinthians 12:7 (NKJV).

God spoke to me very clearly one morning when I was on the treadmill at the gym. I audibly gasped, so stirred by the sound of His clear and powerful voice in my cluttered mind. As I once again asked Him to heal Redmond of all the physical challenges that he faces as a result of that extra copy of the 21st chromosome – He told me NO. He told me that He loves Redmond more than I ever could, but He will not take away the daily struggles we face with him. Maybe Redmond is so anointed and powerful in the Spirit realm that God allowed him to have this thorn in his flesh to keep him from becoming conceited. I will watch and pray over him every day for the rest of my life, begging God for healing anyway, expecting greatness to continue to rise in this child as he shows us why we named him something that means "wise protector."

> *"The Lord says, 'I will rescue those who love me. I will protect those who trust in my name. When they call on me, I will answer; I will be with them in trouble. I will rescue and honor them. I will reward them with a long life and give them my salvation'"* - Psalm 91:14-16 (NLT).

I always understood that to mean that I wouldn't suffer like those who don't love the Lord. I felt protected from storms – from NICUs and PICUs and breathing treatments and heart defects. I felt protected from Down syndrome. My intentions were good. I attempted to have faith that what Scripture said is true. I also ignored the part that says, "I will be with you in trouble." It doesn't say – "You will have no trouble." It says He will be with us IN TROUBLE.

Jesus said, "Peace, be still!", and the storm stopped suddenly. Another time Jesus allowed His dear friend Lazarus to get sick and die. Jesus allowed his family to mourn and bury him. Then four days later He showed up, wept with them, and then called that friend out of the grave. Jesus made him hop out of the tomb because his body was all wrapped up!

This God we serve is the same one who shook the chains off Paul in prison and sent an angel to help him escape, yet let Herod behead John the Baptist. God shut the mouths of the lions when Daniel was put in their den overnight, but He allowed Pharaoh to kill newborn Hebrew babies. God allowed Stephen to be stoned, Peter to be crucified upside down, and John to be exiled; and this same God healed ungrateful men of leprosy, protected Paul from the bite of a deadly snake, and sent tongues of fire to rest on the heads of His followers.

How can we ever understand the mighty God of the universe who knows far better than we do what this old world needs?

There were moments in the NICU when I was calm despite all that doctors and specialists told me. There were moments when fear threatened to take over. Satan came to tell me that God would take this child from me like He had taken so many other dreams. But Satan is a liar.

Long before these children were born, God removed me from situations I wasn't meant to be in by hardening the hearts of those who made the decisions. Just like God told Moses to tell Pharaoh to let His people go, knowing that Pharaoh wouldn't do it – He guided me. God didn't take things away from me. God brought me into a peaceful place, a great place to raise my children, a wonderful place to write, and a redemptive place for my family. God didn't take my child from me. God gave me my child, a precious gift, and with him a rare glimpse into the character of Jesus.

As Redmond began to get better and life started settling down, I felt a familiar stirring in my soul. God prompted me to tell our story. My heart raced when I thought about it. Questions flooded me. When will I find the time with everything I have to do for our family? Where will I tell it? How can I get on stage after I've been sedentary for so long that I'm embarrassed to be seen, much less stand in front of crowds?

The worst one of all hammered away at me: do you just want an audience? Do you want to be famous badly enough that you'd expose your disabled son to the world? Is this really all about you? I wondered if I imagined God's voice in my head because I couldn't embrace my own motives.

But the idea wouldn't leave me alone. It felt like something was pressing down on my chest. Then a friend sent me an email advertising an upcoming women's event at a local church. She wanted me to go with her to hear a special speaker. The speaker lost a disabled child and she shares a message of hope with women, speaking about praising God even through very hard things. I could barely get through the publicity email for the feeling that wouldn't stop pounding in my brain – *this should be me*! I replied to my friend that I didn't think I would go. She pushed back gently, encouraging me to make time for the event. I reluctantly agreed.

A week or so later my friend was making dinner for us at her house when she turned to me and said, "I'm helping out with that event I invited you to. I was at a meeting today and the organizers asked me who I had sitting at my table. When I said your name, they all got excited. They said that if they hadn't been able to get this speaker to come, they were going to ask you to do it!"

I hadn't realized they were even considering me. I went home on cloud nine, so pleasantly surprised and praying for God's direction.

"Lord, do You really want me to tell my story now?"

In the coming days, God sweetly affirmed the calling I'd felt since I was a little girl. I'd learned over the years that my mother's reaction to public speaking was much more common than mine. Whenever God taught me something over the years, I naturally thought of how to teach it to others. Standing in front of people and sharing those insights didn't intimidate me; it seemed exciting. When I haven't had an opportunity to teach the things I'm learning to a live audience, I write it out and post it on my blog. If I don't get it out, I feel like I'll burst.

It was time. Rick and I agreed that I could reasonably do two speaking engagements a month. Since his parents are so supportive with the kids, we talked to his mom. She encouraged me to go for it. I felt God prompting me to let others know that I was ready.

It went against everything in my bones that said I shouldn't promote myself, that if God wanted me to do it then He would open the doors and I wouldn't have to do anything but be available. But what if God calls you to make yourself available and you hide in your house? God didn't bring the Ninevites to Jonah; He made Jonah get in a boat and sail to them. And when Jonah didn't obey, God made sure He got Jonah's attention. I've learned the hard way so many times that I'm not interested in being in the belly of a big fish again.

I spoke with several people I respect and got their input. It would affect them if I started working as a professional author and speaker. Were they okay with that? Did they think I was stepping out of bounds? Every one of them enthusiastically encouraged me to go for it.

With a dry throat and hands that shook so much I could barely type the words, I posted on Facebook something like, "I am prayerfully considering sharing the testimony of Redmond's healing with churches, moms' groups, etc. If you feel like my story would encourage your group, let's get something set up."

I hit "post" before I could change my mind and sat there staring at the screen like it might explode. My friends commented with encouraging messages and I started to calm down a little. The next morning, I got a call around 10:00 a.m. It was Nancy from the church that was hosting the women's event I planned to attend with my friend that night. It turned out that the speaker was ill and wouldn't be able to be there. They'd sold 300 tickets to the event and had no speaker. She wondered if I might be able to fill in at the last minute. She'd seen my post the night before. She told me that they'd considered asking me in the first place but weren't sure if I was ready to do it yet. They were thrilled when they saw what I'd written.

Without a moment's hesitation, I agreed to do it. She was surprised, thinking maybe I'd want to pray about it or talk to Rick. I was giddy when I told her I'd been praying about it for weeks and had already talked to Rick. I didn't know that event was the one I'd been praying about, but I could see how God had been preparing me in advance for it. I even had a new outfit that I thought would be good to wear that night.

Nancy and I finalized some details and hung up. Then it was time to hit the ground running. My mother-in-law watched the kids for the rest of the day so I could prepare. I wrote out everything I wanted to say, praying as I furiously typed. Then I got myself ready, went over my notes again, and it was time to go. That night, I spoke to 300 women about my journey with Redmond. I had to force my feet to walk up on that stage, nearly overcome with self-consciousness that made me want to run away. But God opened my eyes to see the hearts of the women who were there. It wasn't about ME. It was about THEM. God had a message for them - and He chose to use me to share it. I got over myself and walked up on that stage.

It was one of the best hours of my life. It felt so good to share our journey and the things God had laid on my heart through it. I felt God's supernatural strength flow through me and His healing balm pouring over broken hearts. The lights were bright enough that I couldn't see many faces, but I heard their laughter and appreciation. I learned later that I had missed the tears. One friend told me that every woman at her table was wiping tears and one was sobbing.

I didn't mean to make anyone cry, but I believe that sometimes the anointing of the Holy Spirit brings with it tears that wash away our pain. In moments when He is close enough to feel His breath on our face, tears of joy well up inside us and spill out. I felt God's presence that night and it blessed me to know that it had been felt all over the room. Without that kiss of God's Spirit, the most gifted orator is just a speaker. When God's presence is felt, there is life.

Afterwards, exhaustion hit me hard and I went home and slept and slept. We had church the next morning and I was surprised to find that word had spread quickly. Women stopped me every few feet and it was hard to get from point A to point B. We went out to lunch afterwards and I was stopped by women in the restaurant who had been there the night before. For weeks, I couldn't go anywhere without being recognized and acknowledged. It was touching and affirming, but it was also really uncomfortable.

I'd been concerned that my heart was in the wrong place, but that experience showed me differently. I was thankful for all the affirmation, but I also wanted to crawl into a hole. I realized how much I like moving through crowds unnoticed, unconcerned with how I did my hair that morning, if I was wearing any makeup, or if I looked frumpy. I'd pretty much standardized the mom look for myself – a pair of jeans, t-shirt, sweatshirt, and a low side bun. I might have swiped on a little concealer and mascara. Suddenly, I felt like I needed to be dressed nicely with hair and makeup in place before I left the house to run to the store. It felt like a spotlight on me everywhere I went, and I wanted to hide.

God's voice came through loud and clear this time. He wanted me to remember that feeling of discomfort. Sharing my testimony is a sacrifice of praise to God. It has nothing to do with getting attention for myself or using the hard story of our young son's life to build my own social media following. It's an act of worship and obedience, so I stopped second-guessing myself. I started trying to build my social media following so I could make His name famous.

As for walking around town always fixed up, my dear friend Kasey snorted and said something along the lines of – "God forbid that they find out you're real." It was exactly what I needed to hear. While I do have the energy to take a little better care of my appearance these days, I don't feel that tremendous pressure to look a certain way before I leave the house. That event highlighted the discomfort I felt with my physical appearance at that time, so I made some changes. I rejoined the gym, did a 6-week challenge to get myself back into thinking about health and wellness, and made a list of goals that didn't include a number on the scale.

I could write another whole book about my challenges with body image, fitness, and food. It's been a lifelong struggle that has brought me to my knees many times. At this point in my life, I've made some major changes to my attitude about it all. I need to feel good in my skin, not look the way someone else thinks I should. I move a lot more, work out at the gym when I can, eat healthy much of the time, and giving myself grace for the times when I can't. I even give myself grace for the times when I'm a little lazy. No one can hit it on every level all the time. Thankfully, I'm no longer confined to that brown recliner. That's a major improvement.

As I struggled through that year, trying to figure out my place in this new world I'd been thrust into with Redmond and the rest of our family, I got to thinking about God's ideas of Down syndrome.

When Jesus walked on the earth, a huge part of His ministry was to heal the sick. Did He ever heal someone with Down syndrome? Back then it wasn't called Down syndrome or Trisomy 21. We'll never know if Jesus ever laid His hands on a person with Down syndrome and caused their number of chromosomes to change from 47 to 46.

When I read Isaiah 53 through the lens of a mother of a child with Down syndrome, I notice something much different than I did when I memorized the chapter in elementary school. Prophetically speaking of Jesus, Isaiah wrote the following:

> *"...He shall grow up before Him as a tender plant,*
> *And as a root out of dry ground.*
> *He has no form or comeliness;*
> *And when we see Him,*
> *There is no beauty that we should desire Him.*
> *He is despised and rejected by men,*
> *A Man of sorrows and acquainted with grief.*
> *And we hid, as it were, our faces from Him;*
> *He was despised, and we did not esteem Him."*
>
> *Surely He has borne our griefs*
> *And carried our sorrows;*
> *Yet we esteemed Him stricken,*
> *Smitten by God, and afflicted" (NKJV).*

Wait. God afflicted Jesus, the man who carried our sorrows? Well, we thought He did, anyway. Do we think of those with Down syndrome as afflicted, stricken, smitten by God?

Despite our views of those with Down syndrome, research shows[3] that they are overwhelmingly reported to have compassion, empathy, and unconditional love for others. They like the way they look and are content with where they live and what they do.

How is that a curse? How is that a life sentence? As I consider this chapter in light of my role as the mother of Redmond, **I wonder if people with Down syndrome are more like Jesus than those of us who have 46 chromosomes.**

What are we concerned with? Success, power, popularity, wealth, money, and health. We don't feel like we've accomplished much in life if we aren't living independently from our parents, married with children, working a job that pays well and gives us a measure of power in our lives. We put on our job title like we put on an outfit. We consider ourselves

---

[3] Skotko, Brian G et al. "Self-perceptions from people with Down syndrome." *American journal of medical genetics. Part A* vol. 155A,10 (2011): 2360-9. doi:10.1002/ajmg.a.34235

successful when our bodies glow with health and vitality. When our bodies begin to fail us, due to disease or aging, we rage against them. We are keenly aware of how they have failed us.

What are people with Down syndrome concerned with? They've often had health issues all their lives and take it in stride. Redmond used to throw up almost every day, but he rarely complained. At two years old, he put his little head into the trashcan, vomited, sat up and waited, did it again and again, then pushed the trashcan away and reached for the napkin in my hand. He wiped his face, then got back to playing with his cars. I can promise you that when pregnancy caused me to vomit like that, I didn't handle it with anywhere near that much grace.

Why would Jesus heal them of the thing that makes them like Him? Jesus wasn't handsome or wealthy, and he didn't own his own house or have an impressive job title. It doesn't appear that he owned much of anything at all. Was he concerned with popularity or romance?

I think it's quite possible that He laid His hands on people with Down syndrome and healed them of heart defects, poor vision, deafness, Leukemia, and so forth. But did He take away the thing that makes them so much like Him?

I don't know the answer. But here's what I do know, without a hint of a doubt: when I prayed and asked God to heal Redmond of Down syndrome, His voice came like a wave crashing over me. It was resounding and deafening and fierce. He said, "It's a gift."

What?

"It's a gift." The second time around, the voice was gracious and tender. It was quiet and comforting, a gentle breeze blowing over my troubled heart.

And so I find Him in the mystery of Down syndrome.

God's grace is sufficient for me, for Redmond, for all of us. His power is made perfect in our weaknesses. Paul not only dealt with his weakness, *but Paul decided to be content with his weaknesses, insults, hardships, persecutions, and calamities. ~Content!~*

God didn't heal the apostle Paul of the thorn in his side. I'm grateful that Paul didn't tell us what the thorn was. The people he wrote to likely knew, but we don't. We can only guess, and it's certainly possible that he desired physical healing and was denied. Did Paul not have enough faith? That is most certainly not the case. Instead of healing him, God gave him the grace to handle it *with contentment.*

1 Corinthians 1:27-31 states,

> *"But God has chosen the foolish things of the world*
> *to put to shame the wise, and God has chosen the*
> *weak things of the world to put to shame the things*
> *which are mighty; and the base things of the world*
> *and the things which are despised God has chosen,*
> *and the things which are not, to bring to nothing the*
> *things that are, that no flesh should glory in His*
> *presence. But of Him you are in Christ Jesus, who*
> *became for us wisdom from God—and righteousness*
> *and sanctification and redemption— that, as it is*
> *written, "He who glories, let him glory in the Lord""*
> *(NKVJ).*

I begged God to lead me where my trust was without borders. Part of me says, "What a dumb prayer. Stop it. Don't pray for that. What are you asking for?" Another part of my heart pushes past the fear and shouts – "Do it anyway! What can be wrong about asking God to help you to trust Him more? He'll handle the details. You will be okay!"

His spirit makes us brave. He lifts us when we are small and silent, unable to speak for the fear of what we see coming. He keeps us safe. He soothes us with His love and great compassion for our weakness.

With the faith He's given us, we step into deep waters, unafraid.

With the assurance He's placed in our hearts, we embrace the mystery that we do not understand. We submit our lives to the will of the One who we trust. We beg Him to help us trust Him more. We have no reason to fear. Even when we feel like we're drowning, He's holding us. Even when it appears that sickness and struggle are a life sentence, we can be content.

The God of the universe could heal Redmond of Down syndrome in an instant, but He has chosen not to. He has chosen to allow suffering and difficulty, on an everyday basis, possibly for the rest of our lives – and He calls it a gift. The gift has already allowed me to see my spiritual pride, my blindness and arrogance, and healed things I had no idea were broken inside me. Perhaps God has allowed this gift in my life to shake me free from fear and self-doubt, from the silence He commanded me to break. I won't know until He chooses to reveal Himself to me fully, but I will do my best to hold onto the gift He's given me and praise Him for it. He gives good gifts because He's a good Father.

In Philippians 3, Paul writes about knowing Christ in the *fellowship of His sufferings*, that he may become more like Christ. Given this gospel that we read and know, how can we believe that health and wellness are all God has in store for those who love Him? We are to join Him in the fellowship of His sufferings. There is fellowship with God – true relationship and friendship – when we suffer.

What if the trouble that's in our lives is actually a gift? Are there things in your life that you've begged God to heal, to fix, or problems you've asked Him to take away – but you still struggle with them anyway? What if they are your gift? What if God wants to use those things to perfect His strength in your weakness? Is it possible that extended singleness, poverty, disability, infertility, sleeplessness, cancer, or asthma are intended by God not to crush you, but to slow you down enough to catch His vision and run with it?

What if?

As you seek after God with all your heart, soul, mind, and strength; as you love your neighbor as yourself; as you study His word and submit to His teachings, what do you hear God whispering in your ear? If He whispers, "I want to heal you of this," then PRAY! Knock on that door until He swings it open wide. But if He whispers, "My strength is made perfect in your weakness," stop banging until your knuckles bleed. Stop wearing yourself out with the effort to "force" God's hand because you won't give up. Look around.

Look up.

What else might God want you to focus on instead? Do you have a wealth of gifting within you that He's waiting to unleash if you can stop focusing on what you do not have?

My dear, dear friends - God has great plans for your life. Yes, yours.

You, a prisoner in your own home as you care for the needs of your medically complex child, fighting every day to keep him alive? YES, YOU. Look up!

You, an aging single woman who thought God called you to be a mother and yet you know that window is swiftly closing? YES, YOU. Look up!!

You, a widow whose health is slipping away as you wonder what God can do through you as you see your grandchildren embrace evil as their way of life? YES, YOU. Look up!!!

You, a single father whose children drift away because their mother has told so many lies about you that it's hard for anyone to know the truth any more. She's caused you to even question yourself. YES, YOU. Look up!!!!

Open your hands and receive the gift God is holding out to you, breathe a deep sigh of relief, and ask Him what He wants you to do with it. There is so much at stake here. There are worlds to change and people to reach. What is your part in that calling? Please, look up, extend your hands, and receive your gift. God will not let you down.

Through Redmond's little life, and so many of the things leading up to his birth, God has taught me to trust in Him and to expect to see Him working even in what appears to be destruction. He uses all things for our good and His glory. Through the challenge of daily trials and the fear that comes with not knowing if all our efforts will lead to the results we desire, God is still working. If what we desire isn't the outcome we receive, God is still working.

We don't have to be afraid.

Look up and ask God what He's doing in this down time in your life. Listen for the answer, even the one that doesn't make sense to you, and then lean into His strength and goodness and find peace. We serve a very good Father. He will give us each the strength to do all that He's asking us to do.

AFTERWORD

LET'S TALK ABOUT
ABBREVIATIONS

When Redmond was a year old, his weight dropped under the third percentile. That's the "Failure to Thrive" category (FTT). That's also when the pediatrician at the hospital threatened to keep him hospitalized until he gained weight. I fought to take him home, showing the doctor that he had gained weight appropriately for a month before he was hospitalized and deemed NPO (no food by mouth) for several days.

I had the strength to fight the doctor and stand up for my son because I made a choice to take care of myself.

Redmond's physical therapist through Early Intervention (EI), Teresa, told me several times in those first few months of his life that I needed to be evaluated for post-partum depression (PPD). Teresa was very cautious, but she sat and listened to me cry every time she came to help Redmond, and I have a feeling she got kind of tired of spending more time helping me process my grief than working with Redmond. I didn't think I had PPD because one of the questions on the screening asks if you think you're over-reacting to the situation at hand. I didn't think I was over-reacting at all. The situation was terrible and I was understandably upset.

When Nurse Jane mentioned it to me, I figured it wouldn't hurt to ask my doctor about it. I didn't want to be medicated, but I was overwhelmed and exhausted. Two women that I respected had recommended that I investigate it. It occurred to me that my ability to evaluate myself at that point might not be as effective as I thought. My midwife asked me the standard questions, then drilled down a little.

She asked me to tell her about feeling overwhelmed. I explained the thoughts cycling through my mind – should we switch Redmond to a g-tube or will he start eating on his own? Should we continue to vaccinate him given the fact that vaccines haven't been tested on children with Down syndrome and aren't indicated in children with immune system disorders? What if we vaccinated him and it didn't work, so he got sick but wasn't tested for the things he'd been vaccinated against, but he actually had one of those issues because he had no immunity anyway? He's ended up in the hospital within a week of his vaccinations every time. What if we vaccinate him again at six months and he goes back to the hospital? What if we don't vaccinate him and he gets some preventable disease and dies because he has low immunity? Also, why am I so tired? I sleep at night these days, but all I want to do is sleep all day. I answered an email the other day and did a few things to follow up with it, but then discovered that I had answered it incorrectly and done all these things that didn't need to be done. I'm losing words so often that my husband is annoyed waiting for me to think of the word I want to say-

Before I could go on, she stopped me and said, "I'd like to try an anti-depressant and see if it helps you. Let's give it six weeks and then you can tell me how you feel."

I stared at her for a moment. "Do you think it will help? Do you think my response to my circumstances isn't in keeping with them? Am I really depressed?"

She said firmly, "I'd like to try Wellbutrin."

She gave me instructions on how to take it, then handed me a list of counselors in the area and asked me to get in touch with someone to process through all these concerns. I left her office and felt like a huge burden had lifted off me. Even though I didn't think I really needed to take it, the idea of having some help to get my emotions stabilized was a huge relief. I immediately drove to the pharmacy and got the prescription filled.

Six weeks later, I felt so much better. The daily crying had stopped, and I could think clearly enough to understand and follow directions. I didn't feel like sleeping all the time, and the decisions I needed to make regarding Redmond's health became much less stressful. Everyone around me seemed relieved too.

When I'd been on the medication for a month or so, a friend had a baby shower. I put Redmond in his car seat carrier, slung the portable oxygen tank in its black bag over my shoulder, and took him along. I was happy to show him off and had a nice time reconnecting with people I hadn't seen in a while. It was wonderful to hear about my friend's excitement for her much-anticipated first baby.

A few weeks after the shower, we heard that she lost the baby. Her daughter was fully formed and the pregnancy progressed beautifully when it suddenly stopped. She was almost full-term and had to be induced and deliver her still-born baby.

At any other time in my life I would have been devastated for her, cried, prayed, and brought their family a meal. I would have fretted about her and showed up to offer support. But at this time in my life I couldn't handle her loss in a way that was typical for me. I became inconsolable. Unable to stop crying, I went to bed and stayed there for days. Rick, our babysitter Kristina, and Grandma took over the care of all three children while I mourned.

After a week, it occurred to me that my response was not in keeping with my relationship with her and this child. Sadness and concern were normal emotions, but the inability to function and take care of my own children was not. I went to my Bible study group and quietly admitted that I was not doing well at all. Those precious women sprang into action. Not only was I covered in prayer, but within a day I had an appointment with a Christian trauma therapist in a nearby town.

My therapist, Stephanie, diagnosed me with Post Traumatic Stress Disorder (PTSD). I thought she might say I had a mild case, but she did not. It was full-blown PTSD and she said she could help me. She said the work would be intense, but I could feel a lot better within a few weeks and be significantly better in a few months. I eyed her suspiciously. This sounded too good to be true. Desperation drove me to agree to do Eye Movement Desensitization and Reprocessing (EMDR) therapy. It sounded so weird, but it also sounded better than years of talk therapy and more medication.

I didn't know anyone who had done EMDR or who was willing to talk about it. It took me a while to trust that Stephanie knew what she was doing and could indeed help me, but I bossed myself around and did the work. She was right. Everything she said was right. Within a couple weeks, I felt a lot better. Within a couple months, I was done with trauma therapy for the events surrounding Redmond's birth and medical issues. It was amazing. I willingly agreed to do more EMDR therapy for traumatic events in my childhood. Nervous that I would discover some kind of horrible abuse or repressed memories, I was more nervous about that then the things about Redmond.

EMDR therapy showed me that the truth is that I was a highly sensitive child and some fairly normal things that happened affected me deeply. I wasn't abused or terribly mistreated. In reality, I had learned very good lessons about kindness and respect for authority, but not learned to defend myself properly when others hurt me. Instead of walking away from uncomfortable situations where I was mistreated, I smiled like I was fine and told myself that I could handle it. But I could not handle it and suffered later. My new statement of truth became, "I can say when I'm uncomfortable." I learned that I could leave. I learned that I could speak up. I learned that it was okay to think more about how I felt than what someone else might think of my feelings. It was sweet freedom.

Around that time my doctor told me that she was concerned about my body mass index (BMI) and that my hemoglobin levels (A1C) were high. I was close to a diagnosis of pre-diabetic. It was time to take better care of my body again.

I renewed my membership at the gym and started going to personal training-type classes. I returned to a high-protein, lower carb diet and made healthier choices. The twenty pounds that I'd gained as I sat on the recliner and tube-fed Redmond slowly came off, returning my bottom to a more manageable size. My clothes fit again and I even had to buy some new ones. My A1C returned to an acceptable level and my BMI went down several points.

I started leaving the house to go to coffee shops and write this book. I also averaged two speaking engagements a month, sharing our story of Redmond's healing and learning to accept the ways that God works that I don't understand. I learned that it's not sinful pride to believe that God has given me a story to share with the world. God opened my eyes to see that when He calls us to do something and we don't do it because of fear of what others will think or because we don't believe the gifts He's given us are enough – that's sin.

So I wrote and I wrote and I wrote. Then I edited and edited and edited. At one point writer's block took over and I stopped for a while. I couldn't get past it. Voices in my head competed for my attention. What would this person or that one think of what I'd written? Who was my audience? What would they think of me?

Our church hosted a weekend prayer conference and I felt compelled to go that first night. I was so sick that night that I really needed to stay in bed, but Rick stayed home with the kids and I gathered myself together the best I could and went. I sat alone, trying not to expose anyone else to whatever virus I had, listening to the fiery woman who stood in front of us. Within the first twenty minutes of her talk she spoke directly to my heart. She said, "Someone here isn't finishing the work God has called you to do because you're more worried about what others think than what God thinks. You serve an audience of One. Stop worrying about what anyone else thinks and finish what He's called you to do."

Well, okay.

I got back to work the next day, free from the competing voices in my head.

As I send this book to the printer, my prayer is that you, my readers, will see beyond our story and hear the heart of God speaking into your story. I pray that you will find the courage to do what God has called you to do, that you will learn to embrace the hard things in your life, and that you will be empowered to trust that God does all things for our good and His glory. I pray that you will thank God for all His blessings in your life and trust Him with all your heart to guide every step you take. Thank you for giving me your time. Know that as you have read, you have been covered in prayer.

September 2, 2019 – UPDATE

Tomorrow I will send this book to the printer, finally finished with the last edit, just in time for the 2019 Rockin' Mom's™Retreat in Nashville, TN. But first, I want to let you know that REDMOND IS EATING.

In April, 2019, Redmond was 100% tube-fed. He took nothing by mouth and hadn't in months. He also vomited constantly. We finally found a physician who helped. Redmond hasn't vomited all summer.

We visited my parents in June, an eight-hour drive that wouldn't have been possible six weeks earlier. Our kids had a blast with their cousins, aunt, and uncles. Redmond sat at the table for his tube-feedings and watched everyone eat. On the way home, we stopped for a meal where the waitress had a niece with Down syndrome. We ordered food for the older kids, and she brought food for all three. I told her that she could take it back because Redmond wouldn't eat. She smiled brightly and said, "It never hurts to try. I won't charge you for it."

To our total shock, Redmond grabbed the straw cup provided and drank from it greedily. Then he actually took a few bites of applesauce. Ever since then, he has been steadily eating more. At first, his muscles were so weak that he chewed the food offered to him, spit it out to take a break, then chewed it some more, then spit it out, then chewed it some more. After a while, he began swallowing. Then, he chewed and swallowed.

Yesterday he fed himself with a spoon over 1,200 calories by mouth. There was no need to tube-feed him anything. We went to church, to lunch, then to a family gathering with no feeding supplies at all.

At 2 ½ years old, Redmond is eating nearly all his calories by mouth. He's walking four to five steps at a time without assistance, and he can really go with the assistance of a little walker. He's reaching all kinds of milestones, which we attribute to him feeling so much better.

The content for this book was finished in early 2019, and I planned to have the editing done in May, but the vomiting slowed me down. We all needed a break, so I took the summer off, focusing my attention on the kiddos. We spent lots of time in the water, visiting fun places, and playing with cousins and friends. We camped out in the back yard, roasted hot dogs and marshmallows in the fire pit, and even visited Aunt Katie for a week in Nashville. The kids *loved* Aunt Katie's pool. (So did I.)

Redmond is healthy and thriving. We understand that kids come with challenges and they aren't over yet, but for now we are soaking in the moment and looking at one another in amazement. Isn't God good?

RESOURCES

Look into your local area for face-to-face Down syndrome support. A Google search will probably be the most effective, but here are some national resources to get you started.

The Down Syndrome Diagnosis Network.
https://www.dsdiagnosisnetwork.org/

The National Down Syndrome Society. https://www.ndss.org/

National Association for Down Syndrome. https://www.nads.org/

Cedar's Story Blog, interview with the author of *Welcome to Holland* and other excellent resources. https://www.cedarsstory.com/

Maribeth Johnson Music. http://www.maribethjohnson.com/home.html

Jillian Benefield, insightful mother of two children with special needs. http://www.jillianbenfield.com/

Trauma therapy, EMDR, information.
https://www.emdria.org/page/emdr_therapy

For Further Reading

The Lucky Few: Finding God's Best in the Most Unlikely Places by Heather Avis. Zondervan, 2017.

Bloom: Finding Beauty in the Unexpected by Kelle Hampton. William Morrow Publishing, 2012.

Unexpected, various authors, Compiled by Jen Jacob. Available for free download at https://www.jenjacob-dsparentsupport.com/unexpected.

The Parent's Guide to Down Syndrome: Advice, Information, Inspiration, and Support for Raising Your Child from Diagnosis through Adulthood by Jen Jacobs and Madra Sikora. Adams Publishing, 2016.

Babies with Down Syndrome: A New Parents' Guide by Susan J. Skallerup, editor. Woodbine House Publishers, 2008.

To book the author as the speaker for your group's next event, or to read more about her journey, visit:

WWW.KIMBERLYWYSE.COM

Bonus content is available!

YouTube channel: search *Kimberly Wyse* for a fun interview with the author's husband, Rick, and for her new vlogs

Facebook: www.facebook.com/kimberlywyse

Instagram: www.instagram.com/kimberly.wyse

Newborn photo. Mommy was standing beside him with the oxygen tubing ready to put back in his nose right away

Six months old! His onsie was given to us by a good friend and says, "I'm proof that GOD answers prayers!"

one year old and not sitting up unassisted, but talking and full of fun

At two year's old, we know THE SKY IS THE LIMIT for Redmond!

Redmond and Grammy

Wedding Day

Two and One
and so much joy.

Three and Two
Years Old

I was so tired that I forgot to find outfits
for everyone. I almost cancelled photos,
but our photographer pulled it off.

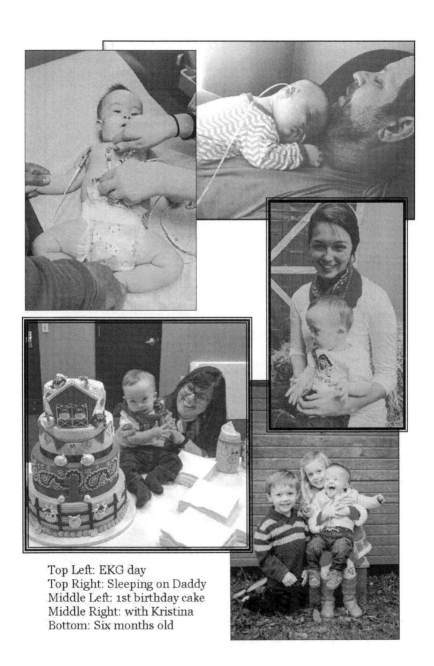

Top Left: EKG day
Top Right: Sleeping on Daddy
Middle Left: 1st birthday cake
Middle Right: with Kristina
Bottom: Six months old

Top: Seeing Redmond's face
for the first time
Middle Left: Six week old
Eliana
Middle Right: Finally preg-
nant

Newborn Charlie
with 15-month-
old Eliana

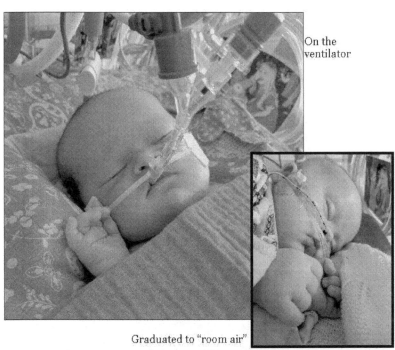

On the ventilator

Graduated to "room air"

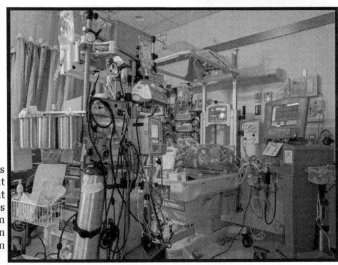

All this equipment meant there was little room for us in his room

Rick and Kimberly Wyse live on a farm in the midwestern United States. Rick grows wheat and soybeans and loves his John Deere tractors. They have fruit trees, vegetable gardens, a large pond, and natural spring water. There's lots of space for the kids to run and play, and they are close to their grandparents, who also help out on the farm. They've been married since 2011, and have three children – Eliana, Charlie, and Redmond. Their children are the light of their lives. When they aren't chasing kids around or changing diapers, they like to watch movies, spend time with friends, visit family, ride around the farm on the four-wheeler (ATV), and if they're really lucky, they get to binge-watch HGTV.

Made in the USA
Middletown, DE
27 February 2020